COMMON GROUND

COMMON GROUND

How to Stop the Partisan War
That Is Destroying America

Cal Thomas
and **Bob Beckel**

wm WILLIAM MORROW *An Imprint of* HarperCollins*Publishers*

HarperCollins books may be purchased for educational, business, or sales promotional use. For information please write: Special Markets Department, HarperCollins Publishers, 10 East 53rd Street, New York, NY 10022.

FIRST EDITION

Designed by Susan Walsh

Library of Congress Cataloging-in-Publication Data has been applied for.

ISBN: 978-0-06-123634-1
ISBN-10: 0-06-123634-9

07 08 09 10 11 WBC/RRD 10 9 8 7 6 5 4 3 2 1

For Ken Paulson, USA Today editor, who said "yes" and made it all possible, and for Brian Gallagher, editorial page editor, and John Siniff, our copy editor, who make the column fit to print and without whose support and encouragement we might not have written this book.

—Cal Thomas

To my children, Alex and Mackenzie, may your generation always seek common ground.

—Bob Beckel

I believe we can find some common ground with the Democrats.
—President George W. Bush answering questions at a press
conference the day following the 2006 election

Extending the hand of partnership to the president—not partisan-ship, but partnership ... [I] say let's work together to come to some common ground where we can solve the problem in Iraq.
—Nancy Pelosi, D-CA, September 8, 2006

CONTENTS

INTRODUCTION 1

PREFACE ▪ WHO WE ARE 15

"Why I Am a Liberal" by Bob Beckel 17
"Why I Am a Conservative" by Cal Thomas 23

PART I ▪ WHERE WE ARE 27

1 The People vs. the Polarization of American Politics 29
2 The Polarization of American Politics 38
3 "The Rest of Us" 46
4 Congressional Stories 55
5 The Parties 61
6 The Press, Fund-raisers, and Myths 69

PART II ▪ THE GATHERING STORMS 85

7 Storm Clouds from the South 87
8 A Circular Firing Squad 94
9 "I'll Never Lie to You" 99

10 *Roe v. Wade*   103
11 The Reagan Revolution   109

PART III ▪ STORMS   115

12 Iran-Contra and Bob Bork: The Peace Ends   117
13 The Politics of Personal Destruction   126
14 Polarization's Poster Children: Bill Clinton
    and George W. Bush   131
15 Clinton Years/Clinton Wars   134
16 Clinton's Revenge   143
17 George Bush Rides In   146
18 War Abroad and War at Home   151

PART IV ▪ THE WAY WE WERE   163

19 A Change of Culture   165
20 When Adults Were in Charge   169
21 Bipartisanship   174
22 The Power of the Parlor   177

PART V ▪ COMMON GROUND   183

23 Common Ground: Slogan or Choice?   185
24 Common Ground: A Campaign Guide for 2008   193
25 Selling Common Ground   204
26 Thoughts and Conclusions   251

EPILOGUE   259

ACKNOWLEDGMENTS   263

INDEX   265

COMMON GROUND

INTRODUCTION

Politics, it seems to me, for years, or all too long, has been concerned with right or left instead of right or wrong.
—Richard Armour, American poet and novelist

IN THE 1994 MIDTERM CONGRESSIONAL ELECTIONS, FOR THE FIRST time in more than forty years, Newt Gingrich led the Republicans to a majority in the House of Representatives. On November 6, 1998, the legendary firebrand from Georgia resigned as Speaker of the House and relinquished his congressional seat. Gingrich had been Speaker for less than four years. He was pushed overboard by the very people he had led to power. In an effort to head off the mutiny, Gingrich placed a call to the House Republican leadership in which he said, "I am willing to lead, but I won't allow cannibalism." The cannibals prevailed.

Nine years earlier, on May 31, 1989, another House Speaker—this one a Democrat—was forced from office. In his farewell address to the House, Jim Wright of Fort Worth, Texas, urged his colleagues to "bring this period of mindless cannibalism to an end." Wright resigned after failing to squelch a relentless ethics campaign concerning allegations that he had received laundered money from organized labor through the sale of a book he had written. In one of political history's great ironies, the campaign to oust Wright was led by Newt Gingrich.

It said much about modern Washington that both Gingrich and Wright invoked "cannibalism" to describe the process that led to their ouster. Both men had become victims of a climate of political polarization, rooted in the 1960s, which by the late 1980s had decimated bipartisanship in national politics. Wright and Gingrich had contributed to the climate, and it ended up consuming their careers.

Forty-four days after Gingrich's resignation, Republican Bob Livingston of Louisiana, chosen by his fellow Republicans to succeed Gingrich, suddenly announced his resignation from Congress. He, too, had become a victim of the "cannibals." In Livingston's case, an extramarital affair with a staff member—which had occurred several years before but was about to become public—placed him in the boiling pot. On that same day, December 19, 1998, the U.S. House of Representatives voted to impeach the forty-third President of the United States, William Jefferson Clinton.

One man who would be instrumental in the effort to oust Newt Gingrich from the Speaker's office, and in the impeachment of President Clinton, was Congressman Tom DeLay of Sugarland, Texas. DeLay was the Republican majority leader (a position he reached after Gingrich was sacked), and a former pest exterminator who treated Democrats the way he used to treat roaches. DeLay was an admitted and unapologetic partisan. His relentless efforts to keep House Republicans in a disciplined and partisan mode earned DeLay the nickname "the velvet hammer."

On September 28, 2005, DeLay was indicted by a Democratic Texas prosecutor for laundering campaign contributions. House ethics rules forced DeLay to resign as majority leader while under indictment. DeLay was also dogged by stories about his relationship with lobbyist Jack Abramoff, who had pled guilty to conspiracy to bribe members of Congress. After winning the Republican nomination for his contested House seat, DeLay resigned from Congress. His "safe" Republican district was won by a Democrat in the 2006 general election. The chief proponent of polarization had become another of its victims.

It could be argued that polarization notwithstanding, these politicians got what they deserved. Perhaps, but in each case polarization played a significant role. It was not at all clear that Jim Wright's book sales were illegal, but the campaign against him was so intense that House Democrats began to feel the "spillover effect" from voters back home. Rather than risk their substantial majority, other Democrats eased Wright out. Similarly, Gingrich was ousted by a cabal of right-wing polarizers, including DeLay, who believed the controversial Gingrich was responsible for Republicans losing House seats in the 1998 election.

Politicians on both sides of the aisle have been pushing the limits of propriety for a very long time. Before the current climate of polarization, these activities, although not condoned, were often ignored. Most players in Washington, including the press, were aware of JFK's sexual escapades, but purposely overlooked them. It is fair to say Bob Livingston's sexual encounters did not reach the excesses of Jack Kennedy's.

Bill Clinton's behavior was certainly reprehensible. But few political observers believe that his sexual activities would have risen to the level of impeachment were it not for the polarizing climate gripping Congress in the late 1990s.

Tom DeLay was indicted for laundering federal campaign contributions to Texas state legislative races. It was a blatant attempt to add to the GOP's already sizable majorities in the state legislature. DeLay needed more Republican legislators to redraw Texas congressional district lines to favor Republicans in the 2004 election. District lines were not scheduled to be redrawn until after the census in 2010. Would DeLay have tried such a dangerous political move were it not for polarization? Indeed, would Tom DeLay have been the House majority leader without raging polarization? Highly unlikely.

James Q. Wilson, the Ronald Reagan Professor of Public Policy at Pepperdine University, is one of the more sober observers of American public policy. In a February 2006 essay for *Commentary* magazine, "How Divided Are We?" Wilson made some observations about the chronic polarization that has overtaken contemporary politics.

Wilson defines polarization as "an intense commitment to a candidate, a culture, or an ideology that sets people in one group definitively apart from people in another, rival group." In other words, the goal of polarization is to knock off the other side before they knock you off. In the last twenty-five years, the political graveyard has been gaining residents at an alarming rate. Our man Wilson, academic tone aside, has got the political players right. To paraphrase Wilson: polarization occurs when the opposing camp regards a candidate as not simply wrong, but corrupt and wicked. The assumption is that one side is absolutely right, the other absolutely wrong, and the wrong side deserves to die absolutely.

Before settling on Wilson's definition of polarization, we considered several others, but rejected them as too broad and extreme. In the latter category, one is worth mentioning. In "The Paranoid Style in American Politics" (1965), Richard Hofstadter wrote, "Polarization in its extremity entails the belief that the other side is in thrall to a secret conspiracy that is using devious means to obtain control over society."

In today's vernacular: "Liberals control the media, the universities, and Hollywood. These commies use their control to force a radical, godless agenda on all God-loving patriotic Amarrricans, especially kids." Or, "Conservatives, working through the religious right and Big Biddness, conspired with their hired neoconservative wing nuts to invade Iraq so the United States and Halliburton could get control of oil."

Now, we know it is a narrow definition, but it raises a question: Could liberals or conservatives who are honestly concerned with the public interest see themselves holding such a belief about the other side? Sure they could, and there are a lot more of these polarizing, conspiracy-believing, boot-stomping members of both parties than you might think. And we're not talking your Al Sharptons or David Dukes here, either. We're talking about members of Congress, party operatives, alternative media bloviators, and think-tank nerds, to name just a few. Sure, only a small (but vocal) number of them publicly embrace the conspiracy theory, but many more secretly agree with them.

When Willie Sutton was asked why he robbed banks, he gave a pretty obvious answer to a patently dumb question by saying, "Because that's where the money is." Using the same logic, this book focuses on Washington, D.C., because that's where polarization first took root and where it has grown, like kudzu vines, into a mighty ugly but powerful species that has entwined itself into every corner of politics.

Washington is the base of operations for the purveyors of polarization who encourage and/or materially benefit from the confrontation it breeds. Although these activists are a small percentage of the population, their fierce partisanship does much more to define politics at the national level than their numbers suggest. Every effort to put these animals on the endangered-species list has failed miserably. They stick around like your mother-in-law after Thanksgiving, with no intention of leaving.

The polarizing community is not monolithic. It is made up of groups and individuals who contribute to polarization to maintain or enhance their particular interests. Their agendas may be different, but for a successful polarizing climate to be sustained, polarizers must practice their trade on a full-time basis. Polarizers generally fit into one of the following categories:

There are the ideologically driven polarizers, who are always agitating, but at least they are driven by firmly-held beliefs. Their issues are ones of conscience: abortion, gay rights, gun control, separation of church and state. These are the true believers, and you have to admire their profound commitment to ideology. These are ideologues who have no interest in, or belief in, finding a consensus position.

Then there are the polarizers, mostly lobbyists and trade associations, who are defending their self-interest by either defending the status quo, or tearing it down. They are corporations, business groups, and various moneyed special interests that polarize to protect, or enhance, profits for themselves or their membership. Few are driven by ideology. They contribute to both parties to cover themselves. They have no difficulty dancing with politicians like Tom DeLay one day and Nancy Pelosi the next. They follow the power.

There are polarizers who are wedded to one party or the other. Labor unions, trial attorneys, health care providers, and highly regulated industries such as energy fall into this group. These are the polarizers that put massive amounts of campaign money and resources behind one party, and rarely do they dance with the other. This crowd has the most to gain or lose in wave-type elections; they are committed to "base-enhancing" campaign strategies. They are also hyperpartisans willing to destroy the other side if necessary, which is why they are among the most dangerous and intimidating of polarizers.

There are party polarizers made up of party apparatchiks and political consultants whose mission is to dirty up the other side enough so their side can win elections. They have less interest in attracting votes to their candidates than in driving votes away from their opponents. This is the crowd most responsible for the death of civil political debate. Worse, these polarizers make a handsome living by destroying the other side, which encourages them to do whatever it takes to maintain their lifestyle.

Self-described intellectual policy polarizers, generally found in the hundreds of think tanks around Washington, are certain theirs is the right policy, and any counterpolicy is wrongheaded and stupid. This is the crowd that provides superpartisans with incendiary talking points and "factual" evidence to defend their usually extreme policy positions.

Finally, there are the "bottom feeders"—polarizers who make money by keeping politics inflamed in order to sell books, maintain readership, sustain ratings, fill speaking schedules, or sell tickets. (None of which are mutually exclusive.)

The membership of these various polarization categories consists of, but is not limited to, the following: individuals or organized groups; trade associations or single-issue groups; corporations and labor unions; grassroots organizations and members of the media; members of Congress and presidents; political operatives and political campaign committees. In fairness, many did not become polarizers for the sole purpose of fomenting polarization, but by their actions and rigidity of agendas, they became agents of polarization.

Who are the polarizers? The following qualify, as do hundreds of others in their respective categories: Among political operatives, Karl Rove on the right and James Carville on the left stand out. In broadcasting, Sean Hannity on the right and Al Franken on the left are leaders of the pack. In Congress, anti-immigrant congressman Tom Tancredo of Colorado on the right and antitrade congressman Dennis Kucinich of Ohio on the left. Among organizations, the NRA on the right and Handgun Control on the left. Among the bottom feeders are Ann Coulter on the right and Michael Moore on the left. Grassroots groups include MoveOn.org on the left and, on the right, Focus on the Family; presidents that stand out are Bill Clinton and George W. Bush; pundits include Paul Begala on the left and Pat Buchanan on the right.

If the primary goal of these activists is to demonize one another, what's the chance of finding unity that could actually be in the country's interest? This raises a more important question: Do political extremists in either party have any interest in unity? Or would common ground alter the status quo that favors their interests (and not necessarily the interest of the country)? Would it hurt their profits, ruin their fund-raising, cut into their political influence, and diminish their sacred power? The answer is painfully obvious. Polarizers could care less about unity. Indeed, finding common ground and consensus is their worst nightmare, especially for the bottom feeders.

But the polarizers haven't lost much sleep over the possibility that common ground could become a viable political option. As we moved into a new century, polarization maintained an iron grip on Washington politics. Friendships between members of opposing parties, which were once numerous and often led to solid legislative achievements, became increasingly rare (and politically dangerous). Invective on the floor of the House and Senate had replaced and debased political debate. Bipartisanship and consensus were increasingly unreachable as Democratic leaders in Congress pressured members to adhere to the party agenda, while Republican members feared retaliation if they opposed the White House.

Polarizers have become major players in the operation, fundraising, and message management of the Democratic and Republican parties. Mainstream politicians of both parties learned that any effort to exclude polarized party activists is nearly impossible; controlling them is completely impossible; ignoring them is suicidal. After all, these activists are the largest bloc of voters in party primaries, and in recent years have not hesitated to challenge incumbents in their own party who have strayed too far from the activist agenda.

Witness the primary victory over Senator Joe Lieberman of

Connecticut in 2006 by an anti–Iraq war candidate supported by Democratic activists. After a thirty-year career as a Democrat, which included being the party's vice-presidential candidate in 2000, Lieberman was denied his party's nomination to the Senate on a single issue; he supported the Iraq war. Certainly tenure should not guarantee a party nomination, but Lieberman had become a target for national Democratic activists who descended on Connecticut with volunteers and money, forcing him to compete against political forces never before involved in Connecticut politics.

Exit poll data from the 2004 election confirm that an uncomfortably large number of voters cast ballots for the "lesser of two evils" for Congress and president. In effect, these voters cast ballots against the opposition candidates rather than for the nominees of their party. Millions of votes were cast for George W. Bush, not because he was the first choice of voters, but because he wasn't John F. Kerry, and vice versa.

Rather than play the extremist game, many centrist voters choose not to vote. Although 127 million voters cast ballots in the 2004 presidential campaign, after the most heavily financed voter turnout effort in history, 80 million eligible voters still chose not to cast ballots. That is more than voted for either George Bush or John Kerry. These included eligible voters who had never voted, but it also included millions of registered voters who had voted in the past, but had left the voting population and turned their backs on politics. James Q. Wilson concludes his *Commentary* essay with this:

> Many Americans believe that unbridgeable political differences have prevented leaders from addressing the problems they were elected to address. As a result, distrust of government mounts, leading to an alienation from politics altogether . . . ordinary voters agree among themselves more than political elites agree with each other—and the elites are far more numerous than they once were.

What Wilson and many other political observers have found is that both political parties have focused less and less on appealing to centrist "swing" voters, and more and more on turning out their activist base to win elections. The base strategy requires that the candidates of the opposing party be transformed into servants of Satan. Karl Rove, the political grand dragon for George W. Bush, took the base-expanding game to new levels in the 2002 midterm election and in the reelection of the president in 2004.

Rove brought the same game plan to the 2006 midterm elections and, in the words of his boss, "took a thumping." In the process, 2006 produced the lowest recorded turnout in party primaries with only 15.7 percent of registered voters participating, according to the Committee for the Study of the American Electorate. In the general election, 40 percent of eligible voters cast ballots, up 1.5 percent from the previous midterm election in 2002. Although most of the disenchanted voters described by Wilson stayed home, some did return to the polls. These "new/old" voters had not suddenly gotten a case of civic-mindedness; instead they had become so frustrated they returned to the polls, not to help Democrats, but to punish incumbents.

We believe there is another way to bring these voters back to the polls, and with them the election of more moderates in both parties. The 2006 election returns clearly identified polarization as the second most potent force behind voter anger (Iraq was first) that propelled the "wave election." In a wave election, the party in control of Congress and/or the White House is rejected after a long period in power. In 2006, the Republicans were ousted after twelve years in the majority. Like the Democrats, who lost congressional majorities in 1994 after forty-two years in control, the Republicans were perceived to be holding on to power for power's sake, while ignoring the nation's needs.

When we began writing our "common ground" column for *USA Today,* in May 2005, the response from the political class, especially the activists, was underwhelming. But the response from readers was overwhelming. "Common Ground" was a direct assault on polarization, and readers responded. By 2006 politicians finally realized that the voters were growing impatient with polarization. As a result, the term *common ground* began appearing in political speeches, in congressional debates, and in the political press. For the first time in decades, politicians began to view polarization as a political liability.

The press, especially, had begun to focus on the "cannibalism" of politics and the dangers of a polarized political culture. Members of Congress, presidents, lobbyists, and even partisan think tanks joined in the criticism of polarization. What had once been viewed as overblown and mostly academic argument about the perils of polarization was now being taken seriously.

Surveys conducted over several years have found that Americans believe even the most partisan issues—from abortion to the Iraq war—can be resolved with an honest commitment by elected leaders in Washington to finding consensus. More important, voters are prepared to punish candidates whose extremist positions make that impossible.

The purveyors of polarization have witnessed periods of voter discontent before, but after the uproar subsides, nothing changes. They believe it's naive to think this deep well of public discontent can be organized into a political movement. The activists know that the only way to organize centrist (and often nonparticipating) voters is for candidates—most likely for the presidency—to carry the message. They're convinced that a message condemning polarization and emphasizing consensus is too difficult to sell.

Given the substantial influence polarizers exert in the nominating process, they are smugly confident that any candidate appealing to common ground would be crushed before he or she got out of the starting gate. They don't think the press will go beyond their current sanctimonious tirades against polarization because it makes good copy, and for media executives polarization makes for good profits. In essence, the polarizers' message is "Sounds good, won't happen."

Yes it can. That's not wishful thinking. We're two guys who spent a lot of years in the polarizing business, but on opposing sides. We helped write the game plan, and we have participated in everything from getting money out of true believers to appearing on television to help spread the contentious messages. In many cases, we wrote the message. We know the gig, and it's just about up.

We believe polarization's domination over politics is coming to an end. To help that process along, we intend to expose the individuals and groups who stoke the fires of polarization. We want to shine a light on the parasites who have a vested interest in the partisan war because it keeps them relevant and rich. We believe that the glory days of the braying radio hosts and mudslinging political consultants are numbered. So, too, the propagandists, who hide out in "think tanks" underwritten by wealthy extremists who get a tax deduction for demeaning the political process.

We recognize that polarizers will always be around politics, but like most bullies, polarizers aren't nearly as tough as their reputation would have you believe. Polarization will remain a factor in national politics, but no longer the dominant factor it has been for the last twenty years. We believe polarization, within the next two election cycles, will be eclipsed by a return to bipartisanship and consensus. Common ground politics will emerge as the preferred territory where smart politics is played, and polarization relegated to the fringe of national politics, where it belongs.

Elections have a way of focusing politicians and the chattering political elites. The roots of the 2006 voter revolt have taken hold and will grow in importance in 2008. The evidence in the early months of 2007 points to a serious (and hopefully lasting) realization among politicians that the public is sick of polarization and polarizers. In 2008, one or two of the presidential candidates will run against the politics of polarization, and a return to bipartisanship. Senator Barack Obama has already embraced the call for common ground (and an end to polarization) in his campaign for president, and others, are attempting to incorporate similar themes in their messages.

The fact that candidates see the need to confront polarization at all is recognition of the voters' negative view of polarization. Ironically, that was part of the Karl Rove strategy in 2000 when George W. Bush decried partisanship and called for "a new tone in Washington." Rove's strategy was not new. Because the public likes compromise over confrontation, most candidates call for a tone change in Washington. But after an election, the public withdraws, and a president is faced with a city full of polarizers. So a change in tone becomes a standard slogan on the campaign trail, but it is not recognized as an issue that attracts a dedicated pool of voters. As a result, it is not seen as a message that carries with it a mandate for change after the election. Until the 2006 election, that was a reasonable analysis.

But what was little more than a slogan in 2000 may well become a necessity in 2008. The politicians who understand the voters' current state of mind will campaign on the simple notion that consensus and common ground will get government moving again; they will campaign on big new ideas to address our nation's neglected needs. Many of these ideas already exist; ideas that will be explored in this book. They have been developed by people whose only agenda is seeking solutions to the daunting challenges facing America. We thank them all for allowing us to present their ideas in *Common Ground*.

This book also looks back at times in America's past when bipartisanship made for good politics. We'll look at some former polarizing politicians who, despite some short-term success, failed in the face of a fed-up electorate, and a few profiles in courage who called their bluff. We'll revisit a time when civility and cross-aisle friendships succeeded in producing consensus. This occurred not through contentious floor debate but sometimes over dinner.

Some of the most immediate and intimate examples of successful consensus politics have come from the dinner tables and drawing rooms presided over by a group of Washington socialites. Their parties provided the settings at which politicians could make deals, settle feuds, and find common ground on issues that had divided them. We will bring you recollections from several of them.

Most important, this book offers a campaign plan, built around a set of creative ideas, to get the nation moving again. *It is a plan that makes polarization the issue and common ground the solution.* We believe the time is right *to challenge polarization and for common ground to become the next dominant strategic force in national politics.*

We believe that common ground as a central campaign message can attract some of the millions of voters who have stopped voting. We intend to put polarization on trial. We will introduce an abundance of evidence detailing the damage polarization has inflicted on politics, and why this insidious culture continues to operate to the benefit of the few and to the detriment of the many.

John F. Kennedy set a higher tone, which might be heard again if enough people demand it: "Let us not seek the Republican answer, or the Democratic answer, but the right answer. Let us not seek to fix the blame for the past. Let us accept our own responsibility for the future."

PREFACE

Who We Are

"WHY I AM A LIBERAL"

by Bob Beckel

> *A Liberal is a man or a woman or a child who looks for-*
> *ward to a better day, a more tranquil night and a bright, infinite*
> *future.*
>
> —Leonard Bernstein

I'M PROUD TO BE A LIBERAL. I ALWAYS HAVE BEEN. FOR MANY YEARS as a guest host for CNN's *Crossfire,* and then for three years as host of *Crossfire Sunday,* I ended each show with this sign-off: "From the left, proud to be a liberal, I'm Bob Beckel, good night for *Crossfire.*" (My cohost on Sundays was Lynne Cheney, whom I liked very much, but I can't remember for the life of me what her sign-off was.) However, I don't presume to speak for all liberals. Liberals represent a broad spectrum of the progressive community that can't be distilled into a single definition, despite the best efforts of the right to do so. That said, I believe I can speak for liberals in response to several misrepresentations that have been consistently advanced (and with some success) by doctrinaire conservatives.

Liberals are patriotic Americans. As my dad, who fought in North Africa and Europe in World War II, used to say, "The blood shed in the war against fascism was not the blood of Democrats or Republicans, it was American blood." My dad is gone now, but I remember those words every time I hear some right-wing radio hosts who have never served a day in uniform, say that liberals want to "wave the white flag of surrender."

Liberals want every American to have an equal chance to achieve the American Dream. That was the clear goal of the Founders when they wrote that all people have a right to life, liberty, and the pursuit of happiness. Like the Founders, liberals believe that equality and democracy are a journey, not a statement; that our democratic institutions must continually promote these ideals if every American is to receive the rewards set forth in the Constitution.

I'm a liberal because I believe in a government of the people, by the people, and for the people—*all* the people, not just some. I believe in the American Dream: a promise that every American has an equal opportunity to achieve his or her greatest potential. Along with protecting our nation's security, that promise must be a priority of the government.

Unlike my friend Cal, I do not believe all people in America have equal opportunities. You can't persuade me that a brown kid born to a poor single mother in the South Bronx has the same opportunity as a white kid born to a wealthy family in Scarsdale. I believe the government, especially the federal government, has a responsibility to ensure that both kids, to the fullest extent possible, have an equal chance to achieve success in America.

To have that equal chance, every child under eighteen is entitled to decent medical care (including prenatal care), housing, clothing, education (including preschool and Head Start), and to grow up, to the greatest extent possible, in a safe environment. As a liberal, I believe unequivocally that if a child's parents are not capable of providing for these basic needs, then the government needs to provide for them. Who should pay for this? You and me and any other American who was fortunate enough to have his or her basic needs met and to have succeeded financially in our society.

Sure, I'd like to believe that a level playing field for success can be provided without government intervention, but overwhelming evidence shows that this will not happen without the influence of a strong central government. My family was privileged to play a small part in the great struggle for civil rights in education, voting, and housing in the 1960s. Looking back, I cannot imagine that progress in these areas could have happened without government action.

Would it have been possible over a period of time for these problems to self-correct? Perhaps, but it would have taken several generations for citizens, particularly in the South, to determine that segregation was wrong, and perhaps several more for institutional change to occur.

In fact, it took the federal courts and strong actions by the executive and legislative branches of the government to mandate that institutional change come sooner than later. Despite the very real progress this intervention created, racism is alive and well in America today. Therefore, we need more, not less, enforcement of federal civil rights laws.

I'm a liberal because I believe in a progressive tax system, wherein higher incomes are taxed at a higher rate than middle and lower incomes. That doesn't mean I am for bashing the wealthy. I don't dislike wealthy people, nor do I envy them. I believe most liberals feel that way. In fact, there are lots of wealthy liberals in America today. The difference in perspectives between liberals and conservatives is that wealthy liberals don't resent a progressive tax system. Most wealthy conservatives do. Liberals take to heart the biblical message "To whom much is given, much is expected."

I grew up in a family with very little income. My father left home when I was fifteen, leaving my family with no breadwinner. My mother, brother, sister, and I were fortunate to find enough work to keep our family together. For most of my adult years, I have been blessed with a sizable income and, as a consequence, pay lots of taxes. But I don't mind paying high taxes if they are used for the right reasons: helping to level the success playing field; assisting the poor and the elderly; and, yes, funding a strong national defense.

It does bother me when my tax dollars go for *wasteful* spending on defense ($200 hammers and no-bid contracts) or for pork-barrel projects. Earmarked contracts and spending projects are a disgrace. The only reason for pork is to help a member of Congress get reelected. Why should I be forced to support an incumbent whom I might not even be willing to vote for? Incumbent members of Congress already have taxpayer-funded advantages over any challenger. On this subject, most conservatives and liberals agree.

Most liberals believe in free trade. We recognize that the economy is now global. However, many, like me, are also "jobs liberals." We believe that good-paying jobs should be kept in this country, not shipped abroad, as so many have been under so-called free-trade agreements. "American-made" means made by American labor. Given an equal opportunity to compete, I believe the performance of American labor can keep the better-paying jobs available in this country, where they belong—in this country.

American workers should not be forced to compete with exploited foreign workers. The only thing cheap about so-called cheap foreign labor markets are the cheapskates running the companies that underpay and often abuse workers. *Fair* trade agreements should be fair for workers and companies alike. Our trading partners should be required to provide the comparable wages and safe working environments that are (or at least used to be) enjoyed by American workers.

Regardless of worker conditions, businesses that ship American jobs abroad to foreign labor markets should pay higher taxes or be subjected to duties on the imports shipped back to the United States for resale.

I know conservatives hear this and think "union sympathizer." Well, you're right; I do favor strong labor unions and have been a union member for twenty years. Conservatives have, over the years, done a good job of bashing and demeaning labor unions. Most of the bashing has not been honest. Americans need to remember that it was the union movement that brought them the five-day workweek, paid vacation, child labor laws, workplace safety rules, the minimum wage, unemployment insurance, and much more.

The reason the union movement had to fight, in many cases literally, for workers' rights and benefits is that many businesses adamantly refused to provide them. Unfortunately, the union movement is currently neither as large nor as powerful as it once was. That's why, as a liberal, I believe the federal government must ensure that these hard-won employee rights remain just that—rights, not merely privileges that can be taken away. Just as we are admonished to defend freedom around the world, we must remember that freedom in America includes labor rights.

As I said previously, I support a strong national defense policy. I initially supported the war in Iraq because I believed the Bush administration's case for the war. We were told there were weapons of mass destruction in Iraq, that Iraq was developing a nuclear weapons program, that Iraq had been involved in the 9/11 attacks. None of these turned out to be true. Some people in our government lied to Congress and to the public, and those who misled us need to be punished. Liberals believe in accountability, a word often used against us by the right. Apparently, to most conservatives, accountability does not extend to the Bush administration.

In hindsight, it is clear the decision to go to war was based on faulty (or altered) intelligence. Liberals are not opposed to going to war, but it should be as a last resort, only after all diplomatic means are exhausted and a clear case is made that any war we fight is to protect our national security interests. As a liberal, I support the war against terrorism, and believe that expelling the Taliban from Afghanistan was necessary to protect our national interests.

The war in Iraq is not a war on terror; it is a civil war. We have no reason to be involved in this war. Our military, despite pathetic civilian leadership, freed Iraq from a brutal dictator and helped the Iraqis create a constitution and elect a democratic government. We have done our part; now it is Iraq's business. Let me be clear on where I and most liberals stand on the Iraq war: if, by the time you read this, the United States still has combat forces actively fighting in Iraq, they should be withdrawn as quickly and as safely as possible. For America, this war must end now so we can get back to the real war on terror.

As a liberal, I believe gay men and women should have the same rights and standing as any other Americans. I believe in reasonable federal environmental regulations. However, those regulations should not be so restrictive that they cost people their jobs, unless a very strong case can be made that irreparable damage will be done to the environment. I believe that we need immigration reform that provides a route to citizenship to those illegal immigrants already in the United States, greater protection of our borders to stop further illegal immigration, and severe sanctions against those businesses that knowingly employ illegal immigrants.

Here are a few outside-the-box beliefs I have as a liberal, which are not universally accepted in the liberal community:

- I believe in nuclear power as an alternative source of energy.
- I believe that a minute of silence should be made available at the beginning of each public school day so that if some or all students choose to use that minute to pray, they be allowed to do so.
- I believe that the federal Department of Education budget should be drastically reduced, with the savings going directly to increase teacher salaries.
- As a former hunter, I believe the government should not restrict guns used for recreational shooting or hunting. However, I support mandatory gun locks on all guns, with criminal penalties for failure to comply.

These may come as a surprise to some conservatives. They shouldn't. Many liberals would disagree with these positions. That makes my point. All liberals are not alike, despite the conservative right's nonstop campaign to convince Americans otherwise.

"WHY I AM A CONSERVATIVE"
by Cal Thomas

What is a conservative? Is it not the adherence to the old and tried against the new and untried?

—Abraham Lincoln

THERE WAS A TIME IN AMERICA—WITHIN THE MEMORY OF SOME— when we encouraged the things we wanted more of and discouraged those things we wanted less of. Somehow, that has been reversed with disastrous results. We now get more of what we want less of, and less of what we want more of. And yet, in too many cases, we won't stop doing the things that produce what we want less of. Does this make sense?

When I was growing up, I never envied the rich, but I did want to know how they became rich so I could do what they did. Today, we are told that if you are rich, or have enough money to care for yourself, you are evil and "owe" government much of the money you've earned so it can be distributed (often badly) to people who haven't earned it. This attitude has created an "entitlement" mentality that serves neither the nation nor those on the receiving end of someone else's money. It also contributes to a permanent underclass because there is little incentive to climb out of poverty when you are getting a check that subsidizes you "in poverty."

I'm a conservative because I believe in principles that work: low taxes, small government (yes, it once existed); self-control and character as primary virtues that must be taught and cannot be caught; hard work as the best ticket to success so you don't rely on government or others to take care of you; a good education that really educates and not the propaganda that is so often taught in too many government schools (this is why I favor school choice, which would especially liberate the poor from this failed monopoly, giving them the chance to escape poverty); strong marriages and responsible mothers and fathers to rear a new generation properly; love of country; love of God; a responsibility and privilege to share freedom (when possible) with others who do not have it because of totalitarian dictators who won't allow it; protecting human life, born and unborn.

These virtues and beliefs were once so prevalent in America that they hardly needed saying. Today, many of these things are in short supply, or they no longer exist, because if someone teaches them, he or she might face the high priests of political correctness who label any appeal to objective truth as a threat to the "inclusive" society they are trying to build. It is inclusive for them, but excludes those who do not accept their doctrines.

I'm a conservative precisely because I want to *conserve* those things that have a track record of working. We know what they are because generations before us practiced them in greater numbers. We have abandoned so many of them that our society now suffers from multiple dysfunctions, and yet the left wants to push on in error rather than return to the root principles that made us great and sustained us through world wars and the Great Depression.

I once thought that politics held the answer—or at least part of the answer—to "binding up the nation's wounds," to use Lincoln's profound phrase. That's why in August 1980, shortly before Ronald Reagan was elected president, I took the only nonjournalism job I've ever held. I went to work as vice president of the Moral Majority, where I stayed until 1985 before leaving to write my syndicated newspaper column.

Among the problems with the Moral Majority and other religious-political movements was—and is—that while they might identify the symptoms of cultural contamination, their proposed solution, politics, falls far short of being a successful treatment. In addition, setting oneself up as more "moral" than people who don't agree with you politically may be great for fund-raising, but it can never contribute to common ground and a commitment to making the grand American experiment work for as many people as possible. It also closely resembles the first and worst sin: Pride.

Yes, I'm a conservative, but I am under no illusions that government—even one dominated by conservatives—will be able to fix the individual and collective problems we face. That's because the source of our problems doesn't begin or end in Washington. It is to be found in our lower nature. If electing conservatives were enough, twelve years of Republican dominance of the Congress would have turned the country around. But as the nation witnessed, many of these "conservatives" became as corrupt as the liberal Democrats they replaced.

A liberal thinks improvements can be made by tinkering with the current system and putting liberals in control. A conservative wants to replace the current system with constitutional government, less federal control and more self-control, less blame and more shame for wrong behavior, less dependency on government and more individual opportunity.

My purpose in joining with my liberal friend Bob Beckel is not to water down what I believe or ask him to dilute his beliefs. Rather, we both look to an objective of far greater importance than which side wins the next election, as important as that may be. At a time when the United States is faced with serious and threatening forces from without and within, we can't afford the "luxury" (if that's what it is) of tearing out one another's hearts in defense of political ideologies. There is too much at stake. Someone has to take the lead by saying "enough" to the old formula of name-calling, to the "take-no-prisoners" mentality.

We want to point to a better way. A way that does not deny that politics is a contact sport, but doesn't require that the combatants feel their opponents are un-American or love country less, a way that used to let us move the ball forward, despite our differences.

It cannot be denied that the "other side" does occasionally come up with some good ideas. Failure to acknowledge that and to benefit from this exchange of ideas makes us all worse off. Moreover, when we call one another names, impugn others' patriotism, and dismiss any ideas but those coming from our own side as idiotic and unpatriotic, we lose what makes us uniquely American.

Compromise is not an ugly word if it promotes the general welfare. The problem is that too many are intent on their own welfare, and that can never lead to common ground, which we believe promotes the best interests of the country and most of its people.

Some might not consider this a "conservative" position, but it is one that can make America stronger. As the sign on Ronald Reagan's desk said, "It's amazing what you can accomplish if you don't care who gets the credit." Not many would challenge Reagan's conservative credentials.

PART I

Where We Are

1

THE PEOPLE VS. THE POLARIZATION OF AMERICAN POLITICS

Politics—I don't know why, but they seem to have a tendency to separate us, to keep us from one another, while nature is always and ever making efforts to bring us together.

—Sean O'Casey

VOTERS WILL TOLERATE POLARIZATION AND EXTREME PARTISANship to a point, especially if it doesn't affect them directly. But by 2006, polarization was paralyzing government. It came at a time when the country was deeply divided over the war in Iraq, and facing a myriad of problems at home. After years of gridlock and extreme partisanship, the public had had enough; polarization ceased to be an insider's game, and voters rebelled in a rare "wave" election.

Wave elections are ones in which the outcome significantly alters the political balance of power. By the fall of 2006, politicians (particularly incumbents) finally caught up with the extent of the voters' anger. Republican incumbents, realizing that their party's strategy of maximizing the base, which had worked in 2002 and 2004, would not work in 2006, tried to persuade voters that they were not partisan extremists. Partisans, yes; extremists, no.

Challengers in congressional races across the country attacked incumbents as members of a "do-nothing" Congress, and they put the blame squarely on polarization. Not to be outdone, even some incumbents who had engaged in the most outrageous polarizing preached the wisdom of "seeking common ground solutions." To enhance this message, candidates reached out to the two most exciting and sought-after politicians in the country at the time, Senators John McCain (R-AZ) and Barack Obama (D-IL). Neither was on the ballot, but both made the evils of polarization a central ingredient of their message. Both are running for president in 2008, and there is no sign that their message will change.

The reelection of Connecticut senator Joe Lieberman in 2006 as an independent provided one of the first campaign tests specifically aimed at polarization . . . and polarization lost. Paradoxically, polarization had forced Lieberman to run as an independent because the Democratic Party denied him the party nomination. For partisans, it wasn't enough that Lieberman had been loyal to their Democratic Party and most of its issues for three decades, or that he had been the party's vice-presidential nominee in 2000. That he differed with them on one issue—Iraq—was enough for the polarizers to dump him.

(We are not suggesting that tenure entitled Lieberman to the nomination, or that the war in Iraq, especially among Democrats, was not a sufficient reason for a primary challenge. But, as we shall see, it was the polarizing tactics in the primary that were destructive and all too commonplace in today's politics.)

Lieberman got his revenge by making party extremists an issue. He won the general election with support from Democrats, independents, and—amazingly—a majority of Republicans. Thirty percent of the antiwar voters, according to Lieberman, voted for him. For these voters, polarizing tactics that attempted to drive a decent man from office were as immoral as the war in Iraq. For several years, many mainstream Republicans had questioned if their party was too associated with religious fundamentalists. In the aftermath of the Lieberman primary, many Democratic Party leaders were raising the same questions about the party's association with a resurgent, cyber-driven left.

Next door in Rhode Island, incumbent Lincoln Chafee, the Senate's most liberal Republican, was challenged by conservative activists who wanted to deny him renomination. The Republican Party leadership in the state supported Chafee but couldn't stop the rebellion on the right, and a primary challenger emerged. Chafee survived the primary, but only after Karl Rove, who might claim a patent on polarization, engaged in a highly publicized effort to save him. Chafee was too liberal for Rove and company, but his primary opponent was too conservative for Rhode Island. In a close race for control of the Senate, saving Chafee was necessary, even critical.

In the general election, Chafee tried to reestablish his independence: "I believe that neither Republicans nor Democrats are always right. I angered Republicans when I voted against the war in Iraq, and Democrats when I voted for legal reform." But the senator's association with the country's most famous polarizer became a major factor in his inability to separate himself from an immensely unpopular president. He lost by a wide margin.

Chafee's message of independence and antipartisanship (echoed by several other incumbent Republicans) could be interpreted as a survival strategy in a bad year for Republican candidates. Such reasoning does not explain why a similar message was adopted by many Democrats, including Chafee's opponent, Sheldon Whitehead, who ran TV ads calling for bipartisanship, and this in a heavily Democratic state where such a message wasn't necessary.

The most telling evidence that polarization may be eroding comes by way of former polarizers who are distancing themselves from the practice. Most political observers agree that Newt Gingrich, former Speaker and architect of the Republican takeover of Congress in 1994, was a skillful advocate and practitioner of polarization. In fact, some, particularly Democrats, believe Gingrich was the founder of the polarization movement.

When we spoke to Gingrich in the summer of 2006, he freely admitted that polarization had been an important component in the Republicans' 1994 victory. More to the point, Gingrich agreed that it was a declining force in politics. Never one to be slow in recognizing the changing political winds, he immediately had ideas about how to end polarization. That's remarkable, considering that before our meeting, he said he hadn't given the topic much thought!

A conversation with the former Republican Speaker is an eclectic tour de force. Love him or hate him, few come away without a sense of awe. That is both a compliment to the man's intellectual reach and a criticism of the confidence and audacity with which his historical revisionism fits so tightly with his Newtonian view of present-day events. Gingrich is a self-taught historian and the author of several historical novels, which may explain his uncanny ability to convince the listener that what he thought he knew about history was simply wrong.

Our first question concerned Gingrich's role in polarization, and his response was predictably defensive:

> If you can skip past Watergate, which some Republicans thought was a sign of [Democrat] bitterness, and get past the destruction of the secretary of labor [Ray Donovan] in the Reagan administration, or get by the destruction of Jimmy Carter's budget director [Bert Lance], which some people thought was a sign of bitterness, though it was by liberals, and skip past the way Iran-Contra was handled and forget the bitterness over Nicaragua, I think it's very easy to think it started with me.

In other words, in order to lay blame at Gingrich's feet, you would have to ignore the evolutionary history of the events he says were at the root of polarization in Washington. Amazing and utterly convincing, until you look closely at the events he cites. Gingrich acknowledges that liberals forced Bert Lance out as director of the Carter Office of Management and Budget; by definition an internal battle, not polarization. He suggests that the Watergate investigation was the result of Democratic "bitterness," not indiscriminate lawbreaking by Nixon. He points to Democrats in the destruction of Ray Donovan, as if it was a partisan lynching of the former secretary of labor, when in fact, Donovan was prosecuted by the Reagan Justice Department.

On Iran-Contra, Gingrich is right about Republican bitterness. What he failed to mention was that he organized the campaign to convince the press and public that Iran-Contra was Democratic revenge over Nicaragua, and not the lawbreaking and subterfuge that originated in the Reagan White House.

After his attempt at self-absolution, Gingrich began to lay out the case against polarization. What followed was classic Gingrich. He proceeded to describe a conference at the respected conservative think tank American Enterprise Institute, where he and former Democratic Speaker Tom Foley were the featured guests. The topic was how Congress had changed over the last two decades. Newt waxed poetic, painting a picture of two former leaders and statesmen reminiscing about a bygone era when, as Speaker, they attempted to avoid polarization.

Who knew? In fact, Gingrich and Foley were über partisans whose battles (including Gingrich's successful effort to recruit a candidate and fund a campaign that defeated Foley in 1994) were at the forefront of the age of polarization. Nevertheless, Gingrich insists that he had resorted to polarizing tactics only because the Democrats forced him to:

> The Democrats toward the end of their reign as they lost popular support were tougher and tougher about using procedures. The two break points in the Congress before me in terms of the rise of Republicans were Representative Tony Coelho's [D-CA] decision to steal the seat in Indiana [he is referring to the 8th Congressional District in Indiana that ended in a virtual tie between the Democratic and Republican candidates in 1984. The election eventually ended up in the House, where the Democrats proceeded to seat the Democrat despite Indiana's secretary of state certifying that the Republican had won], because it led to bitterness on the Republican side that drove people to me; and the second was the day that Jim Wright had two legislative days on the same day, because that drove people like [then congressman] Dick Cheney nuts. It stripped [Republican leader] Bob Michael of the ability to be reasonable because his base was going crazy. There was a procedure that said you couldn't bring something up without passing a two-thirds vote or something unless you laid it over to the next day. So in the middle of the day they voted to adjourn, rose, and came back in. They were driving people to me. Part of what the legislative process has to involve is a minimum level of mutual respect. You can function with each other even when

you're angry and even when you disagree. When I conclude that you will always win because you cheat, then I have to go to a similar level of intensity to offset that behavior. And that was what was happening all during the eighties and nineties.

Gingrich's reasoning seems to be that since the Democrats did it first, he was forced to do it, too. He is certainly correct about the Democrats' abuses; the events he describes are accurate, and in both instances the Democrats used their majority status to abuse the minority Republicans. What Gingrich fails to point out is that he would use these displays of Democratic power politics as evidence of the "arrogance of power" theme that was central to his successful campaign to drive the Democrats from power. Gingrich was brilliant when it came to drawing the Democrats into traps that played to his message. We will leave it to historians to decide if he was the trapper or the trapped.

In any case, Gingrich, ever the visionary, recognizes the importance of disassociating himself from polarization. Three months after we met, Gingrich announced the creation of a new committee, American Solutions for Winning the Future, and pledged to raise millions of dollars to find bipartisan solutions to the nation's problems. To his credit, he continues to be one of the few political figures who explores (and in many cases funds) new policy options, even if those policies run counter to his party's orthodoxy.

Gingrich is also quick to dismiss the so-called get-out-the-base strategy, a principal campaign tactic of polarization:

> I don't buy this "base" mobilizing baloney, which I think is a guaranteed way to minimize long-term survival. It embitters the country and breaks the country apart and creates a profoundly mistaken model. It may work for one or two elections, but the cost you build up doing that bites you for a generation.

What Gingrich is describing is the primary culprit behind the growth of polarization—the practice of both parties to win elections by appealing to their partisan base. In the short term, the base strategy *has* won some elections, but the process has produced elected officials who come to office as extreme partisans beholden to those who are exacerbating the culture of polarization.

Over the two decades that polarization has dominated Washington politics, Republican polarizers have played the game far better than their Democratic counterparts. They have invested far more than Democrats in cutting-edge technologies to identify and turn out their voters (a technological advantage the Democrats had enjoyed for years prior to 1990). As a result, in elections prior to 2006, conservatives have outnumbered liberals at the polls.

Most political experts agree that the overwhelming majority of voters are moderate, but for several years had tilted slightly toward the conservative side. That changed in the 2006 elections, but not because the electorate had made an ideological shift. Most successful Democratic challengers were running against incumbent Republicans in conservative areas. They recognized that the liberal tag would hurt them, and chose to run on very moderate, sometimes conservative, platforms. They pushed Republican incumbents much further to the right on the ideological scale, and in the process won the moderate vote.

The 2006 election increased the number of moderate Democrats in both the House and Senate for the first time since the 1992 elections. The 1994 Republican takeover decimated the ranks of moderate and conservative Democrats, leaving a high percentage of liberals among the remaining Democrats in both houses. Moderate Democrats elected in 2006 are already beginning to move congressional Democrats toward the center. That may be frustrating to their more liberal colleagues (particularity among liberal polarizers), but to the moderates, winning reelection is far more important than supporting liberal positions that would be used against them in 2008.

Polarization may also have taken a hit among Republicans. Many of those reelected in 2006 won by small majorities, and those who were defeated were moderates, mostly from the Northeast and Midwest. The initial analysis of the moderate GOP losses concluded that the Republican caucus would move further to the right. But many of the Republicans who survived, no matter how conservative, seem to be less inclined (in 2007 at least) to pursue extreme ideological agendas. They are trying to seek at least some consensus with the majority Democrats in order to show voters back home that they got the message.

Despite the apparent interest in both parties in achieving consensus on some issues, the deep divisions over the war in Iraq have made efforts at bipartisanship difficult. But on some issues, such as raising the minimum wage, Republicans, who had blocked an increase since 1994, agreed to it in 2007. A minimum-wage increase may seem a small bipartisan step, but in the era of polarization, it is an important one.

How all of this will sit with their respective "bases" is yet to be seen, but if the reactions from groups like Focus on the Family on the right and MoveOn.org on the left to attempts by the new Congress to find consensus is any indication, they will not be pleased. Both groups, among the most powerful forces in their respective parties, promote polarization, believe in it, and need it to continue to raise money to stay in business. We do not expect them to go quietly into the night.

All this indicates at least a crack in the dominance of polarization. One thing that can be counted on in politics is the attention lawmakers give to the results of the previous election. Some will see 2006 as an aberration caused by Iraq and the last-minute Foley page scandal (Foley was a Republican congressman from Florida who got caught exchanging sexually suggestive e-mails and phone calls with former House pages). Some will see it as a referendum on an unpopular president. Most, we hope, will read the election results as the beginning of the revolt by the "radical middle," in a backlash against the "radical right" and "radical left."

Despite the 2006 election results, polarization still dominates national politics. There are simply too many people with vested interests in continuing the climate of polarization. Polarization was the model presented for many years on CNN's *Crossfire*. It was an appropriate name for a show. The problem with cross fire is that people in the middle tend to get shot.

Polarization has always been a factor in politics and always will be, but it has historically been active at the fringes of American politics. Bipartisanship and consensus had been the dominant forces in politics and powerful counterforces to polarization. That changed over the last three decades as polarization came to dominate politics while bipartisanship became increasingly marginalized.

It is important to understand how, as a nation, we got into such a polarized state, and how politics operated before the era of polarization. The time has come to confront polarization, but it is an old rule in politics that in order to to defeat the opponent it is vital to understand where he came from, what strengths brought him to power, and which of his weaknesses can be exploited. Let's start there.

2

THE POLARIZATION OF
AMERICAN POLITICS

Don't vote. It only encourages them.

—Author unknown

AT 7:46 A.M. ON TUESDAY, OCTOBER 17, 2006, THE POPULATION OF the United States reached 300 million, of which approximately 210 million were eligible to vote, according to the U.S. Census Bureau. According to Princeton sociologist Paul DiMaggio, 30 percent of eligible voters identify themselves as "strong Republicans" or "strong Democrats." This means roughly 65 million eligible voters are strong partisans. This minority is at the core of polarization. They are the fierce partisans on the left and right who dominate and define American politics, while the rest of America's eligible voters are at best marginally engaged in politics.

How does a minority of voters, however dedicated, dominate a country of 300 million? First, they vote in much larger percentages than the moderate, less-partisan majority of voters, and many (but far from all) have a deep and emotional attachment to their agendas. They are politically active, and as a result control the management, organization, and funding of the political process.

Strong partisans have vastly more influence than their numbers indicate. In the 2006 midterm election, approximately 80 million Americans, or about 40 percent of eligible voters, cast ballots. If only 75 percent of strong partisans turned out in 2006 (and given their history of consistently high turnout, that is a very conservative number), they would, using DiMaggio's 30 percent figure, account for 45 million voters. That would mean over half of the total votes in 2006 were cast by strong partisans representing less than one-third of all eligible voters.

In contested party primaries (usually for open House or Senate seats), strong partisans represent an even higher percentage of the total vote. Nominees chosen by these highly engaged partisans tend to be very conservative Republicans or very liberal Democrats. According to the nonpartisan Committee for the Study of the American Electorate, only 15.7 percent of eligible voters went to the polls in the 2006 primary elections. That represented the lowest turnout in primaries among eligible voters ever recorded. This pattern of low voter turnout in primaries has been the rule rather than the exception for several decades. It should come as no surprise, therefore, that a large percentage of new members of Congress, elected in the last two decades of polarization, are extreme partisans.

In 2006, despite the low turnout, Democratic nominees proved an exception to the rule. House and Senate Campaign Committees, led by Congressman Rahm Emanuel (D-IL) and Senator Chuck Schumer (D-NY), both liberal but pragmatic politicians, intervened in primaries to support the candidate with the best chance of winning the general election. Congressional campaign committees have historically been reluctant to interfere in primaries, but in 2006 Emanuel and Schumer recruited and funded moderate Democrats, and pressured potential liberal candidates to stay out of primaries. Some liberals refused to back down, and forced a primary anyway. In every case, candidates supported by the congressional campaign committees defeated them.

It helped that the districts and states where Emanuel and Schumer recruited candidates tended to be more conservative, with a smaller Democratic activist base. But the fact that both played hardball with the left was another blow to polarization. The irony is that both Emanuel and Schumer have contributed to polarization in numerous legislative battles in Congress. Both may return to polarizing, but they now have responsibility for newly elected Democrats who ran against polarization. It's unlikely either man will push polarizing issues on their own recruits, knowing that to do so may well cost the new members reelection.

COMMON GROUND POINT TO REMEMBER: *Extreme ideologues in both parties are partisans. Partisans are polarized. These same partisans pick the party nominees from whom "the rest of us" must choose. The vast majority of eligible voters are moderates who lean toward one of the two major parties. The majority of voters are not polarized, but their choices are.*

Robert Samuelson, economist and longtime student of politics, adds:

The result is a growing disconnect between politics—and political commentary—and ordinary life. Politics is increasingly a world unto itself, inhabited by people convinced of their own moral superiority: conspicuously, the religious right among Republicans, and upscale liberal elites among Democrats. Their agendas are hard to enact because they're minority agendas. So politicians instinctively focus on delivering psychic benefits. Each side strives to make its political "base" feel good about itself. People should be confirmed in their moral superiority . . . polarization is really between these politicians and the rest of us.

The polarization crowd goes by many names: extreme partisans, strong Republicans or strong Democrats, political activists, extremists, left, right. We call them, collectively, polarizers. Their mission is to divide the American people along political and cultural lines. Polarizers have intimidated and coerced the press, moderate politicians, and political commentators into believing that polarization is omnipotent. They have done a good job, until recently, in selling their case. But what they are selling is snake oil.

To succeed in their mission, polarizers need to destroy their opponent's agenda. The first step to that end, is to attempt to destroy their opponents. Snake oil notwithstanding, a whole lot of people have bought in. The campaign to sell polarization can be heard in the slogans and certain "revealed truths" that are now taken for granted by the political establishment: "Americans are polarized"; "America is a 50/50 country"; "we are divided politically between blue states and red states"; "Americans are engaged in a great culture war." By repeating these mantras, the establishment continues to perpetuate the conventional wisdom that polarization is an intimidating, unstoppable force.

Intimidating it may be. Unstoppable it is not.

True Believers Versus Secular Polarizers

A certain degree of polarization is to be expected in a democracy. Historically, polarization has been the necessary ingredient for the great ideological battles that have defined America. Our country and our democracy were born out of polarization between the colonies and Great Britain over taxation and home rule. It was polarization between North and South over slavery that led to the Civil War. The polarizing climate surrounding the Scopes trial and the teaching of evolution in the public schools was the preeminent event in the debate over the separation of church and state. All were driven by firmly held convictions by the opposing parties.

But today's polarization has become more than the product of opposing ideologies. For many—let's call them secular polarizers (moneyed interests, party operatives, bottom feeders, etc.)—it has become an artificially stimulated environment for the sole purpose of retaining political power, raising money, or making more money. It is the foundation of a rigged system that benefits a few at the expense of the many. While it may be true that some polarizers remain driven by deeply held ideological principles, they are the minority within a minority.

These ideologues may be the real true believers, but they have chosen to share their bed with secular polarizers. Secular polarizers claim fidelity to the ideologues' agenda, but secretly want to prolong the partisan war, either to maintain the status quo or to shift the power balance in their favor. Recently the marriage is showing signs of strain, as the true believers realize what their bedmate's agenda is, or rather what it is not.

The former president of the Christian Coalition, Ralph Reed, is a good example. After resigning from the organization, Reed set up a political consulting firm. One of his clients was Jack Abramoff, who was then representing the Mississippi Choctaws, a Native American tribe that wanted the government to deny a gambling license to a tribe (and potential competitor) in Texas. Reed was hired to organize Christian activists in Texas to oppose the license. What these good people never knew was that their efforts would not stop gambling, which they opposed, but instead be directed at protecting the gaming profits of the Choctaws.

By promoting polarizing agendas, secular polarizers such as Reed help keep the partisan base motivated for the sole purpose of winning elections or, in Reed's case, to make money. To keep them motivated, secular polarizers oppose any efforts at compromise. To compromise means to lose energy and financial resources provided by true believers. The financial resources keep the polarizers in power, while the energy ensures a large turnout of believers at the polls.

The polarization environment creates conflict, and conflict makes for prodigious amounts of press. The political media, which has its well-studied sets of biases, thrives on polarization. So, too, do the bottom feeders who promote conflict for profit and fame. These are the new kids on the block. They are hucksters and shakedown artists who need polarization to draw suckers to their three-card monte games. Could Ann Coulter sell her factually challenged books or Michael Moore sell tickets to his selectively edited films if America was not polarized? Would the so-called new media, particularly talk radio (right and left), be relevant and profitable absent polarization?

As it is, the combined audience for these shows, on a good week, is perhaps 20 million, virtually all of whom are rabid partisans. They thrive on political conflict. As Rush Limbaugh told Bob Beckel in 1990, "If Democrats manage to elect a candidate to the White House, I would become the biggest talk show host in history." The Democrats did, and to his credit, so did Rush. The fact remains, however, that more than 90 percent of Americans don't tune in to the so-called new media. If ever there was a case of preaching to the choir, it's partisan talk show hosts talking to their audience . . . and laughing all the way to the bank.

COMMON GROUND POINT TO REMEMBER: *Polarization is fueled by ideologues, power brokers, and bottom feeders who gain fame and profit from it. These are not natural bedfellows. Under ideal circumstances with polarization at full throttle, they can exist together. The public's sour mood toward politics, as witnessed in the 2006 elections, is making those circumstances less than ideal.*

A sad reality of polarization is that many decent people are entangled in its web and are desperately looking for a way out. Most fear for their political survival if they dare challenge polarization. They have bought into the many myths polarizers have successfully peddled as fact. Most of these myths would be laughable if they were not so destructive.

Polarizers want you to believe America is split down the middle between the Left (with a big *L*) and the Right (with a big *R*) . . . myth; that Americans are incensed by economic inequality and that class warfare is the solution . . . myth; that the "religious right" is a unified and powerful political force . . . myth; that the unions are a powerful unified force . . . myth; that the blogosphere is a powerful force in affecting voters' choices . . . myth.

Then there are the two hottest myths, whose acceptance is essential if polarization is to maintain a stranglehold on politics. First, polarizers have sold everyone the big myth that America is made up of red states and blue states. They claim red states are controlled by partisans on the right and blue states by partisans on the left. The second great myth is that Americans are engaged in a great culture war over values, competing cultural norms, and God. These are the

Holy Grail, the revealed wisdom, of the polarization movement. We will deal with some of these issues now, but we will later devote a full chapter to these two myths in order to fully expose them for what they are—pure fiction.

Facts are dangerous to polarizers, because they challenge the polarizers' myths. Polarizers want you to believe that the Christian Coalition remains a potent force in politics. Its cofounder, Reverend Pat Robertson, could not win a single primary when he ran for president in 1988, including the primary in South Carolina, where the conservative Christian organization was strongest. Nonetheless, during the 1990s, the Christian Coalition used wedge issues like abortion to turn out voters (almost exclusively for Republicans) and raised lots of money. Its president, Ralph Reed, left the organization to become a grassroots lobbyist. Reed ran for lieutenant governor of Georgia in 2004 and lost. Robertson did not help himself, or the Coalition's deteriorating reputation, when he agreed with Reverend Jerry Falwell that 9/11 was God's judgment on gays and abortion.

Today, the Christian Coalition is little more than an office and a post office box to which the deluded continue to send donations. In 2007 the Coalition recruited Florida megachurch pastor Joel Hunter as its new president. Hunter tried to expand the organization's narrow agenda beyond moral issues like abortion and gay marriage (the hot-button issues at the core of the Christian Coalition's organizing and fund-raising prowess). Hunter believed poverty and the environment are also moral issues.

Hunter was out before he was officially in. Roberta Combs, the chair of the organization's board, said of Hunter, "We're a political organization, and there's a way of doing things, like taking a survey of your membership to see what they want." Apparently, that did not include Christ's many admonitions to help the poor, since the world's impoverished masses are not a good fund-raising message. Hunter said he only wanted the organization to reflect the teachings of Jesus. Is there not a contradiction when a "Christian" Coalition favors a narrower and more political agenda over one that better reflects the teachings and example of the One it claims to represent? Not when the primary goal is fund-raising and people will respond only to "hot-button" issues.

Class warfare is one of the favorite rallying cries among liberal polarizers. They contend that the middle class and the poor share a seething hatred for Americans who are rich. Polarizers on the left are constantly calling on the two groups to join forces and storm the gated communities of the wealthy. There is little evidence to support any interest among the two classes to pick up their pitchforks. There is a difference between the authors about why.

Most of the poor and middle class would like to become, if not rich, then at least better off. Cal believes they mostly have that opportunity through education (if they stay in school), family (if they get married and stay married and do not mother or father children out of wedlock), obeying the law, and refusing to take drugs. Those born into difficult circumstances can still achieve middle-class status if they obey "the rules."

Bob agrees that the poor and middle class obviously want to be better off, but they are attempting to do so on a playing field where "the rules" are rigged toward the wealthy. Those born into poverty are particularly disadvantaged living in neighborhoods with lousy schools and overrun by drugs. For them the rules are mainly survival.

COMMON GROUND POINT TO REMEMBER: *Polarization is a tough game with extremely high stakes. Polarization is still the dominant force in national politics, and has been for many years. It is, however, showing its age. Any minority movement in a democracy that adversely affects the majority cannot last. Eventually the majority will rise up and respond. We believe the majority is beginning to stir.*

3

"THE REST OF US"

Bad officials are elected by good citizens, who do not vote.
—George Jean Nathan, American drama critic

JUST THINKING ABOUT ALL THIS PROBABLY MAKES YOU WANT TO rewrite Willie Nelson's classic so that it reads "Mama don't let your babies grow up to be politicians." Do not despair; turn on your iPod and listen to Bob Dylan's "The Times They Are A-Changin'."

Why are you reading this book? Probably you are weary of the nonstop screaming and yelling by self-important and arrogant politicians, the character assassinations, the blabber that pretends to be political debate, the greed and corruption, the pork-barrel projects that use your tax dollars to help some politician on the other side of the country get reelected. Bottom line . . . you are ticked off at politics.

You are not alone. Surveys, focus groups, academic studies, and circumstantial evidence indicate that the vast majority of eligible voters (eligible is key) are against the politics of polarization. The numbers are rapidly growing.

COMMON GROUND POINT TO REMEMBER: *The vast majority of eligible voters oppose the politics of polarization. Far from being alone, those who are frustrated by the rot of American politics are in the majority. It is a large ma-*

jority. That is the single biggest reason polarization cannot continue, at least at current levels.

"Every place I go I hear people saying the same thing about politics. They hate it. They are fed up. I mean everybody."
—Bill N., focus group, Kansas City, Kansas, Summer 2006

"All the shouting at each other, that's what I mean. Can't they shut up in Washington and do the work? We pay them to work, not yell."
—Pam W., focus group, Memphis, Tennessee, Spring 2006

"The country may be big, and there are a lot of us, but we have to break through a little. Because we're so polarized right now, we're paralyzed."
—Rachel Grady, documentary filmmaker, *Washington Post,*
September 29, 2006

Bill and Pam are two of the hundreds of voters interviewed for this book. Their feelings, like Rachel Grady's, represent 80 percent of the people we contacted. These voters are not naive. They know American politics is—and always has been—a contact sport. They recognize that certain political seasons have been nastier than others and they accept this.

These voters believe that politics, at least the way they remember politics, has changed for the worse. It may be that their memories of politics (and face it, how many people do you know who have memories of politics?) are idealized. Maybe theirs are like memories of the summers of our youth, when days were long and, for most of us, carefree. Then, as we got older, the summer days seemed to get shorter and real life took the "free" out of carefree.

Growing older has not changed our perceptions of the way our summers were, and nothing is going to change the public's perception (and in politics, public perception is really all that matters) that politics used to be different and has now gone bad. It's not that they don't care about the political system, they do. The problem is people don't know what to do to change politics. One of the questions we get most often on the lecture circuit is "How do I change things? Members of Congress only send me form letters when I write them and nothing changes."

> *"Sure it pisses me off, but what the hell I gonna do? The politicians are in the big boys' pockets . . . they don't listen to the little guys."*
>
> —Danny F., focus group, Harrisburg,
> Pennsylvania, Summer 2006

> *"I'd vote for anyone who had the guts to oppose the shit in Washington. But anyone who tries it gets crushed. Look at what those bastards did to McCain right here in SC. They're pros . . . dirty, disgusting people . . . but pros. How you beat that?"*
>
> —William B., Charleston, South Carolina,
> interview with Beckel, August 3, 2006

For Danny, Pam, Phil, William, and the millions of other Americans like them, the political process must look like the great and powerful Oz did to Dorothy—distant, frightening, and very complex. Washington wants us to think that it, like the wizard's Emerald City, is a place where important decisions are made in a system that is complex and difficult for the nonpolitician to understand. By so convincing us, Washington maintains a certain amount of power over our lives, and incumbents mostly enjoy eternal political life. Voters come to feel they are powerless, as Dorothy did, in the face of the Wizard.

COMMON GROUND POINT TO REMEMBER: *Like the Wizard in that classic movie, Washington's political game is mostly smoke, mirrors, and lots of noise.*

The first step is to begin exposing the myths of polarization. The place to start is Congress.

"Congress is rigged to promote partisanship and extremism. Most congressional districts are drawn to favor one party or the other, and contests take place only in primaries, where low turnouts favor candidates who appeal to the motivated extremes. The flow of special-interest money into congressional races adds to this tilt, and now bloggers are pummeling anyone who deviates from their definition of ideological purity."
—David S. Broder, *Washington Post*, September 24, 2006

The Hitler Diaries

The following comments are taken directly from public records. This is what masquerades as debate in Washington's polarized climate:

"Gingrich and the other backers of the 'Contract With America' are 'worse than Hitler,' and his Republican counterpart on the House Ways and Means Committee is a 'Nazi.'"
—Representative Charlie Rangel (D-NY),
Newsday, February 19, 1995

"We, unlike Nazi Germany or Mussolini's Italy, have never stopped being a nation of laws, not of men. Hitler never abandoned the cloak of legality . . . and that is what the [Republican] nuclear option seeks to do."
—Senator Robert Byrd (D-WV), in a speech delivered on the Senate floor, March 1, 2005

"Senator Byrd's inappropriate remarks comparing his Republican colleagues with Nazis are inexcusable. These comments lessen the credibility of the senator and the decorum of the Senate. He should retract his statement and ask for pardon."
—Senator Rick Santorum (R-PA), *Pittsburgh Tribune-Review*, March 3, 2005

"How dare you break this rule? It is the equivalent of Adolf Hitler in 1942 saying: I'm in Paris, how dare you invade me, how dare you bomb my city? It's mine. This is no more the rule of the Senate than it was the rule of the Senate before not to filibuster. It was an understanding, an agreement, and it has been abused."

—Senator Rick Santorum (R-PA), in a speech delivered
on the Senate floor, May 19, 2006

Hitler has been a popular metaphor when Democrats and Republicans are trying to describe each other. So have Joe Stalin, Cambodia's Pol Pot, Mao, Joe McCarthy, O. J. Simpson, and Timothy McVeigh. Along with this rogues' gallery there has also been the resourceful use of sexual innuendo, just to keep things lively.

Few missed Vice President Cheney's comments on the Senate floor in June 2004. After being approached by Senator Patrick Leahy (D-VT), who was attempting to shake the vice president's hand, Cheney told Leahy to perform a sexual act on himself, as in "go f–k yourself." When Neil Cavuto of Fox News gave him the opportunity to express regret over the remark, Cheney said he had none.

During a public hearing by the House Ways and Means Committee, Fortney "Pete" Stark (D-CA) yelled at Scott McInnis (R-CO) "You little wimp . . . You little fruitcake. You little fruitcake. I said you were a fruitcake."

Our high school civics textbooks were never this colorful. Of course, there are the crusty old political veterans who mumble that this kind of tough talk is "nothing new around Washington." They are right. There has been a long history of tough political rhetoric in American politics, but in the age of the 24/7 news cycle, portable recording devices, and YouTube, much of today's tough talk is literally broadcast around the world.

One of our favorite examples of a more classical put-down came from former president John Quincy Adams. When Adams learned that President Andrew Jackson was to receive an honorary degree from Harvard, he refused to attend the awards ceremony. Adams, an overseer for the college, declared, "I would not be present to see my darling Harvard disgrace herself by conferring a doctor's degree upon a barbarian and savage who could scarcely spell his own name."

That was tough talk, but not available on C-SPAN or twenty-four-hour cable news, where such titillating stories are repeated ad nauseam. By the time the news channels tired of the Cheney/Leahy exchange, there must have been several ten-year-olds who happened to catch the story flipping between ESPN and the Disney Channel. Of course, that left parents to explain that "the vice president was only kidding, sweetheart."

In the past, when extreme partisanship surfaced, consensus and bipartisanship would ultimately prevail. Partially this was for reasons of manners and civility, but it was also essential to avoid a complete paralysis of the legislative process. Today, manners and civility, and a functioning government, are often casualties of political warfare. Moreover, there are few moderate voices in Congress to act as an effective political counterforce.

We should be clear about the definition of a moderate in the U.S. Congress. Moderates are not necessarily people without convictions, though some such species exist. Moderates may hold strong convictions, but they are often willing to compromise with someone who disagrees in order to advance a policy that benefits the most people. Today, polarizers would rather have no legislation at all than have a bill that does not reflect 100 percent of their views or protect 100 percent of their financial interests.

Being a moderate voice in Washington these days almost guarantees immediate retaliation by one's own party. Money sources and interests, which thrive in the climate of polarization, cut you off and cut you down. A moderate is viewed as an anachronism, a dinosaur from the old era of politics when being reasonable was applauded. It takes courage to reach across the aisle and seek common ground. It is like lifting the keys to an organized-crime family's garbage truck. Both could abruptly end a career.

Republican polarizers call the moderates among them RINOS (Republican In Name Only). Democrats have no cute name for their moderates. Democratic polarizers refer to their moderates as, simply, dinosaurs.

Thirty years ago, it was commonplace to see as many as 25 percent of the members of one party cross over to vote with members of the other party. Since the late 1980s, however, partisan party-line voting, particularly in the House, has become commonplace. Bipartisan agreement is generally reserved for such critical legislation as the annual Strawberry Awareness Month proclamation.

On serious legislation (and we are being serious), more and more votes are cast along partisan lines. For example, President Clinton's 1993 economic package, which included an income tax increase for the top 5 percent of wage earners, did not get a single Republican vote in the House. In 2003, President Bush's prescription drug benefit plan for Medicare participants passed the House with all Republicans voting "aye"—and only nine Democrats supporting the plan.

Another reason for partisan voting is party-enforced discipline. Party leaders in Congress represent the ideological extremes of their parties. Congressional leaders decide which member sits on which committees, a huge weapon in persuading members to vote the party line. Members want to be on the committees that have the greatest impact on their constituents. It helps, for example, that a member of Congress representing a rural district in, say, Iowa, gets on the Agriculture Committee. Failure to follow the party line could find that same member sitting on the District of Columbia Committee. If he or she has only been a little naughty, the member might be consigned to the Merchant Marine and Fisheries Committee. They have trout streams in Iowa, don't they?

We don't want to close out this chapter leaving the reader with the idea that Democrats and Republicans can't agree on anything. . . .

When it comes to appropriating your tax dollars for designated projects back home (aka "earmarks," "pork," "pork barrel," etc.), there is absolute harmony in the halls of Congress. When appropriations bills containing earmarks come to floor of the House and Senate, you would think you were in a monastery full of devoted and loving brothers, not in the polarized Congress we have come to know. Only a few lonely voices protest the squandering of the taxpayers' money. Their attempts to remove earmarks from legislation have been easily defeated.

During each fiscal year, which for the federal government runs from October 1 to September 30, Congress is supposed to pass the eleven standard appropriations bills to fund the government. The last time that was accomplished, as of this writing, was in 1994. In 2006 Congress passed just two appropriations bills and had to pass a series of temporary spending bills every few weeks to keep the government running. One appropriations bill that usually makes the deadline is the Defense Department appropriation. One would like to think the motivation is national security alone, but, sadly, that is not so.

The defense appropriation comes from the defense subcommittee of the full appropriations committee. The subcommittee has jurisdiction over the largest pool of discretionary spending of any appropriations subcommittee. Most earmarks originate here. You may remember the name of one former chairman of the House defense subcommittee: Randy "Duke" Cunningham, currently serving serious time in a federal penitentiary for giving earmarks to the clients of lobbyist Jack Abramoff in exchange for millions in cash and luxury items.

In the Senate, the chairman of the Defense Appropriations Committee was Ted Stevens (R-AK), and the ranking Democrat was Daniel Inouye (D-HI). When the Democrats took control of the Senate, the two men exchanged seats, but not their love for earmarks. Not surprisingly, in 2006 the home states of both men received the largest earmarks per capita of any other states; Alaska received $1.05 billion, or $1,677 per resident, while Hawaii got $904 million, or $746 per resident according to the New York Times. The Alaska earmarks included $200 million for the infamous "Bridge to Nowhere" to tiny Gravina, Alaska, population fifty.

Stevens's bridge, coupled with the Cunningham/Abramoff scandal, brought much unwanted publicity to the bipartisan earmark pork festival. Government watchdog groups and a few members of Congress had been trying to get the press to pay attention to the pork fest while the number of projects and the billions of dollars raided from the Treasury to pay for them increased under Republican leadership. The bipartisan Congressional Research Service reported that over the past twelve years, the number of earmarks had tripled to more than sixteen thousand with a price tag of $64 billion per year.

One group in Washington has been paying a great deal of attention to earmarks: for lobbyists, pork has become a very big business. Getting earmarks requires lobbyists with contacts on the appropriation committees. If a firm had no appropriations connections, the lobbyists hired relatives of committee members. *USA Today* reported on October 17, 2006, that lobby groups employed thirty relatives of appropriation committee members, which generated more than $750 million for projects in 2005 alone.

A *USA Today* poll, released the day after their story appeared, found that 80 percent of those surveyed believe the practice of hiring relatives was seriously wrong. When the newspaper asked members of the appropriation committee if they had any internal policies to prevent relatives from lobbying them for earmarks, only four members said they did have such policies.

Efforts to make earmarks more transparent were supposed to have been implemented in 2007, but Representative Jeff Flake (R-AZ), who is one of the few members to speak out against earmarks, said, "Transparency would be enough if we had any shame. . . . But Democrats and Republicans have shown that there is no longer any embarrassment."

So bipartisanship as it is currently defined in Washington is spelled PORK.

There is hope. The new Democratic chairmen of the House and Senate appropriations committees, Dave Obey (D-WI) and Senator Bob Byrd (D-WV), announced in January 2007 that all pork projects in the leftover 2006 unfinished appropriation bills would be killed. Despite strong protests (made quietly of course), the bill passed.

It took a few months for the Obey/Byrd freeze to thaw. In an effort to secure wavering Democratic votes for benchmarks and withdrawal time lines in the Iraq war spending bill, the Democratic House leadership added several earmarks to win enough votes to pass the bill. Nevertheless, earmarks are now on the radar screen of the press and the public.

4

CONGRESSIONAL STORIES

In Washington . . . hypocrisy is a perennial crime in both parties; if all the city's hypocrites were put in jail, there would be no one left to run the government.

—Frank Rich

JULY 17, 2003, WAS A TYPICAL SUMMER NIGHT IN THE NATION'S capital. The hot weather matched the political rhetoric. Since he assumed the chair of the powerful House Ways and Means Committee in January 2001, the irascible Bill Thomas (R-CA) had made a second career out of inflaming the committee's Democratic minority. Relations were so bad that the Democrats publicly accused Thomas of being a dictator. His performance was the sort of thing that later caused Senator Hillary Clinton (D-NY) to assert: "[The House] has been run like a plantation. . . . It has been run in a way so that nobody with a contrary view has had a chance to present legislation, to make an argument, to be heard. . . . We have a culture of corruption, we have cronyism, we have incompetence. . . ."

The Ways and Means Committee has more impact on the American taxpayer than any other. From the amount of taxes Americans pay to the protection or altering of Social Security and Medicare benefits, it all starts or ends in this committee. Under Thomas, bills in Ways and Means were written by the chairman and his staff without any input from the Democrats. Thomas would call committee meetings and not inform the minority. When the Democrats managed to attend the meetings, the Republican majority routinely ignored them. Democratic proposals to amend committee bills never succeeded during Thomas's tenure. Committee Democrats complained bitterly to their leadership and routinely blasted Thomas in the press.

On Friday, July 17, 2003, Thomas called the committee to order. The business of the late evening meeting was an important pension bill that would affect millions of Americans and thousands of U.S. companies. In Washington-speak, this type of session is known as a final "markup" of the bill.

The Democrats were fed up with Thomas and itching for a fight. Pensions, which affect so many blue-collar workers, had always been important to Democrats. The revolt was led by Fortney "Pete" Stark, a liberal Democrat from Northern California.

As was his practice, Thomas did not allow the minority to see the bill until the day of the markup. Stark demanded that Democrats be given time to read the complex legislation. Thomas refused Stark's request, and the pot boiled over. The argument quickly escalated, and months of pent-up anger erupted into shouting and name-calling. Chairs were slammed back, fists were cocked, and some members nearly came to blows. The Democrats ultimately stormed out of the hearing room and went to the committee library to plot their next move.

Thomas called the Capitol Police, whose primary job is to protect members of Congress from outside threats, and ordered them to evict the Democrats from the library. No longtime observer or congressional historian could recall the Capitol Police being used this way in that body's two-hundred-year history.

Some Democrats refused to leave, putting the police in the embarrassing position of insisting they either vacate or face eviction. For several minutes it looked as if the police might begin arresting members, but calmer heads prevailed and the Democrats finally left.

As news of the confrontation spread, the next day Democrats descended on the House chamber, demanding that Thomas apologize. Representatives from both parties issued withering criticisms of his high-handed tactics. As terms like *police state* were being thrown around, House Minority Leader Nancy Pelosi confronted the Republican leadership, calling for a formal rebuke of Thomas.

In the end, Thomas had no choice. "It's been said that strengths are our weaknesses," the tearful Thomas declared. "Or as my mother would have put it, 'When they were passing out moderation, you were hiding behind the door.'" He went on to say, "The visions that each of us has for a better America, different though they may be, all have a right to be heard. . . . Each of us is elected by the people to be a member. Each of us has an equal right to be here."

The Democrats were not moved. If anything, they saw his statement as disingenuous and his weeping performance nothing more than crocodile tears. Though seeking to appear apologetic, Thomas stood by his call for police reinforcements: "To reestablish order in the committee, I requested that staff place a call to the sergeant at arms," Thomas said. "That decision in my opinion was proper and appropriate."

His cause was not helped when word leaked to the press that Speaker Dennis Hastert and Majority Leader Tom DeLay had to browbeat Thomas into making a statement. Both men feared the story would make the GOP House majority look like the Democrat majority they replaced in 1994. The ham-fisted tactics of the majority Democrats who were ousted after forty-two years of uninterrupted control prompted Newt Gingrich (like Hillary Clinton a decade later) to compare the House to a plantation.

The "Battle of Ways and Means" will forever stand out as emblematic of this period of bitter polarization. Under the previous Democratic chairman, Dan Rostenkowski of Chicago, the Ways and Means Committee was never a comfortable environment for the then-minority Republican members. But Rostenkowski, even in his most tyrannical days, never called the cops on the minority Republicans.

As anyone who watches C-SPAN or has visited the House in session knows, certain rules of decorum are followed even in heated debates. That's why you hear things like "As my good friend from Nebraska knows . . ." or "The gentlelady from Florida is incorrect when she says . . ." even though you know what they're really thinking is something like "This fool doesn't belong here and should be selling used cars with signs that say 'no credit, no problem.'" So, when this kind of volcanic activity occurs, things are seriously out of hand.

Although the Battle of Ways and Means was colorful and received lots of media attention, polarizing tactics were not limited to the House.

SENATE MINORITY LEADER (NOW MAJORITY LEADER) HARRY REID'S reputation as a highly charged partisan is legendary. Reid, from the tiny town of Searchlight, Nevada, was an amateur boxer in his younger years. Although he left the ring, the instinct to fight never left him. Reid is unapologetic about his partisanship, but on one issue it would come at a high price. It was spring of 2006 and the Senate debated the controversial immigration issue. The House had passed a Republican immigration bill in a special session the previous December that made hiring, or even assisting, illegal immigrants a felony. By spring, the normally restrained Latino community was in an uproar. Demonstrations spread across the country, as millions of Latinos, legal and illegal, protested the House felony bill.

The participation of legal Latinos, many of them U.S. citizens (and voters), raised the political stakes for both parties. George Bush and Karl Rove had aggressively pursued the Hispanic vote in the previous election. Their efforts paid off when Bush received more than 40 percent of the Hispanic vote in 2004. Many believed the House GOP immigration bill was substantially undermining that recruitment effort. Democrats had historically received a strong majority of the Latino vote before the Bush inroads. Republican missteps on the immigration issue, Democrats believed, would bring these voters back.

President Bush had long favored an immigration bill that would allow for a guest worker program and permit most illegal immigrants to pay back taxes and fines, stay in the country, and apply for citizenship. These formerly illegal immigrants would have to go to "the end of the line" behind people who had obeyed the law, but they could hope for eventual citizenship if they worked hard and did not commit any crimes. The GOP base strongly opposed Bush on these provisions, but the outrage in the Latino community convinced Republican senators (and even some House supporters of the felony provisions) to adopt a proposal similar to the president's.

The McCain/Kennedy immigration bill, sponsored by Edward Kennedy (D-MA) and John McCain (R-AZ), was close to what Bush wanted. It was also one of those rare bipartisan efforts, the likes of which had not been seen for years. For a few days before Congress adjourned, McCain/Kennedy was picking up strong support on both sides of the aisle. The White House announced its support for the measure.

The legislation was brought to the Senate floor the day before Congress adjourned for the Easter recess, but Harry Reid was not about to let it pass. The bill had many provisions that President Bush wanted, and the president would get credit for a legislative victory. Reid could not allow that to happen. The stakes in the upcoming election were too high. Arguing that Republicans intended to use amendments to gut the bill, Reid used a parliamentary maneuver and sent the bill back to committee. He anticipated that Republican lawmakers would take significant political heat from home-state voters.

By the time Congress reconvened in early May, it was clear that Reid's strategy had backfired. Democrats told Reid that any further delay could cause serious problems for their party among Latino voters, who expected the Democrats to carry their water on immigration reform. Republican senators told Majority Leader Bill Frist the bill should pass quickly. Grassroots conservatives, who hated the bill, were turning it into a hot-button issue. Latinos were conducting organized voter-registration drives that Republicans believed would produce more votes for Democrats in the fall election. Most Senate Republicans wanted to get the issue off the table and off the front page.

Reid and Frist knew they had to deal. By mid-May, an agreement was reached to bring the McCain/Kennedy legislation back to the Senate floor. Reid dropped his opposition to amendments, while Frist agreed to include additional Democrats on the conference committee that would negotiate a final bill with the House. Partisan stonewalling gave way to bipartisan consensus. Finding common ground, in the Senate at least, provided both sides a political safety net, but then the House refused to sit down with the Senate. An attempt by the Bush administration to pass a "comprehensive immigration reform" bill failed when talk radio and other opponents managed to organize an effective drive that scuttled it. The immigration bill that finally passed, just prior to the elections, called for a seven-hundred-mile fence on the Mexican border, but provided no funding for the fence, and no solution to the millions of illegals in the country. Such is the price of polarization.

Any further efforts at finding common ground on other issues in the 110th Congress failed. There have been occasional moments in recent years in which partisan politics has given way to genuine and unified concern for the public good. For a brief period after the terrorist attacks on September 11, 2001, bipartisanship rolled down like a cool stream on a hot day. Nevertheless, even that "Kumbaya" moment between the two parties had the feel of a shotgun wedding. It took only a few months of war in Iraq to destroy the unity and return to partisan bickering. By the end of 2002 the parties were once more experiencing irreconcilable differences. By 2003 the bipartisan divorce was final.

As America entered the twenty-first century, polarization was well into its second decade. As a result, a generation of politicians and operatives in both parties had never personally experienced cooperation, bipartisanship, or a meaningful search for common ground. They might have heard about it but rarely had they lived it. The vast majority of political consultants and most of today's elected politicians have never functioned in anything but a toxic environment. The national party committees have an interest in keeping it this way.

5

THE PARTIES

Under Democracy, one party always devotes its chief ener-
gies to trying to prove that the other party is unfit to serve—
and both commonly succeed and are right.

—H. L. Mencken

Fools to the Left of Me, Jokers to the Right

In the last three decades, republican political activists have moved further to the right, and Democratic activists further to the left. In the process, what had been a competition of ideas between two great political parties became a destructive climate of polarization. Activists, who are practitioners of the politics of polarization, have replaced mainstream party operatives.

Conservative activists control most functions of the Republican National Committee, while their liberal counterparts direct most of the operations of the Democratic National Committee. Each party's unstated mission is to obliterate the other. The national committees are like two race cars at a NASCAR event trying to push each other into the wall, with their pit crews using every trick, legal or otherwise, to make the cars faster and stronger. The stands are filled with activists screaming for blood, while the political press corps waits expectantly for a fiery crash that will boost circulation and ratings.

Both party cars are covered with the colorful logos of their financial backers. Republican "sponsors" include the National Rifle

Association, National Right to Life Committee (and all the other "pro-life" organizations), the Christian Coalition, the Chamber of Commerce, Focus on the Family, *The 700 Club*, conservative talk radio, the American Enterprise Institute, the Heritage Foundation, and the *Weekly Standard*.

If you think that's a lot, consider the logos behind the Democratic team: AFL-CIO, NOW, AARP, NARAL (and all the other "choice" groups), Greenpeace, the Sierra Club, MoveOn.org, the NAACP, NEA, AFSCME, the trial lawyers, and the ACLU.

These organizations are dedicated to promoting the message that America is divided. They have little interest in common ground because that would blur the distinctions between parties and affect the majority status of one or the other. It would also hurt fund-raising.

COMMON GROUND POINT TO REMEMBER: *If American politics were united and politics was centered in bipartisanship and consensus, special interests would be less relevant, attract far less "conflict money" derived by promoting polarization, and they would have less political power.*

The traditional role of political parties has been to choose candidates, dispense patronage, and get party members to vote on Election Day. Depending on when and where, these responsibilities were well organized, and at other times they were chaotic. As Mark Twain once said, "I'm not a member of any organized political party. I am a Democrat." Whether organized or not, it was generally in the party's interest to keep a low profile since most of their "volunteers" were government patronage workers or the employees of government contractors.

As governments at all levels began to rein in patronage, party organizations lost government workers to do their bidding. When workers owed their jobs to the party and were underwritten by the taxpayer, it was easy for parties to field effective organizations. A party organizer had to perform, or potentially lose his source of income. To the patronage worker, this meant recruiting people to the party and getting them to vote. They had no concern about a particular voter's political ideology, only that he or she showed up to vote on Election Day (or sent an absentee ballot if dead but still on the voting rolls).

Without patronage jobs, party operations had to depend increasingly on unpaid volunteers to do the political jobs patronage workers once performed. Like any other volunteer, a political party volunteer will work harder if motivated by a cause. The more extreme the cause, the more likely the volunteer will be motivated. That's one reason why there has been an explosion of social-issue referendums on election ballots. There's nothing like a referendum on gay marriage or abortion to get election workers motivated and strong partisans to the polls.

To promote the party's agenda and motivate the base, incumbents in Congress are pressured not to deviate from the party line. We have discussed the various punitive measures for wayward members available to the parties' congressional leadership. If an incumbent insists on following his conscience, there is nothing quite like the threat of a primary challenge from a more partisan party candidate to move him to the right or left. If an incumbent refuses to adjust to the party line, it's increasingly likely he will be challenged for the nomination. A prime example occurred in the seventh Congressional District of Michigan in the Republican primary. Republican Joe Schwarz was elected to Congress in 2004. He is a medical doctor who supports the Supreme Court's 1973 abortion decision, *Roe v. Wade*. Schwarz wrote a poignant column for the *Washington Post* on September 17, 2006. Here is some of what he said:

> I am the political equivalent of a woolly mammoth, a rarity heading for extinction. Yes, I'm a moderate.
>
> Our plight today is dire. Even though more than half of all American voters consider themselves centrists, the Republican and Democratic parties are finding themselves controlled to an ever-greater extent by their more extreme elements. On the Republican side, the "religious right," the quasi-theocrats, are infiltrating the party power structure quite effectively. On the left, the moneyed Eastern establishment and California liberals shrilly

tell Americans that the sky is falling, that the world hates us and that Republican policies are all wrong. Yet they offer no viable alternatives. As a result, they have managed to alienate much of the traditional working-class Democratic base, good people caught between Republicans they don't like and Democrats who have abandoned them. What's a moderate to do?

In my case, lose an election. What did me in was voter apathy, and moral absolutist groups supported by a vitriolic negative-ad campaign funded by organizations on the far right.

Schwarz's larger point of a bunker mentality and lack of communication across party and ideological lines is a good one. How can anyone expect to find consensus if people see one another as enemies and won't even consider another person's point of view? This is the reason politics needs a strong middle. However, as Schwarz learned, activists are dominant, especially in the primaries.

Political activists also exert enormous influence on the selection of the party's presidential nominee. Not only do activists vote in large numbers, they also provide a pool of campaign workers for the primaries, and raise much of the "early" money so necessary, particularly in recent presidential campaigns. In the 2008 presidential campaigns, "early" money will play an even bigger role. Since there is no clear front runner in either party, the ability to raise early money will be an important indicator of political strength. Additionally, more money will be needed earlier in 2008 than in previous elections since many large states, including California, have moved their primaries to February 2008, and a few to January.

In the modern presidential selection process, no candidate of either party has been nominated without coming in first or second in either Iowa or New Hampshire. Moreover, the winner of the Iowa caucuses gets a huge boost going into the New Hampshire primary. (In 2008 Nevada will hold a caucus between Iowa and New Hampshire.) Party activists have long dominated the presidential selection process in both states. But even in states where activists have less influence, many are still chosen as national convention delegates (although they must vote in a manner that reflects their state's primary elections or caucuses).

The national party delegates who convene in the quadrennial convention to anoint their presidential and vice-presidential candidates (the nominating process having been concluded by the primary voters months before party conventions) are generally the most partisan of the partisan. Their views are far from the political views of the party rank and file. For two decades, CBS News and the *New York Times* have surveyed the differences between Democratic and Republican presidential convention delegates on key issues. The survey then asks the same issue questions to representative samples of rank-and-file Democrats and Republicans across the country.

In 2004, the CBS/NYT survey asked if delegates agreed or disagreed with the statement "Government should do more to solve national problems." The spread between the delegates to the Democratic and Republican conventions was a whopping 72 percent. The spread between rank-and-file party members on the same statement was only 13 percent, a 59 percent differential between activists and rank-and-file members of the same party.

On the issue of making "all tax cuts permanent," the difference between delegates to the two conventions was 88 percent. The difference between rank-and-file party members on the same question was only 35 percent. That's a 53 percent difference in attitudes between party activists and the members of the parties they purport to represent.

COMMON GROUND POINT TO REMEMBER: *Regardless of the answers to the CBS/NYT questions, the conclusion is obvious—activists of both parties are ideologues, regular party members are not.*

The Gift That Keeps on Giving

By centralizing campaign resources in Washington the polarizers are better able to control elected officials, party operatives, campaign consultants, and especially campaign contributions—providing crucial leverage as the mother's milk of politics. Campaigns have become outrageously expensive.

According to the Center for Responsive Politics, 85 percent of the 2000 Senate candidates who spent the most money succeeded at the polls. The success ratio for big spenders was even higher in that year's House races. Twenty-five financial underdogs were successful, but many of them had spent almost as much as their opponents.

In the 2006 elections, there was not as much disparity between incumbents and challengers. Incumbents still outspent challengers, but in competitive races the differences by historical standards were very small. In 2006 the party campaign committees raised more money than at any time in history. The result was that Democratic challengers, who were thought to have a serious chance at beating an incumbent, were helped with huge amounts of money. Conversely, incumbent Republicans received millions from party committees to retain their seats.

The cost of getting to Congress and staying there requires more money than a candidate could ever hope to raise from family and friends. Campaining for the House routinely costs $1 million or more. Senate races can easily exceed $10 million. All that money for a job that pays $158,103 per year. Those who do not depend on large amounts of money from party campaign committees or Washington special interests are usually multimillionaires who finance their own race. Most candidates for Congress are not millionaires and so are "forced" to turn to lobbyists for campaign contribution. The lobbyists, of course, assume that in return for helping the candidate, they will have access to her after the election. It is a sickening revolving door and the taxpayers are the losers.

Most campaign money, especially for incumbents, is found among the various special-interest groups that swarm over Washington like the occasional locust infestation. Special-interest lobbies grow by the hundreds each year, adding to the thousands already in Washington. The lobby business also provides a source of job security for members of Congress once they retire or lose reelection. Most former members don't go home; instead they become lobbyists. While they once represented their state or district, they now represent themselves, and cash in on the access to former colleagues. (Not to mention lifetime access to the House or Senate floor.)

Campaign Central

In this era of polarization, special-interest groups are encouraged (about as nice a word as we could use) to contribute to the national party committees, and to the House and Senate campaign committees. This gives party committees the ability to control the flow of campaign contributions to candidates, and with it an enormous amount of leverage. With centralized campaign funds has come the nationalization of campaign messages. The parties create their respective messages and expect the candidates to use them. It doesn't matter how different one media market is from another, the campaign ads have the same message. The background may be different and the accents appropriate for the region where the ads appear, but they all seem to say the same thing.

This is due, in part, to the influence over political consultants by the same national committees that control campaign money. Political consultants have multiplied exponentially in recent years. Most of their campaign experience has been limited to the highly charged partisan climate of the past three decades. The results have been negative campaigns, which are now the rule rather then the exception. Consultants, like candidates, rely on the goodwill of the party committees for candidate referrals. The committees become, in effect, job banks for consultants. Consultants, wanting to maintain good relationships, agree to promote the party's agenda with their clients.

> *"The result is that the conventional debate about whether congressional elections are primarily local or national in character is both irrelevant and misleading. Even apparently local developments are often orchestrated from afar, and even personal attacks on individual candidates are largely the work of a cadre of Washington-based researchers."*
> —E. J. Dionne, *Washington Post*, October 2006

Candidates' dependency on partisan sources for money and their addiction to consultants inevitably lead to negative campaigns. Much has been made of the nastiness of modern political campaigns. But it would be a mistake to assume, as some commentators have suggested, that negative campaigns are the primary cause of political polarization. In fact, the opposite is true. The control exerted by proponents of polarization leads to negative campaigns. Polarizers depend on messages that undermine their opponents and cast their differences in the starkest of terms. To accomplish this, polarizing messages by definition need to be negative.

6

THE PRESS, FUND-RAISERS, AND MYTHS

Every two years the American politics industry fills the air-waves with the most virulent, scurrilous, wal-to-wall character assassination of nearly every political practitioner in the country—and then declares itself puzzled that America has lost trust in its politicians.

—Charles Krauthammer, syndicated columnist

MOST OF THE NEWS ORGANIZATIONS, EDITORS, AND REPORTERS who cover modern politics have never worked in anything other than a polarized environment. Most of the older reporters, who at least experienced periods of conciliation and comity, are retiring or have died. It is a cliché, but no less true, that conflict sells, and if harmony broke out, newspaper sales would drop and ratings, especially on cable TV, would decline sharply. Both of us have been called by TV bookers and then rejected because our views were not extreme enough. The networks think people will watch only if they are guaranteed a verbal smack-down.

Why? Because conflict brings ratings; and ratings bring profits. Those profits provide cable television and talk radio personalities with salaries that are among the highest of any profession. Keeping those big salaries is dependent on maintaining good ratings. If conflict ensures ratings success, and ratings success ensures a good income, then on-air talent will provoke all the controversy they can. It is a vicious cycle. Some media outlets, especially talk radio, were created almost entirely for the purpose of exploiting political polarization.

The right argues that conservative talk radio was a response to big media shutting out conservative views and values. Conservatives have a range of programming options today that were not available a decade ago. They can bypass the big media and go to conservative media outlets where their beliefs are being heard and "getting through" what they believe to be a liberal media filter.

This backlash has had many upsides for conservatives, but the one downside is that many people never have to consider any ideas but their own. They can tune in and listen only to what they already believe. It might be argued they get the "other side" in the mainstream media (Rush Limbaugh calls it the "drive-by media"), but most conservatives do not trust what they hear from the mainstream network newscasts between "good evening" and "good night."

The left argues that conservatives have used the so-called liberal bias of the mainstream media as a flimsy rationale for the proliferation of alternative conservative media outlets. They are convinced that the right creates allegations of bias merely as a marketing tool to attract an audience. In some cases that is true, but the success of conservative media formats indicates that a substantial market exists for the product it is selling.

Still, the left believes these outlets are where the real bias exists, and that bias is against the left. Liberals feel outgunned, particularly on talk radio, yet attempts at liberal talk radio formats have met with limited success.

In this contentious environment, political reporting increasingly resembles sports reporting. The focus is on the horse race and the outcome: who won, who lost, and who gets to wield political power. Ideas and thoughtful, reasoned analysis have virtually disappeared. Yes, PBS still engages in lengthy debate and discussion on important subjects, but most conservatives believe PBS tilts left, so few watch.

Increasingly, the Internet is the source for political "news" for polarizers on both the right and left. The proliferation of politically oriented blogs and websites has been enormous, and millions surf them for political information. Most mainstream media organizations (many of which initially hated to recognize the potential of the Internet) have now invested millions on web pages of their own. Newspapers, especially, which have suffered a substantial loss in daily readership, have turned to the Internet to regain readers and advertisers. A growing number of "net-only" newspapers and magazines have followed the pioneering Internet magazine *Slate.*

Many TV and radio pundits, including Arianna Huffington on the left and Ann Coulter on the right, have used their exposure to launch successful websites. Most talk radio and cable-TV political hosts use their web pages to blog and simulcast their shows. Every legitimate candidate for president (and most other political offices) has a web page that provides a daily blog; most with streaming video content. But the greatest impact from the Internet on political news and commentary is coming from daily blogs written and produced by people who never had exposure in either broadcast or print. Their sites are highly partisan, with endless polarizing commentary and chat. Younger people, especially, now go to the net for virtually all their political information.

The impact of the Internet on politics is growing exponentially, but not always in favorable ways. Balanced, nonpartisan, nonpolarizing sites on the net are few and far between. *Newsweek, Time,* the big-four networks, and prominent daily newspapers will argue that their sites are balanced and their news impartial. But for political junkies, partisan extremists, and other polarizing communities, mainstream media outlets are not their first (or even last) stop for political information. Conversely, the left and right blogs are rarely visited by impartial, undecided voters, and certainly not by each other. These sites often portray themselves as news sources, but are in fact forums with partisan editorial views.

The "news" components of these sites are the most troubling. Bloggers on the net are not subject to editorial review, nor are they subjected to any form of fact-checking procedures to ensure the accuracy of the daily information they provide. This leads invariably to abuse of the Internet by polarizers and their followers. News is presented as fact, and the viewer simply accepts the content as factual. Generally, visitors to these various sites are not looking for fair reporting, but rather political information from sources whose political philosophy they share. It is unlikely that many liberals visit Rush Limbaugh's site; the same with conservatives' rare visit to the Huffington Post.

Polarizers, who can say whatever they want, dominate the Internet in contemporary politics. Many produce nonstop and usually unsubstantiated rumors. The good news is that the Internet audience for political information, though growing, is not the source for political information for the vast majority of voters. The bad news is that this vast number of polarized sites encourages more polarization. The result is sort of a "polarizer's gas station." It is where people on the right and left go to get their minds filled and fine-tuned with whatever polarizing agenda the sites are presenting, and when they leave they are primed for battle.

The Money Changers

Unlike the younger operatives who run the day-to-day campaign operations, political fund-raisers tend to be older people with successful careers. They have large networks of friends and associates, which provide a built-in source for political contributions. Many have had the experience of raising money in a more civil political climate before polarization infected politics. Most will admit that raising campaign money is much easier in a polarized climate.

That is the dirty little secret about the role polarization has played in the massive increase in campaign contributions over the last two decades. Money is easier to solicit with a negative approach to the other candidate. Absent a strong negative, it is more difficult to raise money for a candidate who runs a positive campaign, and has only an optimistic vision and positive agenda. Polarization allows fund-raisers to play off fear, and fear in politics is a mighty motivator.

According to the Federal Election Commission, the 2006 midterm elections broke all records for political contributions for a nonpresidential election. When it began to look like the Democrats could win the House, the money poured into Republican and Democratic campaign committees. The business community, which had enjoyed twelve years of support from a Republican House, raised millions to protect the GOP majority.

It wasn't a tough sell. The possibility that the next chairman of the powerful Ways and Means Committee could be the liberal, African-American Charlie Rangel from Harlem, and not the big-business-loving Bill Thomas of California, sent shivers up the spines of corporate America. When the Senate suddenly came into play in October, big-business lobbyists couldn't get their checkbooks out fast enough. When asked about the fear factor, one prominent fund-raiser told us bluntly, "Fear is a wonderful thing."

But if you think the Democrats raised money in 2006 from a well-spring of hopeful anticipation, and not fear, you'd be wrong. Every union, liberal-issue group, environmental organization, and New York and Hollywood deep-pocket liberal, not to mention thousands of trial lawyers, got the same message: "If we don't win it now, we'll be shut out for at least another decade." Fear is a wonderful thing in the political fund-raising business.

Fund-raising for the party in power (and incumbents in general) has become a "protection racket," right out of the organized-crime handbook: "Give me money and I'll protect you from the guys who want to ruin your business." For the party out of power (and challengers in general), fund-raising has taken a page from the military manual on successful guerrilla warfare. In a year like 2006, the fund-raising message for Democrats was the equivalent of "Give me resources while they're weak, and we can attack before they regroup."

Even today's social life in Washington divides along partisan lines. Social occasions (as we shall discuss further) once provided civil settings for discussion and the building of consensus between political opponents. Now people patronize the fancy restaurants or bars that cater to their fellow liberals or conservatives. Call it political segregation. At the dinner parties that remain in Washington, hosts generally avoid inviting people with clashing viewpoints for fear the china might be broken.

Polarization has infected every aspect of politics from press coverage, to fund-raising, to where politicians eat. The goal of polarizers is to make these changes permanent. The key to realizing that goal is to sell the notion that polarization is ubiquitous and ingrained in the body politic. To make that sale, polarizers have relied heavily on two myths, and they have done a masterful job of selling both. As former members of the polarizing sales force, we want to break down the sales pitch for you.

Myth One: Red State/Blue State This!

Let me raise a red flag about the "red and blue states," which is the reigning theory of U.S. politics. All those blue states (heavily urban and mainly on the East and West coasts) voted for Al Gore. The red states (more rural, Southern and Western) voted for George Bush. Presto, the map defines us. We're a country geographically "polarized" by values and lifestyles. This is a masterful explanation for the increasing nastiness of politics, with only one big drawback. It's wrong.

If the country were more polarized, you'd expect to find it in the polls. You don't. After scouring surveys, sociologist Paul DiMaggio of Princeton University concluded: "the public actually has become more unified in attitudes toward race, gender and crime since the 1970s." One standard poll item asks respondents to react to this statement: "I don't have much in common with people of other races." In 1987, 23 percent agreed; by 2002, only 15 percent did. Of course, strong disagreements (on abortion, for instance) remain. But these disguise large areas of consensus (80 percent of Americans regularly support environmental regulation). What's even more absurd is the idea that regions have—after jet travel, interstate highways, air conditioning, TV and mass migration—become more different. Texas and New York have more in common now than in 1961.

—Robert Samuelson, *Washington Post*

During presidential elections extending back to the 1988 contest between Michael Dukakis and George H. W. Bush, all visual media coverage has used the same color coding to illustrate which presidential candidate had won a state's electoral votes—red for states captured by the Republican candidate and blue for states won by the Democratic candidate. The imagery quickly became the standard not only for characterizing how states vote for presidential candidates but for defining the politics and values of the entire state.

Red state/blue state has become a widely used stereotype for our political differences. To characterize an entire state as Republican or Democrat based on the popular vote for a presidential candidate (giving the state's entire electoral vote to one candidate) is absurd. Perhaps the media's intent was to limit the color designation to presidential races. If so, and we doubt it, they failed miserably. What they did accomplish was to provide a visual image that produced a public relations windfall for polarizers.

Once tagged red or blue, a state inherits the simplistic definition associated with the two colors. Depending on which side you talk to, people in "blue states" have loose moral values, while those in "red states" promote family values; or the "red state" mentality is intolerant and mean-spirited, while the "blue state" mind-set is intellectually tolerant. Therein lies the problem. As a political theory, the red/blue division, at least among average Americans, is largely a myth. Life is complicated; the political philosophies, morals, and ethical standards of real people are just not that black and white (or red and blue for that matter).

Ohio is a prime example of this flawed labeling. Because it voted for the Republican presidential candidate in several election cycles, Ohio has inherited a "red state" designation, and thus, to the casual observer of politics, it is presumed to be a solid Republican state. The red color of presidential politics allows for no distinction between national politics and state and local politics. Even the presidential designation is misleading. In 2004, 49.5 percent of Ohio voters cast ballots for John Kerry, 50.5 percent for George Bush.

The result is that Ohio, an evenly divided state, joins such heavily Republican states as Mississippi, Utah, and Wyoming under the same red designation, and all that it implies. It is irresponsible and laughable that red/blue has become commonplace in America's political vernacular and is taught as serious political science in many high school civics classes. Not only does Ohio have several Democrats in its congressional delegation, in 2006 it elected a Democratic governor and dumped a Republican incumbent U.S. senator and replaced him with an unabashed liberal. Using a more accurate standard, Ohio should be considered a swing state that is leaning blue.

Nor is Ohio unique. Michigan and Minnesota are considered "blue states." During the 2004 presidential elections, John Kerry won each state by a 51 to 48 percent margin. That's fairly weak for states colored all blue. Iowa was designated a red state after voting for George W. Bush in the 2004 presidential election, yet a majority of Iowans voted for the Democrat in the three previous presidential elections. It has a conservative United States senator, Chuck Grassley, yet he serves alongside Tom Harkin, who is among the most liberal in the Senate. In 2006 Iowa elected a Democratic governor, and defeated twenty-two-year Republican House veteran and chairman of the House Banking Committee, Jim Leach. Is Iowa really a red state? Politically bipolar might be a better designation.

The so-called red state of Colorado has two senators who are polar opposites—Wayne Allard, a conservative Republican, and Ken Salazar, a moderate-to-liberal Democrat. In 2004 Bush carried the state 52 to 47 percent, at the same time as Democrats were making gains at the state level. Previously serving senators were William Armstrong, a conservative Republican, and Gary Hart, a liberal Democrat. In 2006 Colorado elected a Democratic governor. How can one paint Colorado a single color?

New Hampshire, the most reliable red state in New England? In 2006 New Hampshire reelected a Democratic governor with 74 percent of the vote, and the New Hampshire legislature became Democratic for the first time in history. Don't put that paint can away!

What of the bluest of blue cities, New York? The last two mayors, Michael Bloomberg and Rudy Giuliani, have been Republicans, though liberal. Blue state? Blue city?

Are such states suffering from voter split personalities, or is it simply that the voters in these states select their leaders based on factors other than the stereotypical labels and perspectives advanced by political extremists and the media?

To the average American, the divisiveness of the red state/blue state theory makes no sense. Most people (whether in red states or in blue states) like their neighbors and their community. They carpool together. Their kids play together. Some of them actually go to the same church together. They realize their state has committed voters in both parties. They also know a voter who is a "blue" in one election might switch to red in the next election. Alternatively, a voter can split his or her ticket, voting for some Democrats and some Republicans.

While they may know neighbors who are members of another party, they are also aware that they all live in the same state and that it takes working together to ensure a quality of life that promotes the common good. What "color" does that make them—purple? It gets a little confusing.

What is the motive behind the promotion of the red/blue divide? How could you take advantage of a network graphic that has turned into a political theory, dividing a nation? How could you further refine the message to get maximum value from it? Conservative Republicans were first to mine the red/blue division with a refining message that was emotional, personal, and threatening, and that resonated with "red" voters. They believed the "values issue"—by which they meant God, abortion, guns, same-sex marriage, bad movies, and worse TV—belonged to them. They saw (and see) themselves as the defenders of the *Father Knows Best* families, even though according to the latest figures from the U.S. Census Bureau, "traditional families" have slipped to just under 50 percent of the population.

That government alone, or even government principally, was not responsible for whatever "values" had been lost was a concept Republicans misplaced in their hunger for a base of voters that might lead them to the electoral promised land. They began to paint all who disagreed with them as godless heathens bent on destroying the country only Republicans truly loved. There was no doubt in the minds of GOP extremists that if you opposed a Republican policy, it was the same as being a terrorist because you were in favor of weakening the country. If your neighbor disagreed with you, he was on the "other side," which often meant he must be working for the devil.

Not to be outdone, liberal Democrats jumped on the "red state" message to rally their base. "Blue state" partisans used the "red" message to underscore the intolerance of extreme conservatives. Theirs was a defensive, but no less polarizing, message. They accused Republicans of being "moral interventionists" who wanted to dictate values and morality. This became a particularly frightening message to the left after the Republicans took control of Congress in 1994. Polarizers on the left charged that Republican extremists in Congress were trying to legislate morality and deny individual liberties, especially "a woman's right to choose."

The irony is that for years conservatives charged that the (then majority) Democrats were "government interventionists." The right alleged that the Democratic Congress wanted the government to intrude on state and individual rights and, in the process, undermine "traditional" American values.

This is the same thinking that gave birth to the term *culture war.*

Myth Two: The Culture War

In a speech to the Republican National Convention in Houston on August 17, 1992, Pat Buchanan declared that America was engaged in a culture war. Buchanan was addressing the Republican delegates as an insurgent candidate challenging the incumbent president of the United States, George H. W. Bush. It didn't take Buchanan long to make his point:

> My friends, this election is about much more than who gets what. It is about who we are. It is about what we believe. It is about what we stand for as Americans. There is a religious war going on in our country for the soul of America. It is a cultural war, as critical to the kind of nation we will one day be as was the Cold War itself.

Buchanan, a controversial character by anyone's definition, was in his element. He is a long-standing member of the reactionary pundit club. His roles have included White House speechwriter for Richard Nixon, columnist and television commentator, communications director for President Reagan, talk radio host, author of several controversial books, and ardent conservative warrior. For the record, we both know Buchanan, Bob from appearing with him on CNN's *Crossfire,* and Cal as a colleague over many years.

The leaders of the Republican Party had not wanted Buchanan on the podium that night. He had already embarrassed President Bush by finishing a strong second to him in the New Hampshire primary. Despite being soundly defeated by Bush in later contests, Buchanan refused to abandon his insurgency before the Houston convention. He had attracted a small but ardent following among social conservatives with his cultural values message. Buchanan was determined to use the national spotlight provided by the convention to proclaim the culture war message to a large television audience.

Never known to shrink from confrontation, Buchanan enjoys a good fight. With his communications background, he also knew that cultural division was an issue that guaranteed controversy and press coverage. We are not suggesting that Buchanan invented the culture war for political purposes. He had been talking about the subject the year before he faced Bush in New Hampshire. Buchanan has told us that one of his inspirations for announcing the culture war was sociologist James Hunter's 1991 book, *Culture Wars.* Hunter suggested the cultural divide is so deep in America that actual physical violence was almost certain to break out at any moment. The term caught on as descriptive of a widely held belief among mostly conservative Republicans.

Pat Buchanan didn't invent the culture war, but he is a firm believer that a war exists and that the stakes are enormous. He is not alone. Millions of political extremists on both the left and the right believe in a culture war and they have enlisted in it. The culture war is primarily being waged over the issues of abortion, gay marriage, school prayer, and, more recently, stem-cell research. Because of the prevalence of these issues and the controversy and fervor they have generated, the term was embraced by the press corps, which pursued the story with the ferocity of a pack of lawyers chasing an ambulance.

With its endless potential for controversy, excitement, and political intrigue, "culture wars" makes for good ratings and high interest. The culture war gets covered with as much intensity as Paris Hilton or World War II on the History Channel. It never ends because the media won't let it end. Politicians from the polarized left and right do not want to see it end either, as long as there are votes and contributions that can be gained by the war. There is one small problem . . . the so-called culture war is really a small battle, being fought between polarizers on the right and left, while the vast majority of Americans refuse to be involved.

The cultural war is crucial to the proponents of the red state/blue state theory. The conclusion is that Americans are divided along cultural lines, with red states committed to traditional cultural norms, and blue states to tolerance and individual expression. That is simply not true.

COMMON GROUND POINT TO REMEMBER: *The so-called culture war is being fought on the fringes between ideologues from the right and left. It does not divide the majority of Americans, and it certainly does not divide along state lines.*

The nonpartisan Pew Research Center for the People and the Press and the Pew Forum on Religion and Public Life released a survey on August 3, 2006, about Americans' attitudes on key cultural and social issues. The study is titled "Pragmatic Americans Liberal and Conservative on Social Issues." In the summary of its findings, Pew reported, "Americans can not be easily characterized as conservative or liberal on today's most pressing social issues . . . the public remains reluctant to move too far from current policies and practices on many key social policy questions. Despite talk of 'culture wars' and the high visibility of activist groups on both sides of the cultural divide, there has been no polarization of the public into liberal and conservative camps."

To Pat Buchanan and his like-minded fellow Americans on the right, this war is serious business. They have come to see the "moral issues" (in addition to those mentioned earlier, they include flag burning, illegal immigration, and keeping "under God" in the Pledge of Allegiance) as central to the continued freedom and prosperity of the nation. To their opponents on the left, the stakes are equally grave. They see the culture warriors on the right bent on stripping away their constitutional rights. These include the freedom of individual choice (abortion), lifestyle (gay rights), expression (flag burning), and separation of church and state (school prayer).

The passions among culture warriors are deep and profound. The confrontations are often mean and sometimes violent, both rhetorically and sometimes physically. But these small incidents of violence are not on the scale that Hunter predicted in his book. However small (although if you accept DiMaggio's 30 percent, there still are millions in the war), they are loud enough to garner endless press and political analysis. And this attention encourages the extremists and their financial supporters to keep the battle going. The extremists on both sides need each other. If one side were to win, the other would go out of business. Success is the great enemy of culture warriors.

One of the more astute warriors in the culture crusade is Rush Limbaugh. Limbaugh stokes the fire of resentment in his listeners, attacking liberals who Limbaugh believes are trying to destroy certain virtues that have made America great. That, of course, is not the intent of liberals, but every dog needs a fireplug on which to relieve himself, and Limbaugh sees liberals as that fireplug and himself as that dog.

Rush Limbaugh—the country's king of talk radio—is a subject on which we disagree. Cal believes Limbaugh is the greatest thing since the Founding Fathers because he gives voice to a significant number of people who have long felt disrespected and disregarded by the elite. Cal also believes that Limbaugh simply comments on what liberals say and do, exposing their agendas in ways that were not possible before he and others managed to circumvent what Limbaugh calls "the drive-by media."

Bob thinks Rush is the greatest self-promoter of his generation. He admires his ability to attract millions of listeners a day with, in

Limbaugh's words, "half my brain tied behind my back," thus explaining the type of listener Rush attracts. Bob also thinks Limbaugh could care less about cultural issues and simply uses them as a platform to keep his audience riled up, thus perpetuating the culture war for ratings and profit.

We both agree that talk radio—left and right of the dial—has a special interest in keeping the war going. They make gobs of money off the conflict.

Despite the millions of Americans on either side of the culture battle, we stick with our view that it is nevertheless a myth. It is a myth because its proponents insist that the entire country is on one side or the other of the culture divide, despite the fact that most Americans refuse to take sides. As the Pew study suggests, the majority of Americans are firmly rooted between the combatants. They understand the cultural issues, and believe there is a middle-ground (and thus a common ground) solution to the divisions. What people on both fringes of the political spectrum don't understand (or don't want to understand) is that gradualism will more likely help them reach their goal than a "neutron-bomb" approach; that cooperation produces greater and more felicitous results. But culture warriors are not seeking cooperation or consensus, and "gradualism" is not in their vocabulary.

We realize that it was the Supreme Court that dropped its legal "neutron bomb" on the country with the Roe decision in 1973. Until that 7–2 decision, some states were modifying or eliminating abortion restrictions with no interference from Washington, but not rapidly enough for the pro-choice movement or for women in states where abortion remained illegal. More than any other ruling—even more than the prayer-in-schools decision a decade earlier, or *Brown v. Board of Education* a decade before that—Roe has becoming the biggest divider and loudest rallying cry on the right and left. Abortion has become the penultimate polarizing issue. Both sides consider any compromise on abortion, or any of the other social issues, to be politically traitorous.

The cultural warriors refuse to accept that most Americans are conscientious objectors in the culture war; which is not to say most

Americans don't care about social issues. They do, but they believe sensible common ground solutions are preferable.

> *"What are those people in Washington doing? All they do is yell at each other about a bunch of stuff no one out here gives a rat about. I'm a conservative, but as far as gays . . . so what? Leave 'em alone. They ain't bothering anyone."*
> —A white male, forty years old, Independent, Kansas City, Kansas, during a focus group interview by Beckel

> *"I think abortion is killing, but I don't go out and shoot abortion doctors like some of 'em has been doin'. That's murder, too. We don't want that* Roe *thing, but it's the law and not changing. Let's get as much for the unborn as we can, get real."*
> —A white female, fifty-six years old, registered Republican, Kansas City, Kansas, during a focus group interview by Beckel

Regrettably, these pleas for restraint, which are reflective of the majority opinion, fall on deaf ears with polarizers in the culture war. To be fair, most participants hold their views strongly and with conviction, but many secular polarizers simply prey on these emotions to continue the climate of polarization we have witnessed over the last twenty-five years.

How did it come to this? Why did American politics, which has produced so many great leaders, and the world's oldest democracy allow the muck of polarization to gain center stage? When did it all start? The storm clouds that produced the climate of polarization were a long time coming, but many of us either missed them or chose to ignore them.

PART II

The Gathering Storms

7

STORM CLOUDS FROM THE SOUTH

I think it's about time we voted for senators with breasts.
After all we've been voting for boobs long enough.
—Claire Sargent, Arizona Senate

IN LESS THAN TWO DECADES, CLOUDS OF DISCONTENT, SPAWNED BY a series of unanticipated events, converged. A type of geomagnetic storm sprang up, causing fluctuations in the political field that affected our public discourse and overwhelmed our politics. Both political parties would be dislodged from their historic foundations. The voter base of each would be profoundly changed. The climate of bipartisanship and consensus that had anchored American politics since the Civil War would be shattered, radically altering the political landscape. What followed has been a quarter century of political polarization, which continues to this day.

The first storms appeared in the South as the struggle for civil rights moved from the courts to the streets. Television carried pictures that transported the evils of segregation from small Southern towns into living rooms and challenged consciences across America. The storm then moved north, igniting riots in the inner cities of Detroit and New York. In the Watts section of Los Angeles, a single incident between white cops and a black man triggered the largest race riot in American history. In 1968 Martin Luther King Jr. and senator Robert F. Kennedy were assassinated. Vietnam War protests erupted on college campuses, revealing a youth counterculture that had Grandma fleeing to the basement in horror.

Conservative supporters of Arizona senator Barry Goldwater wrenched control of the Republican Party from GOP moderates, only to give it back when Goldwater lost the 1964 presidential election in a landslide. Alabama's segregationist governor George Wallace left the Democratic Party, making it easier for white Southern voters to abandon their lifelong commitment to the party that had dominated the South since the Civil War.

America lost her first foreign war, while at home the Supreme Court struck down state laws banning abortion. The exodus of Southern whites from the Democratic Party intensified as Congress and the federal courts overturned Jim Crow laws. A break-in at the headquarters of the Democratic National Committee led to a scandal that came to be known by a single word: *Watergate*. Richard Nixon became the first president to resign from office. A farmer from Georgia was elected president, and replaced four years later by an actor from California.

The women's movement emerged as a political force. The importing of foreign oil became a major economic, as well as a political, issue. Rachel Carson's book *Silent Spring* spawned an environmental movement that would clash with corporate America, while inflation in the 1970s eroded wages and profits. The Cold War between the United States and the Soviet Union continued, while China emerged as a serious economic and political power. A fragile peace in the Middle East was brokered by the United States, as a nascent and dangerous Islamic fundamentalism began to build.

The size of the federal government grew under both Democratic and Republican presidents. These new agencies and departments created a substantial increase in government rules and regulations, impacting citizens and businesses alike. The growth of government produced cadres of political activists who would descend on Washington, demanding (and getting) access to policy makers. Activists working for change were countered by an increase in the number of people who worked to protect the status quo. The result was a tenfold increase in the number of lobbyists and lawyers. Campaign donations became the means of access, as campaign costs skyrocketed. The federal budget, which would grow to more than $1 trillion by the end of the twentieth century, brought even more players to Washington. They sought jobs, government contracts, and a share of the fiscal pie.

American culture had dramatically changed. The 1950s *Ozzie & Harriet* and *Leave It to Beaver* TV image of America gave way to the 1960s "Summer of Love." Elvis faded (temporarily), the Beatles were in, beer drinking gave way to LSD tripping, and the sexual revolution supplanted submarine race watching at the drive-in. Condoms were out, the birth control pill in. Summer camp took on a whole new meaning at Max Yasgur's Woodstock farm in upstate New York. Valium helped some people in the seventies "make it through the night."

Well-behaved black students on college campuses suddenly grew Afros, wore leather coats, and thrust clenched fists into the air. Nice, well-scrubbed white students grew their hair long, burned their bras, and took to the streets to protest the war in Vietnam. In rural America, guys in pickups played Sergeant Barry Sadler singing "Fighting soldiers from the sky, fearless men who jump and die. These are men of the Green Berets." In VW campers from Ann Arbor to Harvard Square, Country Joe and the Fish could be heard singing "Be the first one on your block to have your boy come home in a box."

Across America, the two-fingered peace sign was answered with a one-finger response. Everyone wanted power: black power, white power, brown power, red power, women's power. Meanwhile most folks were just trying to pay the power bill.

Helicopters played a big role in the 1970s and early '80s. One flew an American president away from the White House in disgrace. Another flew an American ambassador off an embassy roof in Saigon, fleeing for his life. Iranians seized the U.S. embassy in Tehran, taking Americans hostage; U.S. military helicopters collided and burned in the Iranian desert trying to free them. Movie lines were long, but not as long as gas lines. Blockbuster movies like *Jaws* and *The Exorcist* reflected the fearful public mood. Eight percent inflation helped to propel a new president to office, while nearly 14 percent inflation helped drive him out four years later. In 1980 a deadly virus began to infect the gay community.

The political storms from 1964 to 1980 upended much of our political and cultural past. For the next twenty-five years, America's dominant political parties agreed on less and fought more. Like aging boxers past their prime, the parties kept pulverizing each other, seemingly oblivious to the pain they caused to themselves and to the country. Congressional bipartisanship and consensus broke down. It was replaced by a growing climate of polarization that threatened America with a civil Cold War.

No single event in the twentieth century changed the Democratic Party more than the civil rights movement. The dramatic shift occurred in 1960 when an overwhelming number of black voters— many loyal to the Republicans since Abraham Lincoln issued the Emancipation Proclamation a century earlier—moved their allegiance to the Democrats. After the Kennedy assassination, President Lyndon Johnson sealed that allegiance by signing the Voting Rights Act, the Fair Housing Act, and the 1965 Civil Rights Act.

Johnson recognized the consequences of the civil rights bills by telling an aide he was signing away the South to the Republican Party. With his signature came the beginning of the end of the coalition that had made Democrats the dominant political party in America since 1932. Trickles of Southern Republicans were elected to Congress. By the 1970s, the trickle became a stream, and by the 1980s, the floodgates had opened.

To underscore how profound the political change was in the South after 1965, consider this: in 1960 JFK received 50 percent of the Southern white vote. By 1968 the white vote for Hubert Humphrey had shrunk to 10 percent. In 1960 there was not a single Republican senator in the thirteen states of the Old Confederacy. By 2007 only five Democrats remained in the Senate from the same thirteen states. The Democrats' former stronghold had become the Republicans' new base.

Politics in the South were changing even before the sweeping civil rights laws. A region that had been economically dependent on agriculture increasingly became more attractive to companies seeking cheaper, nonunion labor. The year 1965 marked the first year that more American workers wore white collars than blue collars. White-collar workers who followed companies south were mostly conservative in their politics and culture. The South provided a heritage and a history that reflected their values and viewpoints. Southerners attended church more often than citizens in other parts of the country and the churches they attended were mostly conservative and Protestant.

Strong support for the military has a long tradition in the South, going back to the Civil War. There is hardly a town in Dixie without a war memorial to a Confederate hero and a monument to fallen soldiers in every subsequent American war. Southern congressional Democrats—whose longevity in office assured them powerful positions on the Armed Services Committees—made the South home to more military bases and personnel than any other region of the country. As a result, the military became a dominant economic force in the region. But that mattered less to Southern white voters than the unraveling of American traditions embodied in the growing number of Vietnam War protesters and their counterculture movement. Since Democrats were "in charge," they were blamed.

Just as the civil rights crisis appeared to recede after sweeping national legislation striking down Jim Crow laws was enacted, America's involvement in Vietnam escalated. As the number of American "advisers" grew, so, too, did the antiwar movement. The South, on a per capita basis, sent more soldiers to Vietnam than any other region of the country. As a result, the South would experience the largest share of casualties.

Television, which brought pictures of Southern segregation into millions of homes, was now doing the same with antiwar protests. TV coverage of racist Alabama sheriff Bull Connor, with his fire hoses and dogs, inflamed non-Southerners. TV coverage of hippies burning the American flag and marching on the Pentagon evoked a similar reaction in the South. "America: Love It or Leave It" became the slogan of the traditional preservationists. "America: Save It or Screw It" responded the hippies and yippies.

As unacceptable as it was to oppose the war, to most Southerners the protesters' assault on America was more than unpatriotic—it was ungodly. Their counterculture lifestyle profoundly and deeply offended citizens who affectionately referred to their region as America's "Bible Belt." The dominant churches in the South were Baptist and Methodist, the most conservative of the Protestant denominations, at least in that region. There were conservative Roman Catholic strongholds in Louisiana and among Latinos in Texas and Florida. Some pockets of Jews could be found in the few progressive cities of the South, like Charleston, South Carolina, and Atlanta. But it was conservative Protestants who dominated the cultural agenda, and increasingly the political agenda.

Disgust with the antiwar movement wasn't limited to the South. In the vast ethnic blue-collar enclaves of the Midwest and Northeast, the counterculture lifestyle was just as unacceptable. Blue-collar workers, many still living in urban areas and who mostly voted for Democrats, would see their sons go off to war, while most children of suburban white-collar workers would go off to college. In the 1960s, the massive baby boom generation had swelled enrollment in the nation's colleges and universities. As students, they were exempt from the draft until graduation. Despite their college deferments, thousands of suburban kids did, in fact, go to war, but the perceived disparity caused significant resentment among blue-collar families.

As the civil rights battles of the 1960s escalated in the South, more blacks migrated to Northern cities looking for work. The migration threatened blue-collar workers who feared competition for jobs and an increase in crime in their neighborhoods. Race riots in Detroit and New York, coupled with court-ordered school busing in the Northeast and Midwest, heightened fears of a dangerous breakdown of law and order.

For Democrats, all of these storms came to a head in 1968. The antiwar movement was growing and protests were spreading. In a March 1968 nationally televised address from the White House, Lyndon Johnson announced that he would not seek another term as president. The relatively peaceful and optimistic mood of the fifties and early sixties had given way to anger over the Vietnam War. The counterculture movement associated with the antiwar demonstrations provoked outrage and disgust in older Americans. Both the antiwar and counterculture movements would increasingly become associated with the Democratic Party. (This was a real culture war, not the culture war fabricated by polarizers two decades later.)

Doubts about the Democrats grew among voters in the sixties and seventies. Opposition to the Vietnam War raised questions about Democrats' patriotism and commitment to national security. The party's apparent indifference to, or involvement in, campus protests and street demonstrations, coupled with race riots and (as conservatives charged) liberal judges who gave light sentences or probation to violent criminals, prompted critics to suggest the Democrats were soft on crime. The support of labor unions, minority groups, and the growing feminist and environmental movements gave Republicans an opening to label Democrats as the party of special interests. All of these charges would haunt Democrats for decades.

The assassination of Dr. Martin Luther King Jr. caused radicals in the black community to challenge his tactics of nonviolence. The Black Panthers, who rejected passive protests and encouraged confrontation, were among the most vocal of the extremist groups. King's death was followed within months by the assassination of Senator Robert F. Kennedy, who sought the Democratic presidential nomination on an antiwar platform. With the deaths of their heroes, the hope that burned within many of the "love generation" turned to despair and then anger. Protests became increasingly violent and TV caught it all.

8

A CIRCULAR FIRING SQUAD

How come we choose from just two people to run for president and fifty for Miss America?

—Author unknown

IN 1968, ANTIWAR ELEMENTS OF THE DEMOCRATIC PARTY, INCLUDing many who were supporters of Bobby Kennedy prior to his assassination, rallied around Eugene McCarthy; Democratic Party leaders supported Hubert Humphrey. This left Democrats deeply divided as they approached their national convention in Chicago. It was a convention that resembled a train wreck. When antiwar protesters descended on Chicago, they were met by the Chicago Police Department commanded by the legendary "boss," Mayor Richard Daley, who supported the Vietnam War and had little patience with demonstrators.

Daley ordered the police to keep the protesters away from the convention site. The confrontation that followed caused hundreds of injuries, and thousands of protesters were arrested. Ultimately, Humphrey won the party's nomination, even as those outside the convention center and hundreds of liberal antiwar delegates inside screamed in opposition. Humphrey felt obligated to support Johnson's Vietnam policies, but finally did criticize the war during the final weeks of the campaign. It was too late, and Humphrey narrowly lost the election to Richard Nixon. Party regulars blamed the antiwar left for Humphrey's defeat, while liberal Democratic activists ignored the regulars and began a campaign to seize control of the party.

Nixon's the One

In 1968, Kevin Phillips, a Republican political consultant and author of the seminal political book *The Emerging Republican Majority,* was a Nixon campaign strategist. Phillips argued that the FDR/JFK coalition of Southern Democrats and ethnic blue-collar Catholics in the industrial cities of the North was now fertile ground for Republicans. Nixon's call for "law and order" exploited the racial and cultural fears of these voters, who saw lawbreaking and disorder play out on the nightly news and more ominously in their own neighborhoods. They wanted order restored and believed the campaign slogan, "Nixon's the One."

It worked. Nixon won the presidency, but he faced a Democratic Congress and a liberal press corps that interpreted the race as a Humphrey loss, not a Nixon victory. Nixon did his best to win them over. Many of Nixon's domestic programs were liberal, but he talked conservative, and for most Republicans, that was enough. It was Richard Nixon, for example, who became the first president to propose a minimum income for all Americans of working age, employed or not. Suspicion of Nixon ran so deep among liberals in Congress and the press (both of which had wanted a minimum income program) that Nixon's proposal was defeated.

Nixon did other unconservative things. He expanded welfare benefits, created the Environmental Protection Agency, and nominated Harry Blackmun and Warren Burger to the Supreme Court. The "Minnesota Twins," as they were called (because both came from Minnesota), voted as part of the 7–2 majority in *Roe v. Wade,* which ushered in legal abortion nationally.

On Vietnam, Nixon was determined (like Lyndon Johnson before him) not to be the first president to lose a war. To blunt domestic opposition to the war, he instituted new regulations that put fewer young men at risk of being drafted after college. Notwithstanding the new draft rules, the antiwar movement and particularly the counter-culture movement continued to grow. When these young protesters reached voting age, they overwhelmingly registered Democrat.

After repeated confrontations, Nixon abandoned any pretense of trying to get along with the Washington establishment. In the 1970 midterm election, he adopted a polarizing strategy of dividing Democrats along the demographic fault lines Kevin Phillips had outlined in 1968. Nixon and Spiro T. Agnew (Nixon's vice president and a former governor of Maryland) crisscrossed the country denouncing liberals and calling the press, in Agnew's immortal phrase (written by William Safire), "nattering nabobs of negativism."

A growing number of Southern Democrats and Northern blue-collar workers began to vote Republican for the first time. Conservatives in the Republican Party welcomed the new recruits, with good reason. There had been an ongoing struggle between moderate and conservative forces within the GOP that had been brewing since Dwight Eisenhower's second term (the roots of the struggle went back to Teddy Roosevelt's campaign against William Taft). The new Southern recruits, however, would ultimately tip the balance for party supremacy in the conservatives' direction. Moreover, this new conservative supremacy seemed to be permanent.

The Liberals' Revenge

By 1972 the antiwar movement had spread well beyond college campuses, providing liberals with enough votes to elect a majority of delegates to the Democratic Party Convention in Miami. This time, party regulars were on the outside looking in, as antiwar senator George McGovern of South Dakota won the nomination. The Democratic Party was in disarray, and Nixon was reelected in a landslide. The Republican Party, expecting long coattails in Nixon's forty-nine-state romp, got none. In the Senate, the GOP actually lost seats. Voters split their ballots in every region of the country, opting to continue divided government and maintain the status quo of checks and balances between the White House and Congress. With the country so divided, voters were reluctant to put their trust in one party, a voting pattern that would repeat itself in future elections.

Watergate

The Democrats' gloom was quickly overtaken by an emerging scandal that had been almost overlooked during the tumultuous 1972 campaign. That June, the headquarters of the Democratic National Committee was the scene of a break-in. Enough has been written about the Watergate scandal and the subsequent resignation of Richard Nixon that we will give it only a passing mention here. Nixon resigned the presidency on August 9, 1974, and Gerald Ford was sworn in as the thirty-eighth president. In his first address as president, Ford said, "Our long national nightmare is over." As it turned out, it wasn't quite over.

It would take the Republican Party several years to recover from Watergate. President Ford was left with a stagnant economy, the withdrawal of American forces from Vietnam, and a number of other challenges and problems not of his making. One problem that was of Ford's making was his decision to pardon Richard Nixon. On September 8, 1974, Gerald Ford signed an unconditional pardon of Richard Nixon, which meant Nixon would never have to face trial for a range of potential charges emanating from Watergate.

The reaction to the pardon was quick, negative, and huge. It wasn't that voters wanted to see Nixon handcuffed and sent to prison (although a few Democrats would not have shed tears), but at a minimum they wanted him to be subjected to the judicial system in some way. People vented their rage in the only way they could, by voting in historic numbers for Democrats in congressional races across the country. Seventy-five new Democrats were elected to the House, making the Democratic majority 290 to the Republicans' 145. It was the Democrats' largest margin since 1932. In the Senate, Democrats gained four additional seats to add to their already solid majority. The combined House/Senate Democratic majority was the largest since 1936.

The Presidential Campaign of 1976

Prior to Watergate, Republicans (at least at the presidential level) had been starting to draw a new electoral map. The traditional Republican states in the Rocky Mountain West and the lower Midwest and Plain states were now anchored by a solid base in the South. The central question going into the 1976 race was whether the voters had finished venting their anger over Watergate.

President Ford had other problems. In July 1975 Ronald Reagan, the newly retired governor of California, authorized his supporters to establish a campaign committee. In November, Reagan officially declared he would challenge Ford for the Republican presidential nomination. Reagan had been governor of California for eight years. He came from a state the size of a midsize country. His tenure and the size of California were assets in the minds of Republican voters who preferred a president with experience. Reagan had once been an FDR Democrat, who left the party to support Barry Goldwater's 1964 campaign for president. He liked to say, "I didn't leave the Democratic Party, the Democratic Party left me."

Reagan trailed Ford by substantial margins in the polls. Washington insiders and political experts considered him a lightweight. But Reagan's candidacy kept the nomination a cliffhanger all the way to the convention. Ford won virtually all the early primaries and caucuses, most in the North and East. But when the nominating process turned south, Reagan caught fire. What the political experts missed was that the Reagan campaign had become the rallying point for the fast-growing conservative movement within the Republican Party.

Ford did secure the nomination, but the coming of Reagan and the conservatives ensured that future Republican nominees would no longer be moderates like Jerry Ford.

9

"I'LL NEVER LIE TO YOU"

When I was a boy I was told anybody could become president; I'm beginning to believe it.

—Clarence Darrow

"I'M NOT A LAWYER, I AM NOT A MEMBER OF CONGRESS, AND I'VE never served in Washington," said Jimmy Carter as he traveled across the country from 1974 until 1976 seeking the presidency. It was a long march for the peanut farmer, turned governor of Georgia, turned candidate for president. But a long march was perfectly suited to a Carter candidacy.

Carter was served well by not being a product of the Washington political crowd. Vietnam and Watergate, combined with a general feeling that the federal government was not the omnipotent force it once was, had soured voters on establishment candidates. Being a Washington outsider was now "in."

The anti-Washington themes Carter and Reagan used in 1976 would be embraced by many other candidates for president and Congress in years to follow. It is fair to suggest that both contributed to the polarization that would explode a decade later. The core of the polarizers' message today inevitably begins with the evils of the Washington political establishment, which is a variation on the Carter/Reagan message. The irony, of course, is that the polarizers have become the political establishment in Washington.

Carter's message was perfect for the times. He was a former naval submarine officer; a small-town farmer from tiny Plains, Georgia; a Sunday school teacher; and the first openly born-again Christian to run for president, with a record without a hint of scandal, all of which reinforced his campaign theme, "I will never lie to the American people." This appealed strongly to conservatives and moderates who had been appalled by the Watergate scandal and the seemingly endless erosion of bedrock family values.

Carter's election gave Democrats a false sense of optimism that their old base was being restored. The election was close, with Ford closing the gap in the final weeks, much as Humphrey had done against Nixon in 1968. The electoral map in 1976 resembled 1960. It appeared that Kevin Phillips's prophecy of an emerging Republican majority of presidential electors had been short-lived. In fact, it had only been delayed. That Carter won (in part because of Watergate) is true, but it is also true that his style suited the times.

Despite having large Democratic margins in the House and Senate, Carter and the Congress never got on the same page. The president's plans to reorganize and streamline the federal government met fierce resistance on Capitol Hill, especially among liberal special-interest groups that depended on government to fund their pet programs. Liberal activists increased their number to defend their agenda. This growing body of liberal activists (during a Democratic presidency) would provide recruits for the coming polarization wars with conservative Republicans.

Something else happened on Carter's watch that would feed polarization. Congress, especially the House, began to change the structure of its committees. Important committees, including Ways and Means and Appropriations, established subcommittees with new chairmen. New subcommittees meant more staffers and congressional hearings, which meant more lobbyists and special-interest groups would descend on Washington. The new subcommittees also meant new power centers that would help raise campaign funds.

On foreign policy, Carter had some successes, but these were overwhelmed by far too many political setbacks. He succeeded in ratifying a controversial Panama Canal Treaty and in bringing

American pressure on some nations guilty of human rights abuses, but neither was politically popular. The OPEC countries drove up oil prices, keeping Americans in long gas lines, while Carter's energy program was crippled by special interests, leaving consumers with virtually no relief. To his credit, Carter was the only president to forge a peace treaty between Israel and Egypt, but that accomplishment was soon overshadowed by the seizure of the American embassy in Iran by Islamic terrorists.

The embassy takeover, coupled with the Panama Canal Treaty, an unexpected Soviet invasion of Afghanistan, and opposition to Carter's human rights policies, underscored a growing perception that the Democrats were weak on national security issues. Conservative Republicans pounded the message home, while conservative think tanks made the case for the Democrats' appeasement of America's enemies. The result would be a significant step toward the polarization of foreign policy between the two parties.

The last thing Carter needed was a fight for the Democratic nomination, but he got one from the liberal wing of his party in the candidacy of Massachusetts senator Edward Kennedy. Kennedy ran a hapless campaign that only served to highlight the Democrats' far-left wing and undermine moderate Democrats. But the Carter/Kennedy contest went all the way to the Democratic convention in New York. Carter prevailed, but he entered the fall campaign weakened by the economy, hostages, and a divided party.

Ronald Reagan easily won the GOP nomination, and in the process put a new and endearing face on the conservative movement. Despite efforts by Democrats to demonize Reagan, his genial personality and optimism won over a majority of voters. What looked like a close election turned into a blowout. The emerging Republican majority was back on track.

This was the first "wave election" since FDR ran in 1932. (Some argue 1952 was a "wave election" when the Republicans took the White House and Congress. However, it only lasted two years.) One ingredient of a "wave election" is a sense that the politicians currently in control in Washington have ceased to understand the needs and desires of the average voter. They usually occur when one party has been in control of the White House and Congress, as was the case in 1980. One-party control that can't produce results garners very little sympathy from the voters. If you can't make progress when you control everything, when can you? As we shall see, a similar fate would confront presidents whose party controlled both houses of Congress in 1994 and 2006.

The years 1976 to 1980 became a significant benchmark in the growth of polarization. Both Carter and Ford faced intraparty challenges by candidates on the extreme left and right. Party unity and discipline had given way to ideological division. In both cases, the challenge to Ford in 1976 by Reagan and to Carter in 1980 by Kennedy weakened each president and contributed to his defeat in the general election.

In the end, both parties became dominated by their political extremes, as moderates became increasingly irrelevant. With the demise of moderates came the erosion of bipartisanship, especially in foreign policy. An unwritten rule accepted by both parties had been that "partisan politics end at the water's edge." No more.

10

ROE V. WADE

Some men change their parties for the sake of principles;
others their principles for the sake of their party.
　　　　　　　　　　　　　　　　—Winston Churchill

IN 1973, WHEN THE SUPREME COURT DECIDED, BY A 7–2 MARGIN, that state laws restricting or outlawing abortion were unconstitutional, some on the secular, religious, and political left believed they had once again socked it to the religious and political right. As with the Scopes "monkey trial" fifty years earlier, *Roe v. Wade* (and the companion *Doe v. Bolton* decision) was a triumph of reason over faith and a victory for personal choice of the many over dictatorship by the few. But unlike Scopes, when religious conservatives left the political playing field in favor of the "catacombs," this time they began to mobilize with the intention of fighting back.

The left failed to anticipate this revolt by religious conservatives because most liberals do not "hang out" among those they view as uneducated. To the secular and religious left, religious conservatives were unwashed, trailer-park-living, pickup-truck-driving, white-socks-wearing, nondancing, nondrinking, nonmoviegoing, noncard-playing know-nothings who believed if you were having a good time you must be engaging in sinful activity.

The problem for these disgruntled conservatives was that they lacked a leader. Politically, there was no one who excited them. Richard

Nixon cared little about culture or what came to be known as "social issues," and his charisma level had the depth of floor wax, but without the shine. Nixon had his own problems in 1972 that would ultimately lead to his resignation. Gerald Ford, who replaced him, was regarded by conservative Republicans as a RINO (Republican In Name Only) who, along with his wife, Betty, was pro-choice.

By 1976 many conservative Christians saw in Jimmy Carter a presidential candidate around whom they could rally. Carter spoke their language. He had been a Southern governor and was a Baptist who openly told of having been born again. He attended church and even taught Sunday school. Enough conservative Christians voted for Carter in the 1976 election to give him a narrow victory over Gerald Ford (Carter got 50.1 percent of the vote to Ford's 48 percent with slightly more than one and a half million votes dividing them). Had Ronald Reagan managed to beat Ford for the nomination, he might still have lost to Carter, who could talk in the religious language that appeals to evangelicals probably better than Reagan did at the time.

Conservatives were quickly disappointed in Carter when he failed to convert his religious language into political action. He hired Sarah Weddington—the attorney who argued in favor of abortion before the Supreme Court in the *Roe* case—to be one of his top aides. He also stocked his administration with people who were mostly secular liberals. Conservative Christians were appalled and many felt they had been duped by Carter. They expected something more from him because they incorrectly believed that the language of faith translates into agreement on their policy issues and political agenda.

The frustration level continued to build among this still-unorganized group. As inflation and interest rates grew, along with unemployment, conservatives began looking again at Ronald Reagan, a divorced man whose church attendance record was spotty compared to Carter's, but who could arouse them as no potential candidate had in their lifetime. It was with Reagan that the shift began. Evangelical Christians were about to accept someone who may have been personally flawed, but who they believed could deliver them to the electoral promised land and give them the respect they felt they had not received from the elites. Reagan's most serious flaw in the eyes of evangelical voters was that he had been divorced. That could be easily forgiven because increasing numbers of Christians had experienced marital breakup and evangelicals were becoming pragmatic. Reagan's second flaw was a bigger obstacle to overcome.

As governor of California, Reagan signed a bill on June 15, 1967, liberalizing that state's abortion laws, six years before *Roe*. Reagan later said he regretted that decision and many conservatives were happy to forgive him and accept his "repentance." This was an important and strategic shift for conservatives, who until then would put a "mark of Cain" on someone they believed was outside "biblical norms."

Political sophisticates knew it was not enough to have secular and economic conservatives for Reagan. They needed another demographic, one that could be brought into the arena only if one of their own gave them permission.

Enter Jerry Falwell, a relatively young pastor of what the press and even Falwell called a "fundamentalist" congregation in Lynchburg, Virginia. Lynchburg is located about 180 miles southwest of Washington, D.C., but in the late 1970s, it was another world in terms of culture and political sophistication. Old homes dot tree-lined streets, and the trees are older than most residents. *Sleepy* would be an appropriate adjective. This was old Virginia (as in "Carry Me Back to Old Virginia"), where people knew one another's names, folks didn't move too often, and lots of people went to church on Sunday. It was also the home to several well-known colleges and universities, including Randolph Macon Women's College, Lynchburg College, Sweet Briar, and the soon-to-be-famous Liberty University (then called Liberty Baptist College).

Falwell had preached for years against a too-close association with politics. For the Christian, he taught and believed at the time, politics was about another "kingdom" headed in another direction. It was also about a "King" who doesn't stand for election. One of Falwell's most famous sermons was delivered in 1965. It was titled "Ministers and Marches" and was a response to the civil rights movement and the pronouncements and political activism of Dr. Martin Luther King

Jr. In that sermon, Falwell laid out a seemingly uncompromising position on the relationship between church and state. It is worth quoting one of its most important lines because it shows how far Falwell would have to turn (a complete 180 degrees) in order to lead the Moral Majority fourteen years later. Falwell said at the time, "We have a message of redeeming grace through a crucified and risen Lord. Nowhere are we told to reform the externals. We are not told [in the Bible] to wage war against bootleggers, liquor stores, gamblers, murderers, prostitutes, racketeers, prejudiced persons or institutions, or any other existing evil as such. The gospel does not clean up the outside but rather regenerates the inside."

That seemed about as clear as one could get. The greater power came from a King and Kingdom not of this world. Politics was a lesser power, and besides, according to Falwell circa 1965, it wasn't something in which real Christians should be involved anyway. Not only were they not "called" to be in politics, getting into politics would sully their primary message and do little, if anything, to reform the culture.

By early 1979, Falwell had become increasingly frustrated with the social and moral direction of America. His "Liberty Singers" were involved in patriotic rallies around the country and Falwell himself was speaking more from the pulpit and on his televised *Old Time Gospel Hour* program (which was mostly a broadcast of his Sunday-morning church service) about cultural and social issues.

Two men who were known less for their religious ties than their political experience decided to meet with Falwell to see if an alliance might be formed to change the political direction of the country. They were Paul Weyrich, a Roman Catholic, and also president of the conservative Committee for the Survival of a Free Congress, and Howard Phillips, at the time a Jew, who was president of the Conservative Caucus.

All three agreed that something had to be done and, in fact, could be done if a new alliance might be established between the fundamentalist and conservative churches of America and the conservative political movement, mostly embodied within the Republican Party. Conservatism within the GOP had not been much of a force since the disastrous defeat of Barry Goldwater at the hands of Lyndon Johnson in 1964, but the rise of Ronald Reagan and his near miss at capturing the Republican nomination from Gerald Ford in 1976 gave them hope that in 1980 the conservative triumph might be achieved. But it would not be complete without religious voters abandoning their reluctance and tearing down the wall they had helped to construct between church and state.

Falwell agreed to lead, or at least be a part, of such a movement. What to call it? It was Weyrich who suggested there was a "moral majority out there in the country."

"That's it," responded Falwell. "We'll call it 'The Moral Majority.'" The organization hired direct-mail wizard Richard Viguerie to help raise funds and Falwell abandoned whatever reluctance he once had to preach on politics and began devoting entire sermons to political issues—from abortion, to the Supreme Court, to Jimmy Carter, to the homosexual rights movement. People began to send him money in response to those sermons and a sophisticated direct-mail campaign.

In August 1980, Falwell joined with a large group of pastors and political activists in Dallas, Texas. Reagan attended and delivered his famous line, "You can't endorse me, but I can endorse you." Bill Moyers of Public Television was at that gathering and wondered on his program "where all these people had come from." Like many other Americans who didn't "hang out" where these people did, Moyers had failed to see the movement coming. Like other liberals, he thought of religious conservatives as an endangered species who had been extinguished in the 1920s. That they were back and ticked off was a surprise to him and much of the rest of the media.

Some fundamentalists—like Bob Jones III, president of Bob Jones University in Greenville, South Carolina—stuck to their belief that Christians should stay out of partisan politics for all the reasons Falwell once stated. But others joined the movement. Fifty state Moral Majority chapters were set up. What most of the media didn't know (because, again, they didn't hang out among these people) was that Falwell was perpetrating a giant hoax on the media and the political establishment. Many of these "chapters" were little more than a separate phone line on a pastor's desk. And none of the money raised by the national organization would "trickle down" to the state level. That was kept in Lynchburg. State chairmen (and they were all men) were expected to raise their own funds.

Training sessions were held in many states to teach people how to talk on television and how to dress. This was a crash course in entry-level politics for a people who mostly knew they were mad and weren't going to take it anymore, but needed direction to channel that anger. That meant getting behind Ronald Reagan and pushing.

It wasn't long after Reagan's inauguration that the compromising of principles an earlier Falwell had warned would come for conservative Christians were they to marry into politics took place. But Falwell and those who would make the leap with him would soon be high on the narcotic of political power and there would be no turning back. He would continue to back Reagan even though Justice Sandra Day O'Connor, whom Reagan named as the first woman to sit on the Supreme Court, turned out to be the swing vote upholding *Roe*. Reagan had assured Falwell in two phone calls that O'Connor would be okay on abortion. To Falwell, that meant she would vote to overturn *Roe*. When she did not, Falwell held his tongue.

Since Falwell had repeatedly called abortion "America's national sin," it was difficult for some to reconcile such a statement with his uncritical support of Reagan. What it was about, of course, was access. Like Fred Astaire and Ginger Rogers—Ginger gave Fred sex and Fred gave Ginger class—Reagan gave Falwell access, which is power, and Falwell gave Reagan a "moral covering" for his policies, even some policies that many conservative Christians did not like. They mostly remained silent, because by then it didn't matter. They had the illusion of power (which fueled fund-raising) rather than power itself, and that was enough.

Falwell died in May 2007. His legacy will not be politics but his university and the people he introduced to God through his pastoral ministry.

11

THE REAGAN REVOLUTION

Politics is supposed to be the second oldest profession. I have come to realize that it bears a very close resemblance to the first.

—Ronald Reagan

THE DAY RONALD REAGAN WAS SWORN INTO OFFICE, JANUARY 20, 1981, the Iranian regime of Ayatollah Khomeini set fifty-two American embassy employees free after 444 days of captivity. It was a bittersweet moment for Jimmy Carter, who had spent over a year negotiating the hostages' release. The timing was clearly an affront to Carter, but the embassy staff, like Carter himself that day, was finally going home.

To his credit, Reagan took no responsibility for the release of the hostages, but he benefited nonetheless. The embassy captives had become emblematic of the last year of the Carter administration. The public saw a great superpower being held hostage by soaring gas prices, runaway inflation, towering interest rates, and Iranian thugs. The entire nation was in a sour mood. Now the hostages were free and a new, optimistic president was heading to the White House. Americans seemed ready for almost anything but the status quo.

Reagan's signature legislation involved cutting federal spending while at the same time lowering federal tax rates. At the core of the Reagan plan was an economic theory called "supply-side economics." This view claimed that cutting income taxes would eventually increase federal receipts. More money, the proponents argued, would be available for spending and investment, creating a "trickle-down" effect throughout the economy, producing more income for individuals and thus more tax revenue. To make up for revenue losses in the short term, significant budget cuts would be required to avoid further federal deficits that were already too high for most conservative Republicans. Reagan got most of the tax cuts he wanted, but the budget cuts were mostly accounting smoke and mirrors. In any event, Democrats (and many congressional Republicans) restored most of the Reagan budget cuts, especially money for entitlements.

Democrats didn't like Reagan's tax cuts. The major beneficiaries were in the high-income brackets and most of them were Republicans. They resisted rich people getting tax cuts while Social Security benefits were reduced. Social Security, the most important program that remained from the New Deal, affects more Americans than any other federal program. As far as Democrats were concerned, it was their legacy.

The battle between Democrats and Republicans over Reagan's tax and budget cuts caused taxes and Social Security to dominate domestic politics, becoming polarizing issues for years to come. While taxes would serve as the rallying cry for Republicans, protecting social Security was at the heart of the Democrats' domestic agenda.

The 1982 elections marked the twenty-eighth consecutive year the Republicans were a minority in the United States House of Representatives. Aging House Republican leaders had grown accustomed to this status. But in 1978 and 1980 a number of younger GOP members had been elected who were decidedly more conservative and impatient than their elders. These young conservatives were led by a firebrand congressman from Georgia named Newt Gingrich.

As their nominee for the 1984 presidential election, the Democrats chose former vice president Walter Mondale, but not before he faced a stronger-than-expected challenge from Colorado senator Gary Hart and the Reverend Jesse Jackson.

Hart pounded Mondale as an old-fashioned liberal beholden to the party's interest groups, especially organized labor. This was audacious considering that Hart had been George McGovern's very liberal campaign manager in 1972. Jackson was the first black to run a major campaign for president, forcing Mondale to emphasize big government programs in order to appeal to Jackson's base. Despite making a historic decision to choose the first female vice-presidential candidate—Congresswoman Geraldine Ferraro of New York—Mondale came to his convention tired and bloodied after a yearlong battle against Hart and Jackson.

Reagan was reelected in one of the greatest landslides in history. The Democrats lost seventeen seats in the House and two seats in the Senate. Despite the landslide, 1984 had the largest incumbent reelection percentage of any in history to that point. Of the 435 House members, 392 were reelected. In the Senate, 93 of 100 members returned to the next session of Congress. As we shall see, the reelection of incumbents would grow to unbelievable levels as Democrats and Republicans, in one of the few areas they could agree on, colluded to fix district lines for incumbents.

One Senate race that year in North Carolina pitted incumbent Jesse Helms—the unreconstructed right-wing Republican—against Democratic governor Jim Hunt. It was the first campaign in which negative television advertising by both sides outpaced positive ads. The ads of one candidate would be answered within twenty-four hours by the other. In the end, Helms, who won, spent nearly $17 million. Hunt spent almost $10 million. Both were records for a Senate campaign. The Helms–Hunt race led to the growing force of consultants and negative messages that were early indicators of the polarization in American politics.

The new Congress elected in 1984 would preside over the last major bipartisan legislative achievements before extreme partisanship settled in and stayed. Budget legislation for the first time set limits on federal spending with requirements to find cuts to match any spending increases. The most significant tax reform bill since 1961 dropped the highest tax rate on income to 25 percent, and closed major loopholes in the tax code. The Social Security Trust Fund, which was rapidly being depleted, was salvaged when President Reagan and Congress agreed on increasing Social Security taxes and gradually raising the retirement age. When Ronald Reagan signed this legislation, the president who hated taxes would approve the largest tax increase in history.

In 1986 an immigration bill that granted amnesty to the roughly 3 million illegal immigrants already in the country, and put sanctions on employers who hired illegals, was signed into law by President Reagan. Ironically, twenty years later immigration would reemerge as a pivotal issue in the polarization of politics. Amnesty, applauded by the conservative hero Reagan, would become the poll-tested, conservative catchword used to undermine immigration reform.

An important event in 1985 underscored a growing tolerance in America for different lifestyles. Actor Rock Hudson, the handsome leading-man heartthrob of millions of aging American women, announced that he was gay and dying of a then relatively new disease called AIDS. The public reaction, from Nancy Reagan to Americans across the country, was one of sympathy and support. Hudson's announcement brought the AIDS virus to the public's attention at a time when very few outside the gay community had even heard of the disease.

Prior to Hudson's public disclosure, the Reagan administration had been under fire by liberals for ignoring AIDS. When the HIV virus began to spread in the early 1980s, it was thought to be a disease contracted only by gays. Given that gays were a solidly Democratic voting block and anathema to Christian conservatives, liberals charged that the administration had little interest in devoting resources to combat the disease.

There is some truth to the allegation, but Reagan himself was not at fault. He had been an actor for decades in California and counted among his good friends many gay actors. Reagan was never as intolerant as the left portrayed him. On the other hand, he did cultivate the conservative Christian community, which made their feelings known about AIDS, or the "gay plague," as the Reverend Pat Robertson and some other Christian leaders referred to the disease. Given the influence of conservative churches, liberals might be excused for suggesting a conspiracy of silence by some in Reagan's administration.

The cultural tolerance that pervaded America in the 1980s was in stark contrast to the great cultural divides of the sixties and seventies. The public seemed to adopt a disposition of live and let live. America was becoming more culturally diverse and people were much more accepting of different lifestyles as long as those lifestyles did not negatively affect them, their families, or their community.

What Americans were witnessing in these few years was not the end of the storms that had swept across the country during the previous two decades, but rather a brief respite before the unpredictable turbulence that would follow. Like the eye of a hurricane, which can give an amateur a false sense that the storm has passed, Americans began to convince themselves that they were secure. In fact, they had survived the dangerous outer bands that precede a hurricane's calm center only to be catapulted back into the storm still raging just beyond the calm of the eye.

PART III

Storms

12

IRAN-CONTRA AND BOB BORK:
THE PEACE ENDS

There are many men of principle in both parties in America,
but there is no party of principle.

—Alexis de Tocqueville

THE 1985–1986 BIPARTISAN AGREEMENT ON THE BUDGET, TAXES, and immigration was applauded by mainstream politicians and the press, but the extremes in both parties viewed it as capitulation to the other side. Conservative activists, especially, thought the new tax cuts had not gone far enough. Liberal activists believed conservatives had gone too far. The brief period of bipartisanship following the 1984 election posed a real threat to the polarizers. Neither side had the slightest interest in reaching consensus. Both were itching for a fight, and they found one in Nicaragua.

In 1979, the socialist Sandinista movement seized control of Nicaragua. The Reagan administration, in a classic Cold War reaction, feared the Sandinista ideology would spread to neighboring countries. President Reagan went so far as to declare "a red tide is spreading in the Americas." The administration asked Congress for money to help the Contras, an anti-Sandinista militia group.

After a long and contentious debate, Congress approved aid to the Contras in August 1986. The Contras demonstrated little prowess on the battlefield and even less skill in accounting for how they used U.S. taxpayers' money. Congress eventually became wary of a commitment that might repeat the debacle in Vietnam a decade earlier and halted military aid to the Contras.

Contra supporters in and out of government were outraged. The Contras had become a central rallying cry for Reagan administration hawks, as well as a celebrated cause for several conservative think tanks and wealthy conservatives. A private fund-raising operation was initiated by Colonel Oliver North, who worked on President Reagan's National Security Council staff. Substantial private funding initially kept the Contras going, but even with aid from these deep pockets, Contra supporters couldn't fund a war.

A scheme was hatched within the White House to raise money from the illegal sale of American weapons to the regime of Iranian mullah Ayatollah Khomeini. The proceeds would be used to subsidize the Contras. This operation was also coordinated by North, with the knowledge of Reagan's NSC adviser, Admiral John Poindexter, and Secretary of Defense Caspar Weinberger, and with the suspected knowledge and complicity of CIA Director William Casey.

The plan unraveled after an obscure Beirut newspaper revealed the arms sale the day before the 1986 midterm elections. The story seemed so outrageous that only a few press outlets pursued it. Selling arms to Iran in itself was a blockbuster story, but when Attorney General Edwin Meese confirmed the sales, the story rose to the level of the bizarre.

Not only had weapons been supplied to Iran, which had held U.S. embassy employees hostage only six years earlier, but the weapons were transported by Israel from its stockpile of American missiles. Meese then dropped this blockbuster: the proceeds from the missile sales had been laundered through European bank accounts and sent to the Contras.

Within a month, Poindexter and North were gone, and President Reagan had appointed a commission to investigate Iran-Contra. It was chaired by former Texas Republican senator John Tower. But congressional Democrats, now in control of the House and Senate, conducted their own hearings. Unlike Watergate, the Iran-Contra hearings had a far more partisan tone. The Democratic committee staff ignored their Republican counterparts, infuriating GOP members.

Many Republicans believed, with good reason, that the Democrats used the hearings as a platform for attacking Republicans before the 1988 presidential election. Vice President Bush, the front-runner for the 1988 Republican nomination, came under heavy fire from Democrats for attending meetings on Contra funding.

Iran-Contra led to the appointment of an independent prosecutor, Lawrence Walsh, to determine if any laws had been broken. The Walsh appointment was the result of a law, enacted after the Watergate scandals, that allowed federal judges to appoint a prosecutor independent of the Department of Justice. The Independent Counsel Act would become one of the prime contributors to polarization.

Walsh proceeded to prosecute and convict key players, including North, Poindexter, and Weinberger, the latter shortly before the presidential election of 1988. President Reagan's approval ratings, which had been in the high sixties, plummeted to the forties. On October 19, 1987, the Dow Jones Industrial Average lost 508 points, or 23 percent of its value, in the largest single-day decline in the history of the stock exchange. Legislation in Congress began to stall as partisanship, ignited by Iran-Contra, deepened.

The rancor generated by Iran-Contra carried over into Ronald Reagan's second Supreme Court nomination. Reagan nominated the former solicitor general in the Nixon administration, Robert Bork, who was to replace retiring justice Lewis Powell. Bork was the type of strict constructionist the conservative movement had been longing for. Reagan's first selection, Sandra Day O'Connor—who became the first female jurist on the high court—was historic, but many on the right did not consider her conservative enough.

For most conservatives, Bork was the ideal choice. Not only was he conservative, Bork was also vocal in his opposition to "activist judges." He believed that nothing in the Constitution permits abortion, and he was not afraid to mix it up in his confirmation hearings. Rather than kowtow to senators, Bork was blunt.

It was his bluntness that would cause him trouble. Democrats saw his unsmiling persona as arrogance. Bork's demeanor was more likely caused by his anger following an unprecedented assault by

Senate liberals and outside liberal interest groups. On the day Reagan announced the nomination, Senator Edward Kennedy went to the Senate floor and gave a scathing denunciation of Bork. Kennedy's "In Robert Bork's America" speech infuriated Bork and his conservative supporters.

Bork was defeated in October by a vote of 58–42 with virtually all Democrats and a handful of Republican senators voting no. The Bork battle rewrote the rules for future nominees. No longer were a potential jurist's qualifications paramount; ideology and personal issues were now fair game. After Bork, no Supreme Court nominee (or for that matter any federal judicial nominee) would be as candid in confirmation hearings as Bork had been.

The Bork defeat, as much as any other event, helped launch a new era of "the politics of personal destruction." A new verb emerged from the Bork debacle. From the day of his defeat until today, whenever political nominees for the courts or high administration posts were denied confirmation, they were said to have been "Borked."

G. H. W. Bush and the Willie Horton Diaries

Of all the politicians associated with the politics of personal destruction, George Herbert Walker Bush seemed the most unlikely. The senior Bush had developed many friendships, including some with Democrats, during his long tenure in Washington. Before becoming president, he had been a member of the House of Representatives, director of Central Intelligence, chairman of the Republican National Committee, ambassador to the United Nations and China, and vice president under Ronald Reagan.

Bush was the clear front-runner in 1988, but Iran-Contra and sagging poll numbers for Reagan raised serious doubts that any Republican could win the presidency that year. That didn't stop a full field from trying. Among them were Kansas senator Bob Dole and a preacher who had never been elected to public office named Pat Robertson. Robertson was the head of the Christian Coalition, a grassroots organization of conservative, mostly Protestant churches.

Running a far-flung religious organization while simultaneously seeking the presidency seemed both improbable and audacious. Robertson, however, was host of a daily Christian television show, *The 700 Club,* and was comfortable with the most influential medium in contemporary politics. He was a curiosity who generated large press coverage. The media seemed to love covering religion and politics and the resulting debate over the separation of church and state. The Robertson campaign was good for ratings, but the church–state battle it spawned contributed mightily to polarization.

Bob Dole was thought to be the front-runner in Iowa, but Bush had a superior ground operation and the support of many in the Iowa Republican establishment. At a minimum, the Bush campaign expected a strong second-place finish with a shot at beating Dole. Bob Beckel was in Iowa the day of the caucuses in 1988. "I was covering the race for a number of television outlets with my Republican counterpart, Haley Barbour, now governor of Mississippi. We had gone to a large caucus site in Des Moines to get a feel for the Dole–Bush race and noticed dozens of church buses in the parking lot. I asked Haley about all the church people. Since Haley had been involved in several Iowa presidential caucuses over the years, I assumed there was an explanation. Haley said, 'I've never seen that crowd before.' What we were seeing was an upset in the making by Pat Robertson."

As expected, Dole won the caucuses, but in a stunning and embarrassing defeat for George Bush, Pat Robertson came in second. Bush was a distant third. Far from ending the contest early, Bush now had to slug it out for several months. He won the New Hampshire primary, but he "won it ugly." Bush had to go negative, something he didn't like and wasn't accustomed to. The negative attacks were directed at his principal opponent, Bob Dole, who was not afraid to "go ugly" himself.

Bush finally got the Republican nomination he had sought his entire political life, but he was battered and bruised by the time of the Republican convention in New Orleans. Meanwhile, Bush's Democratic rival, Governor Michael Dukakis of Massachusetts, benefited from a rarity: a united Democratic Party and a thirty-point lead in the polls heading into the fall campaign. Perhaps if the

Republican nominee had been Dole and not Bush, the negative campaign that followed would not have surprised or angered Democrats as much as it did . . . but this was George Bush, Mr. Nice Guy, a consensus player. However, the campaign he ran was anything but nice. His manager was the legendary hard-knuckled veteran of political combat, Lee Atwater (who would die tragically from a brain tumor only two years later). Atwater was an expert at destroying political opponents.

Dukakis's inexperience at national politics caused him to repeatedly stumble. It especially showed in the way his campaign refused to respond to the Bush camp's negative attack ads. Dukakis was put on the defensive on several fronts, but none had the impact of Willie Horton.

Massachusetts had a state law that allowed criminals to take furloughs from prison to explore employment opportunities following release and to be with their families. The law was passed under Republican governor Francis W. Sargent in 1972. Republicans connected Dukakis to the law because in 1976 he vetoed a measure that would have made inmates convicted of serious crimes ineligible for furloughs. One of the prisoners furloughed while Dukakis was governor was convicted murderer Willie Horton. While home in Maryland on furlough, Horton committed a brutal rape. A Maryland judge refused to return Horton to Massachusetts, fearing he might be released again. Horton was sentenced in Maryland to two consecutive life terms plus eighty-five years.

In a TV commercial produced by a committee supporting Bush, responsibility for letting Horton out of prison was placed squarely on Dukakis. The impression left with voters was devastating. Dukakis lost the race, but the Democrats didn't lose their resentment over the Bush campaign's negative tactics. If George Bush would go down this trail, the Democrats surmised, they could, too.

Shortly after Bush was elected, Iraq's dictator, Saddam Hussein, invaded Kuwait. Employing his consensus-building experience and foreign policy expertise, Bush assembled a coalition to force Hussein out of Kuwait. Nicknamed Desert Storm, the war lasted a phenomenal one hundred hours. Hussein was routed and Bush was exalted.

For a brief time, the Democrats rallied to Bush in a show of bipartisan support. It wouldn't last.

Clarence Thomas, an African-American, was nominated to be an associate justice by George Bush in 1991. The liberal establishment, led by the National Organization for Women, furiously attacked Thomas. The left accused Thomas of sexual harassment when he was a lawyer with the Equal Employment Opportunity Commission during the Reagan administration.

One of his employees at the EEOC, Anita Hill—also an African-American—accused Thomas of sexually harassing her and engaging in lewd sexual behavior while they both worked there. Hill, a professor of law, became the liberals' key witness against Thomas. Republican members of the Senate Judiciary Committee assailed Hill. They wanted to know why she had come forward at virtually the last minute when she might have spoken up sooner. Hill's supporters claimed that she had little to gain from appearing before the committee (other than defeating the nomination of a conservative justice). They cited authorities on sexual harassment who say most women don't come forward out of fear and embarrassment.

What about Clarence Thomas? Hill might well have lied. There was no significant evidence produced at the confirmation hearing or during the FBI background check on Thomas that came close to proving him guilty of the sexual harassment of Anita Hill. Thomas suggested he was the victim of "a high-tech lynching," a rejoinder that put even some white liberals in fear for their political lives. An article by David Brock in the conservative magazine the *American Spectator* ravaged Hill, underscoring how polarized the political climate in Washington had become. In the article, Brock called Anita Hill "a little bit nutty, and a little bit slutty."

Cal Thomas talked to former president Bush in October 2006 for this book. The senior Bush was decrying the state of polarization today. His answer reflected how polarization had played out in the Clarence Thomas nomination.

> You take the judges, Cal, and it's almost like when you send up
> the first nominee, batten down the hatches because we're going to

destroy people. That seems to me to be the attitude a lot of them are taking. And I'm not sure it's all one-sided, either. We have some hip-shooters on our side as well.

The euphoria over Desert Storm made President Bush a heavy favorite for reelection in 1992. But the good feelings about the war gave way to concerns about the economy. The Democrats mounted a furious attack on the president's economic policies, particularly budget deficits. The Bush budget pending before the Democratic Congress was in trouble, and he was forced into a deal with them. While Bush's intention was to cap spending, part of the deal included a tax increase.

Republican activists were apoplectic. Tax cuts were the hallmark of Renaldo Maximus (as talk show host Rush Limbaugh affectionately nicknamed former president Reagan, who, by the way, also raised taxes after first cutting them—we guess he must have been against them before he was for them). The right never fully trusted Bush, viewing him as a member of the party's moderate "Rockefeller wing." They regarded his deal with Democrats as a sellout and confirmation of everything they had feared about him.

The last two years of the Reagan presidency and the four years of the Bush 41 term will be remembered for a successful war in the Middle East and the breakup of the Soviet Union. But it will also be remembered for Iran-Contra, titanic battles over the federal budget and tax policies, and bitter division over judicial nominees, especially the Supreme Court nominations of Robert Bork and Clarence Thomas.

On October 15, 1991, Clarence Thomas was confirmed by the Senate 52–48, giving Bush a much-needed victory. Despite the Thomas success, conservatives were still burning over the Bush deal with the Democrats allowing tax increases. By the time the 1992 presidential campaign began to heat up, Desert Storm and Clarence Thomas were almost an afterthought in a political year dominated by bad economic news. The reelection of president Bush was no longer a sure thing.

After the polarizing battles over Iran-Contra and Bork, voters appeared ready to turn the Republicans out of the White House in 1988. However, Dukakis turned out to be the wrong Democrat to take advantage of the public's discontent. In effect, the race was a referendum on Dukakis, not a mandate for George Bush. But in 1992 Bush faced a very good Democratic candidate in Arkansas governor Bill Clinton. Texas billionaire Ross Perot entered the race as an independent who focused on the dangers of the exploding federal deficits under Reagan and Bush. With voters generally tired of Republicans, Democrats desperate for the White House after a twelve-year drought, and Perot drawing a surprising 19 percent of the vote, Bush faced too many obstacles to win a second term.

Clinton won the election with only 43 percent of the vote, a historic low for a victorious presidential candidate, while George Bush also set a record for a sitting president, getting just 38 percent. Clinton's victory enraged an already polarized conservative base. They were appalled that a man they believed lacked family values, and was on the wrong side of the culture war, would occupy the Oval Office. The right never considered Clinton a legitimate president and immediately set out to prove it. The political climate, already ugly, was about to get a lot uglier.

13

THE POLITICS OF PERSONAL DESTRUCTION

Why pay money to have your family tree traced; go into
politics and your opponents will do it for you.
—Author unknown

SCANDALS HAVE ALWAYS BEEN A PART OF AMERICAN POLITICS. MOST
have involved money, sex, or treason. Scandals are not the exclusive
property of Republicans or Democrats, though each party tries to
cast itself as more moral than the other. Following a scandal involving one party, the other party promises to usher in a "new era" of
honesty and integrity. Somehow it never quite works out that way.
Scandals have been as big as Watergate (Republican) and as small as
a stripper jumping into the Reflecting Pool with a congressman
(Democrat), though there have been bigger scandals involving Democrats (Abscam) and smaller ones involving Republicans (the late
senator John Tower's drinking and philandering).

Politicians in this era of polarization have little margin for error.
With an aggressive and ever-expanding media pool including twenty-
four-hour cable news, left-wing blogs like the Huffington Post, and
right-wing bloggers like the Drudge Report, accompanied by permanent opposition research teams from both parties, politicians are
under intense scrutiny.

Many of the tactics employed by polarizers against their opponents bear a striking resemblance to the methods used by the notori-

ous Republican senator Joseph McCarthy of Wisconsin. During the 1950s, McCarthy led a campaign that falsely accused many public figures of being communists or communist sympathizers. There probably were a few communists embedded in the United States government (e.g., former spy Whittaker Chambers fingered a midlevel State Department official, Alger Hiss, who became a stepping-stone for Richard Nixon's rise to power).

But McCarthy's scattershot approach, virtually accusing everyone who had as much as shaken hands with a communist of being afflicted with the "disease," would lead to the senator's political and, ultimately, personal destruction. Before McCarthy's reign of terror ended, the reputations of many innocent men and women would be destroyed. The McCarthy era was one of the bleakest periods in American history.

To avoid the fate that ended McCarthy's career, today's members of Congress practice rules of etiquette that border on the pristine. They are forbidden to engage in personal attacks on one another, or on witnesses testifying before committees. Such behavior is also forbidden during floor debates.

By the mid-1980s, polarizers in Congress found plenty of outside groups to do their dirty work. For example, on the left, pro-choice groups, including NOW, eagerly took the lead in muddying Bob Bork. On the right, the National Rifle Association bashed liberal gun-control advocates in Congress as soft on crime. Both parties contributed to these most polarizing of tactics. Given the speed at which information flows today, inaccurate information moves too quickly to control, and corrections or retractions come too late to undo the damage. It is a cliché, but no less true, that "a lie can travel halfway around the world before the truth can get its shoes on."

Both parties—and especially their interest-group allies—justify their contribution to the politics of personal destruction on pious ideological grounds. Polarizers argue that they undertake this wanton personal destruction to protect politics from ideological forces bent on imposing their extreme agendas on the "rest of us." This allows the character assassins to portray themselves as defenders of the faith, raising the question (that should have been asked of Joe McCarthy when he used a similar argument): What and whose faith are they defending?

We would like to reintroduce the term *McCarthyism* in its proper context and apply it to every bottom-feeder and polarizer in Washington who has participated in this most cowardly form of personal destruction. To be specific: some allegations leveled at Bob Bork and Bill Clinton deserved to be heard and investigated. But those organizations that unfairly used unsubstantiated hearsay and manufactured "evidence" in an attempt to destroy the careers of these men were guilty of McCarthyism.

Many congressional observers believe four events set the table for the politics of personal destruction:

The Ethics in Government Act was passed by a Democratic Congress in 1978 following the Watergate scandal. Its purpose was to curb the powers of the president and other senior executive-branch officials. The law provided for a "special prosecutor," later changed to "independent counsel." This office had nearly unlimited powers and resources. It became the weapon of choice in the politics of personal destruction. Like many laws passed after a crisis in Washington, the Ethics in Government Act was well intentioned, but flawed.

Its first test came during the Carter administration. The issue was whether government officials had used cocaine at the Studio 54 nightclub in New York. No one was prosecuted, but the targets had their reputations sullied, and were forced to pay enormous legal fees out of their own pockets. The law has provisions for most, but not all, legal fees to be paid by the government, but only if the person charged is acquitted.

Many more government officials would suffer unnecessarily at the hands of overzealous independent counsels. Most were cleared of charges, but sometimes only after years of investigations, costing millions of dollars. The government can dip into a bottomless pit of money, giving it an unfair advantage over an individual with limited resources.

Two examples stand out. One is the case of the Clinton administration's secretary of Housing and Urban Development, Henry Cisneros. In 1995 Attorney General Janet Reno asked a three-judge panel to appoint an independent counsel to determine whether Cisneros criminally concealed information from the IRS or conspired with his mistress to do so. He later admitted to paying the mistress more than $250,000 in hush money and was forced to resign. What makes this case particularly egregious is that as of this writing in mid-2007, the independent counsel has not yet closed this investigation and issued a final report. What a waste of taxpayer dollars!

The other case involved Ronald Reagan's first secretary of labor, Raymond Donovan. Prior to joining government, Donovan had been a successful contractor. One of his company's projects was the construction of a new subway line for New York City. The construction contract required Donovan's firm to subcontract part of the work to minority firms. Some of the minority contractors Donovan used were accused of being fronts for real owners who were not minorities. Donovan was charged with larceny and fraud. After a protracted, high-profile trial, he was acquitted. After his acquittal, he was famously quoted as asking, "Where do I go to get my reputation back?"

The law was allowed to lapse in 1992, but was reinstated two years later after Republicans, who had wanted the law to expire, suddenly began to consider the many potential scandals of Bill Clinton. Despite political advice to the contrary, President Clinton went along with the law's reinstatement. It would later be used to investigate him and lead to his impeachment.

Democrats and Republicans often abused the intent of the law by using it to harass political opponents. The act ruined reputations and in one case may well have affected the outcome of a presidential election. George H. W. Bush believes to this day that Lawrence Walsh, the independent counsel for Iran-Contra, contributed to his defeat by indicting Defense Secretary Caspar Weinberger on June 16, 1992, less than five months before the November election.

The second factor contributing to the politics of personal destruction was the Senate's rejection of Robert Bork. Bork was not the first court nominee to be turned down, but the campaign against him was unusual. Most, though not all, nominees who had failed to win confirmation in the twentieth century were defeated for reasons unrelated to their judicial philosophy. Generally, conflicts of interest, financial improprieties, or personal misconduct were the reasons cited. The only reason a Senate majority rejected Bork was his conservative view of the law, especially his dislike of *Roe v. Wade*. The Bork case showed the pro-choice interest lobbies to be formidable (and polarizing) players in the confirmation battle.

The third factor contributing to the politics of personal destruction has been a generation of political consultants in both parties who have plied their trade almost exclusively in the genre of negative campaign ads. They have turned the process into the political equivalent of pornography. The 2006 campaign was the zenith in negative advertising in terms of record dollars spent to purchase TV, radio, and newspaper space for a slew of negative ads. A climate of polarization leads naturally to heavy reliance on negative campaign messages.

A fourth contribution emerged in the campaign cycles of 2004 and 2006 in which the Internet and individual "blogs" began to play important roles in the politics of personal destruction. Increasingly, what is carried on the blogs—from President George W. Bush's alleged use of cocaine to the Swift boat veterans' allegations against John Kerry—has had an impact on our political dialogue. Thus far the information (or should we say, "disinformation") from these Internet sources probably has not had a direct impact on the outcome of an election. Nonetheless, if future presidential elections are as closely decided as those of 2000 and 2004 and the Internet continues to grow as it has in the last decade, a presidential election might well turn on just such inaccurate "facts."

14

POLARIZATION'S POSTER CHILDREN: BILL CLINTON AND GEORGE W. BUSH

We'd all like to vote for the best man, but he's never a candidate.
—Frank McKinney Hubbard (1868–1932), Indiana humorist

POLARIZERS NEED CONTROVERSIAL ISSUES TO KEEP THEIR SUPPORTers energized, and they need enemies to keep them angry. If the early era of polarization got its energy from civil rights, Vietnam, abortion, and "family values," Bill Clinton and George W. Bush came along later to provide the enemies. Each man stirs a well of resentment in the opposition party that runs deeper than any witnessed in modern American politics.

Some argue that these two presidents "coincidentally" came to power during a time of polarization and paralysis in national politics. In this theory, after two decades of increasingly disruptive partisanship, presidents elected at the end of the twentieth century were bound to inherit a growing and highly charged political climate. It was the times, rather than the people in power, that brought on polarization.

The trouble with this theory is that political personalities actually do matter. Of course Bill Clinton and George W. Bush were elected during a time of extreme partisanship. However, during their terms the climate grew increasingly toxic. Some argue that neither Clinton nor Bush could control the political environment they inherited, but that is doubtful. Both men had personalities and agendas that exacerbated and intensified polarization. Worse, both came to realize that the polarizing climate could enhance their own political fortunes.

Initially, both men recognized that governing in a polarized environment was not in their interest and that an atmosphere that might lead to some consensus on their respective agendas would be much more effective. Two things conspired to ensure that this would not happen.

Clinton and Bush were elected to their first terms under circumstances that raised questions about the legitimacy of their victories. Both presidents began their terms with a majority of voters having opposed their election; in Clinton's case by an historic margin. Clinton won his first election with only 43 percent of the popular vote in a three-way race. Although Clinton won the electoral college by a wide margin, he was the first president since 1968 to receive less than a clear majority of the popular vote. The third-party candidate, Texas billionaire H. Ross Perot, won 19 percent of the popular vote, the highest total for a third-party candidate since Teddy Roosevelt in 1912.

Bush won his first term after losing the popular vote to his Democratic opponent by 500,000 votes. Not only did Bush lose the popular vote, but his electoral-college victory was challenged in the courts for over a month until the Supreme Court, dominated by Republican appointees, ruled that the Florida secretary of state, Katherine Harris, was within her constitutional rights in deciding that Bush had won the state's twenty-seven electoral votes. A hard core of Democrats still believes that Bush's victory was illegitimate.

The second factor that doomed any chance for compromise was that neither man's party leadership was interested in bipartisanship. When Clinton was first elected, Democrats controlled both houses of Congress; when Bush was elected, Republicans were in control of both chambers. Events that had preceded the election of each man had caused much rancor in Congress, particularly in the House. In both cases, the minority party in Congress frustrated efforts by the majority-party president to enact much meaningful legislation. The goal was to ensure that the president would be unable to enact anything that the opposition party considered extreme. More important, the minority did not want the president to succeed.

Ironically, the reversal in standing, with Republicans now in the majority, seemed to bring more cohesiveness to each party. The Democrats needed a united front if they were to thwart the Republican agenda, and the Republicans rallied together, knowing that whatever bills they passed would be with few, if any, Democratic votes. They also knew they faced Clinton's veto pen until the 2000 election. That election and the controversy over it would further strengthen the Democrats' partisan cohesion.

In the end, both Clinton and Bush chose to be polarizers. After the Democrats lost control of Congress in 1994, Clinton adopted a strategy for his reelection that depended on constant confrontation with the Republican Congress. Bush simply ignored the Democrats, while Republican congressional leaders kept their thin majorities together and steamrolled the Democrats on issue after issue. With Bush as president, the Republicans on Capitol Hill no longer feared a veto pen. As a result, the divide between the parties grew ever wider and more polarized.

15

CLINTON YEARS/CLINTON WARS

Instead of giving a politician the keys to the city, it might be better to change the locks.

—Doug Larson, author and humorist

AT THE BEGINNING OF 1992, REPUBLICANS COULD NOT IMAGINE the prospect of a Democratic president. After Jimmy Carter's failures, the success of Ronald Reagan, and, under George H. W. Bush, the end of the Cold War and the victory in Desert Storm, Republicans began to think of the White House the way Democrats used to think about Congress: it was their personal entitlement. Republicans also assumed that the Democrats would continue to dominate the House, making control of the Oval Office that much more important.

With Bill Clinton in the White House, the Democrats would control both the executive and legislative branches with the prospect that Clinton would get to nominate at least one Supreme Court justice (he named two). This made finding ways to cripple the new president an imperative among the extreme partisans, who by now virtually controlled the GOP. These Republican operatives, who had used Willie Horton to eviscerate Dukakis in 1988, needed ammunition to attack the new president. Bill Clinton gave them plenty.

During the 1992 campaign, Clinton was dogged by allegations of sexual indiscretions, evading the Vietnam-era draft, and, along with his wife, Hillary, exploiting the Arkansas governor's office for personal financial gain. All of this and much more would provide Republicans with a rich vein of material with which to launch a relentless campaign to destroy Clinton. Republicans would argue that Clinton's behavior was self-destructive, and they merely pointed it out.

The attack was launched on multiple fronts. They included the Clintons' involvement in an Arkansas development project called Whitewater, Clinton's long history of sexual indiscretions, his use of Arkansas State Police officers to facilitate his sexual escapades, and Hillary Clinton's use of the governor's office to enhance her private law practice.

The Washington press corps gleefully jumped on the Clinton-bashing bandwagon, proving to some that even though the media is mostly liberal, they are equal-opportunity muckrakers when it comes to a good political scandal. The media wallowed in the Clintons' misery. Even the liberal *New York Times,* which had endorsed Clinton, seemed to leave journalistic standards behind in its quest to expose the president and first lady. The scandalmongering became so blatant that the *Times* lowered itself to reprinting rumors and wild charges by people with questionable motives and suspect reputations. The *Times* quoted stories that had first appeared in the *National Enquirer* and other tabloids normally given to fantastic revelations about alien visitations and two-headed women.

Clinton's troubles were exacerbated by the emergence of conservative talk radio. The Clintons were the ideal targets for the conservative audiences attracted to the new radio format. It could be argued that without Bill and Hillary Clinton, the shows might not have enjoyed the success they have today. (However, we do not expect Rush Limbaugh or Sean Hannity to rush out and thank the former president and first lady.)

By June 1994, the multiple allegations against the Clintons had reached a politically critical stage. With President Clinton's approval, his attorney general, Janet Reno, appointed an independent counsel to investigate a number of allegations, collectively known as "Whitewater." Reno named Republican lawyer Robert Fiske, deputy attorney general in the George Bush 41 administration. The Independent

Counsel Act (ICA), which had caused so much trouble for both Republicans and Democrats, was about to do so again.

Fiske issued an interim report on Whitewater and intended to release several other conclusions concerning additional allegations. Virtually the same day Fiske published his report, the ICA was reinstated. That wasn't enough for some conservative Republican senators, who thought Fiske had been far too moderate during his tenure at the Justice Department, so they asked for a new counsel. The judge in charge of the Special Division, the three-judge panel that appointed independent counsels, was David Sentelle. Sentelle was a devout conservative and a close friend of Senator Jesse Helms (R-NC), who was one of the Senate's most notorious polarizers. The Special Division selected former federal appeals judge for the District of Columbia Kenneth Starr. The choice was controversial, but well within the Special Division's guidelines for independent counsels. In the several years he was special counsel, Starr would prove to be Clinton's greatest nemesis and the most controversial independent counsel ever selected under the ICA.

The allegations that dogged Clinton from the beginning of his term did not deter him from pursuing a legislative agenda that flew in the face of the Republican mantra on taxes. Clinton's first major legislative proposal was an economic plan to deal with the budget deficit that included a tax increase on the top 5 percent of taxpayers. Republicans strongly opposed the proposal.

When the House and Senate voted on Clinton's economic package not one Republican supported the bill, but Democrats rallied around Clinton, though for many it was a dangerous political vote. They knew the Republicans would use the tax increase against them in the coming midterm elections. Nonetheless, all the Democrats stayed with Clinton's economic plan, and as a consequence, some were defeated in the 1994 election on their tax-increase vote alone.

That not a single Republican supported the bill was a bigger story than the immediate political fallout. The vote on Clinton's budget would set a pattern of party-line voting in the House—and to a lesser extent the Senate—that continues today. The days when members voted for local interests over party interests were coming to an end. In the years since 1993, Congress—at least on politically charged issues—has begun to look more like the British Parliament than a representative democracy.

With party-line voting enforced by increasingly partisan leadership in both parties, the negative aspects of a parliamentary system followed. Those downsides are best described in a book written by British authors Michael Schluter and David Lee: *The R Factor*. In Chapter 9, the two discuss the British system of political confrontation. Many of the same practices and principles in the British system now apply to contemporary American politics.

Consider the similarities: the authors lament the "confrontational style which one finds expressed in the House of Commons" (and in the House and Senate in America), saying that "it is institutionalized in a two-Party [system]" that "leads to sometimes paralyzing discontinuities of policy and not infrequently turns important policy issues like education and health into political footballs. The politicizing does little to benefit the ordinary citizen. Indeed, as a Swahili proverb has it: 'when the elephants fight, it's the grass that suffers.' "

After 230 years, the British have found their revenge! What has happened in the American Congress over the last two decades has, indeed, turned important issues into partisan footballs with "little benefit to the ordinary citizen." It would get worse after 1993.

The extent to which party-line voting is becoming the norm was displayed in the 1999 impeachment of Bill Clinton. No vote cast in Congress is more important under the Constitution than a vote in the House to impeach a president and one in the Senate to convict and remove a sitting president from office. No president has ever been convicted, but President Andrew Johnson was the first to be impeached. Bill Clinton would be the second.

The vote on Clinton's impeachment underscores the extent to which polarization had affected politics at the end of the twentieth century. At the time of Clinton's impeachment, there were 228 Republicans and 206 Democrats in the House. The first article of impeachment on perjury passed 228–206 along straight party lines.

Health Care Reform: Clinton's Mission Impossible

Bill Clinton's pledge to reform the American health care system had been the centerpiece of his campaign for the presidency and it became the signature issue of his first term. To underscore the importance of health care reform, Clinton put his wife, Hillary, in charge of the task force that would develop the administration's plan. If any one initiative could be described as encapsulating all the ills wrought by polarizing politics, it was the Clinton health care reform proposal.

Health care represents 17 percent of the American economy. It encompasses some of the highest-paid professions and employs millions of workers. As a result, the health care industry is well represented in Washington and is a major source of campaign contributions. The industry's premier advocacy group is the American Medical Association, one of the most powerful and influential in Washington. The AMA is also overwhelmingly Republican, as is the U.S. Chamber of Commerce and the American Insurance Association. Both the chamber and the AIA represent huge corporations that provide products and services to the health care industry.

Even before Hillary Clinton convened the first meeting of the health care task force, these massive special-interest groups were planning a campaign to undercut reform. They simply took it for granted that any proposals coming from a Clinton White House would not be in their interest. After all, the status quo was providing enormous profits for the health care industry, much of which came from the federal Medicare and federal-state Medicaid programs. What followed was a textbook example of just how powerful and destructive special interests have become in Washington.

Health care reform gave congressional Republicans an opportunity to derail Clinton's agenda early in his term. Their message was that the American health care system was the best in the world and any effort to change it significantly was dangerous. They floated the idea that under a Clinton plan, Americans would have to change their primary care doctor, that Clinton wanted health care taken over by the federal government, which would create a "single payer" plan similar to Canada's. They charged that a Clinton plan would benefit uninsured Americans at the expense of diminished quality of care for those who were covered. All this before Clinton even began to draft a health care reform package!

This frightening message was widely disseminated through a massive advertising campaign paid for by the health care industry. The infamous "Harry and Louise" TV commercials showed a young, white suburban couple holding hands and telling each other that the Clinton health plan would be devastating and would force them to leave their beloved family doctor and not pay for important new medical advances or new breakthrough drugs. Thus, they would be forced to accept either mediocre health care or face the poorhouse if they opted for the best health care.

The ad became a classic and a model for future advocacy advertising on a range of issues (and a potent weapon for polarizers). Political pressure continued to grow, and even health care reform advocates in Congress were getting cold feet. By the time it was sent to Congress, Clinton's health care reform proposal was DOA—dead on arrival.

By the 1994 midterm election, the Clinton tax increases had passed, but the advertised benefits of the president's overall economic plan were not yet in place. With Clinton under siege by the independent counsel, Democrats were left with few accomplishments to bring to voters that November. The press and pundits were quick to point out that this lack of productivity was surprising since the Democrats controlled the White House as well as the House and Senate. Was this a "do nothing" Congress (a phrase coined by Harry Truman in his upset election in 1948) or a "can't do" president, or both?

The election would have historical and unanticipated consequences. Republicans, for the first time since 1952, took control of the House of Representatives, and also regained the Senate for the first time since 1986. The election, the crown jewel of the Republican conservative revolution, was a stunning repudiation of Clinton and the Democrats. The newly elected Republicans, especially in the House, were a very conservative lot and had run their campaigns as much against Clinton as against their respective Democratic opponents. Their unquestioned leader was Newt Gingrich.

Republican Crusaders Successfully Storm the Gates

Like Moses wandering with the ancient Israelites in the wilderness, House Republicans wondered whether they would ever reach the "promised land" of a majority. After forty years in the minority (the same number of years that Moses led the Israelites, so the analogy is apt), Republicans seemed resigned to the prospect of remaining in the minority for decades to come.

At least those ancient Israelites had a leader who told them he knew where he was going. House Republicans had a leader, of sorts: Representative Bob Michel (R-IL), who was an amiable but not a forceful man. To many Republicans, Michel appeared content with his minority leader role. After all, the Democrats allowed him to have a nice office and certain perks, so long as he knew his place and didn't get too "uppity."

If this sounds like slaves on the Southern plantations of the nineteenth century, that is exactly how many Republicans felt about their status. Newt Gingrich and his fellow Reaganites believed that their only hope of moving forward was through confrontation, not conciliation, with the Democrats. These conservative firebrands believed Bob Michel's strategy of going along to get along doomed Republicans to permanent minority status, and no conservative agenda could be enacted under such an arrangement. The confrontational strategies worked, and in 1994 the GOP finally found the promised land.

Now Gingrich and the Republicans had the power. Gingrich was savvy enough to realize that his working majority of Republicans (232) to Democrats (202) was not large enough to carry on an all-out war while simultaneously passing their long-sought conservative agenda. So Gingrich tried to find some areas of consensus with the Democrats. He wasn't ignorant of the benefits of consensus; Gingrich simply hadn't been in a position to practice it during the scorched-earth campaign he and the conservative activists waged in their quest to wrest power from the Democrats.

The campaign for Republican power deepened polarization to such an extent that very little, if any, legislation was going to pass the House without bloodshed. Republicans could stick together, steamrolling the Democrats on straight party-line votes, but that strategy was certain to be met with a Clinton veto. The House Democratic leadership, particularly Speaker Tip O'Neill, hated Gingrich. There were precious few Democrats in the House who had any personal, or even professional, relationship with Gingrich, and none trusted him.

Gingrich did try some consensus building with the Democratic Black Caucus on trade with Africa and sanctions against South Africa. Gingrich told us that his motives in these, and a few other instances, were not altogether altruistic. The African free-trade bill was supported by the business community, the source of much GOP campaign money. The South African sanctions bill gave Speaker Gingrich an opportunity to take some of the edge off the antiblack image of the GOP.

Let's be careful not to be revisionists. Yes, Gingrich sought some consensus, but for the most part he remained the devil incarnate to Democrats. At the same time he was seeking bipartisan consensus on some things, he was ramming his conservative agenda through committees headed by handpicked chairmen, setting up confrontation after confrontation with Bill Clinton.

Conservative think tanks were sprouting up all over Washington. The business lobby finally had a pro-business Congress, and they would go to any lengths to maintain it. Conservative special interests, from the NRA to the National Right to Life Committee, saw an opportunity to push their most polarizing agenda items. Rush Limbaugh was joined by several new conservative talk show hosts, including Sean Hannity, Laura Ingraham, and Tony Snow (currently the White House press secretary). In 1995, Fox News Channel was launched. It would become the most viewed cable network and arguably the most influential conservative media outlet.

Republican polarizers and their polarizing friends were in power. The Democratic polarizers in Congress (and their polarizing friends) were getting a quick lesson in the guerrilla tactics of the minority. The Democrat-controlled Congress was now gone, but Bill Clinton remained. He was about to become an even larger target for conservative polarizers.

16

CLINTON'S REVENGE

We hang the petty and appoint the great ones to public office.

—Aesop

AFTER THREE YEARS OF INVESTIGATING THE CLINTONS, INDEPEN-dent Counsel Kenneth Starr was at a standstill. Republicans in the House were frustrated with the lack of evidence against the Clintons and urged Starr to keep digging. Starr had plenty of potentially damning information, but none could stand the scrutiny in a court of law. This did not stop the Office of the Independent Counsel from getting it out to the public.

Starr's team was caught leaking raw, unsubstantiated documents to the press. Public opinion began to turn against Starr and his right-wing cohorts. In the spring of 1997, Starr decided to quit. He had accepted an offer to become dean of the new public policy school (funded by Clinton nemesis, millionaire Richard Mellon Scaife) at Pepperdine University in Los Angeles.

Clinton then proceeded to snatch defeat from the jaws of victory. An allegation had surfaced that he had had an affair with a twenty-three-year-old White House intern, Monica Lewinsky. The scandal became public when Linda Tripp, who worked in the Bush 41 White House and was now employed at the Pentagon, surreptitiously re-corded phone conversations with her "friend" Monica Lewinsky about her affair with Clinton. The tapes also referenced attempts by Washington Democratic superlawyer Vernon Jordan to secure a private-sector job for Lewinsky away from Washington.

Washington was now in full polarization mode. Some predicted the end of the Clinton presidency. The House Judiciary Committee began organizing what would be a spectacular impeachment hearing. Many conservative columnists, conservative talk radio hosts, Republican operatives, and even a few liberals not only doomed Clinton's presidency, but also predicted the addition of twenty to thirty Republican gains in the House in the 1998 midterm election.

Once again, the public took a different view of the scandal from the Washington crowd. It was noted that Clinton's enemies in Congress had lower approval ratings than Clinton. Three weeks after news of the Lewinsky affair broke, the president's approval ratings shot up from 59 to 66 percent favorable in a CNN/Time poll. A CBS poll showed an increase from 57 to 72 percent.

The House impeachment hearings were badly managed. The average TV viewer saw the proceedings as driven more by politics than by evidence. Besides, the public seemed to feel "everybody does it" (the "it" being engaging in sexual indiscretion), and as long as the wife didn't mind, most of the public appeared not to care either. In the 1998 midterm election, Republicans lost five House seats, instead of gaining up to thirty, leading to the resignation of Newt Gingrich as Speaker and subsequently from Congress.

The House passed two of four Articles of Impeachment against Clinton on nearly straight party-line votes. The Senate trial was a bit more orderly, with Chief Justice William Rehnquist presiding. Although almost all Republicans voted to convict Clinton, they never came close to the three-quarters vote necessary to remove him from office. Clinton's indiscretions were unforgivable, but the party-line votes in both Houses once again underscored the polarized divide between activists in Washington and the average voter.

Clinton's Houdini-like escape from his enemies infuriated Republican activists in Washington and across the country. Many in the press who had staked their future advancement on the demise of Bill Clinton were likewise beaten and angry. Conservative commentators were apoplectic. The polarized climate got worse, guaranteeing that consensus could not be reached on any issue during Clinton's final two years in office.

17

GEORGE BUSH RIDES IN

George Washington is the only president who didn't blame the previous administration for his troubles.

—Author unknown

DESPITE THE CONTROVERSIAL DECISION THAT MADE GEORGE W. Bush the forty-third president, he came to the White House with his party controlling both the House and the Senate. This would be a blessing and a curse for the new president. The blessing was his party's control of Congress, meant a conservative agenda might finally become a reality. The curse was that with his party controlling Congress and the White House, Republicans couldn't blame Democrats if something went wrong.

George Bush had run for president describing himself as a "compassionate conservative." Although not many people understood exactly what that meant, it sounded warm and fuzzy compared to the hard-edged reputation the Republicans gained during the impeachment proceedings against Bill Clinton. Running as a Washington outsider allowed Bush to distance himself from the growing polarization in Washington. Sensing the public's weariness with partisanship, the Texas governor called for a return to civility and bipartisanship.

Despite his New England patrician roots, George W. Bush was a Texan at heart. He didn't care much for Washington and its pretentiousness. He rarely entertained, went to bed early, and would escape

1600 Pennsylvania Avenue as often as possible to his beloved sixteen-hundred acre ranch in Crawford, Texas. When he couldn't go home, he made regular use of the Camp David presidential retreat. Bush's inner circle was small. With the exception of Chief of Staff Andy Card, most had been with him in Texas.

Bush was loyal to a fault, and expected the same in return. Like most presidents, he was disdainful of the political press corps and hated leaks. The players in the Bush administration took the "no leak" policy to heart and were surprisingly successful in keeping internal discussions out of the media. But leaks are inevitable in Washington, especially when a large group has access to information.

His record as governor of Texas provided evidence that Bush could work with Democrats to pass legislation, and his first proposal to Congress, the "No Child Left Behind" education reform proposal, was an effort to achieve consensus. The White House developed the bill with two of the most liberal Democrats on Capitol Hill, Senator Edward Kennedy of Massachusetts and Representative George Miller, a liberal House Democrat from California.

This attempt at bipartisanship did not sit well with the leadership of either party. Democratic leaders were still chafing from the 2000 election, and were none too pleased with Kennedy for giving the president a legitimacy they felt he did not deserve. Had it not been for Kennedy's stature as *the* liberal lion of the Senate, these concerns might have been more public. Miller, like Kennedy, had been the Democratic go-to guy on education issues for nearly thirty years. But as is the case in so many convoluted Washington power games, there was another story behind the story of the education legislation. It was Miller's Republican co-sponsor for No Child Left Behind, House Education Committee chairman (now House minority leader) John Boehner of Ohio, who was causing real problems for the leadership of both parties.

Democrats didn't like Boehner, and Republican leaders were wary of him because he was one of the few Republican legislators who strongly supported public education. He also was somewhat critical of vouchers that would allow public school students to attend private schools. Tuition vouchers were the most important program in the education reform package supported by the House GOP leadership.

As recounted by Juliet Eilperin in her book, *Fight Club Politics,* when Boehner and Miller negotiated a compromise education bill with Kennedy, the Republican leadership considered it far too liberal. They appealed their case to the president. Bush convened a meeting in the Oval Office with the Republican leaders and Boehner. The meeting was hastily arranged, catching the perpetually tanned Boehner on a golf course. He had to rush to the White House, borrowing a tie on the way.

President Bush went around the room giving each side a chance to make its case. In the end, he said, "I'm with Boehner; meeting over." Thus, Bush got his first (and his only) bipartisan domestic-policy victory. It was a promising start after several years of growing partisanship and polarization between Democrats and Republicans. It would not last.

As much as George Bush wanted his public education bill, he wanted his tax-cut package even more. Like Ronald Reagan, he believed in supply-side economics, which assumed tax cuts, especially on high incomes, would "trickle down," benefiting the entire economy. The Bush tax-cut plan was ambitious. It would take trillions in revenue from the government and return it to taxpayers. The issue was who would get the greatest tax relief.

Democrats argued that the Bush tax cuts would unfairly benefit the wealthiest Americans, provide far too little relief for the middle class, and do virtually nothing for low-income workers. Democrats said Bush wanted to give the surpluses to wealthy Republicans in the form of tax cuts that Democrats argued they didn't need or deserve. Bush countered, accurately as it turned out, that under his plan, millions of low-income workers would be exempt from federal taxes altogether. In the end, he got his tax cuts, but with only a handful of Democratic votes. What had been a good start on consensus domestic policy with the Bush education package ended after a rancorous debate over tax cuts.

Tax cuts came early in Bush's first term and with them the partisan divide between Democrats and Republicans that continued to worsen. George Bush soon learned that Washington Democrats were not like Texas Democrats. In Texas, Democrats controlled the legislature, which required Bush to compromise. With a Republican Congress, the president did not need to seek common ground.

That was just fine with Hill Republicans, particularly in the House. They weren't interested in bipartisan cooperation with Democrats. After forty years under what they perceived as Democratic oppression, Republican Speaker Dennis Hastert, and specifically Republican Majority Leader Tom DeLay, instituted their version of political "get-back." Democrats were mostly ignored and their efforts to influence legislation stymied. At times, Democrats were even shut out of committee hearings, especially during the final drafting of legislation. Republicans controlled the House floor debate and rarely allowed Democrats to offer amendments to pending legislation.

The climate in the Senate was slightly better for the Democrats, given the 50/50 split between Republicans and Democrats. Republicans became the Senate majority by virtue of Vice President Cheney's vote as constitutional president of the Senate. Nonetheless, with such a divided Senate, Republicans were forced to work with Democrats. Then, in the spring of 2001, Vermont Republican senator Jim Jeffords declared himself an independent and announced he would vote with the Democrats. That put Democrats in the majority, 51–49.

Now the Republicans were furious. The change in the Senate brought even more heavy-handed Republican tactics in the House. Republican House members were pressured by DeLay to stay in line since any House bill would face a Democratic alternative in a House/ Senate conference to reconcile differences. Hastert and DeLay insisted on passing the most partisan and conservative bills possible. That tactic, they reasoned, would put the House in a stronger position when the bills went to a conference committee.

(The years Tom DeLay served as majority leader [1999–2005] of the House will be remembered as the high point of the polarization cycle. Perhaps a Democrat, had he or she been a majority leader during this period, would have contributed as heavily to the polarized climate as DeLay did, but we will never know. What we do know is that Tom DeLay was the most extreme partisan in Congress since Lyndon Johnson was majority leader in the Senate in the 1950s).

September 11, 2001, provided the one brief period when the freeze between the Republicans and Democrats in Washington would thaw. Few who witnessed the events that followed 9/11 will forget the evening of September 20, when George Bush addressed the Congress and the world on the response by the United States to the horrors of that fateful day. The president, who sometimes has trouble communicating, was as eloquent as anyone had ever heard him. Democrats embraced him, figuratively and literally. For one brief shining moment and for many weeks and months to follow, America united in common purpose. Despite the agony of 9/11, that unity would not last.

President Bush asked for and received a broad mandate from Congress to pursue the terrorists responsible for 9/11, declaring war on terror. With virtually no oversight and only a handful of dissenters, legislation was quickly approved allowing Bush to pursue terrorists anywhere in the world if he thought they might pose a threat to the United States. What became known as the Bush Doctrine would allow the president to engage in "preemptive" actions to stop terrorists before they could strike America.

President Bush said, "You are either with us, or against us," and that line would become the governing philosophy for the Bush administration, not only on terrorism, but on his entire foreign-policy agenda. It was also a doctrine, as it turned out, that would be applied to his critics at home. This was hardly a domestic political message that encouraged consensus.

This "my way or the highway" attitude backfired because it united Democrats. If they were not allowed in the game, they would have to stick together and find ways to stymie the majority wherever possible. The Democrats' embrace of the war on terror was sincere, but their resentment at the Republicans' polarizing tactics was just as real. No Child Left Behind and the war resolution would be the only bipartisan legislative consensus reached between George Bush and the Democrats, although he did receive considerable Democratic support for the Patriot Act (a bill that would become the source of major divisions between Bush and the Democrats).

18

WAR ABROAD AND WAR AT HOME

Politics is the art of looking for trouble, finding it whether it exists or not, diagnosing it incorrectly and applying the wrong remedy.

—Ernest Benn (1875–1954), British publicist

WHAT FOLLOWS IS WRITTEN BY BOB ALONE BECAUSE CAL STRONGLY disagrees with the conclusions. The Iraq war is one issue on which the authors, despite their best common ground efforts, cannot agree. We do agree that a bipartisan consensus should be pursued by President Bush in consultation with Democrats and Republicans in Congress. The facts concerning the content of the Patriot Act and the campaign attacks described below are accurate.

The Patriot Act was submitted by the White House to Congress in the immediate aftermath of 9/11. The Patriot Act gave the executive branch broad powers to pursue terrorists at home and abroad. It suspended habeas corpus for terror suspects and refused to accept the rules of the Geneva Convention on treatment of prisoners of war, to which the United States was a signatory, by creating a new category of enemies called "enemy combatants." Most of these prisoners were held at the U.S. naval base at Guantánamo Bay, Cuba.

In an extremely controversial move, other terror suspects were sent to Eastern European countries, where they were placed in secret (and perhaps illegal) prisons set up by the CIA. Still others were turned over to our Arab allies in Egypt, Saudi Arabia, and Jordan, where they were tortured for intelligence that was then handed to U.S. officials. Documents have since surfaced indicating that the United States was aware of the torture by its allies, which was widely reported by European and Mideast press outlets. The United States Supreme Court ruled that the confinement of prisoners without habeas corpus was unconstitutional. Congress rewrote the Patriot Act shortly before the 2006 election to comply with the court's ruling.

The domestic provisions of the Patriot Act gave the FBI wide-ranging authority to create roving wiretaps of suspected targets and allowed the Bureau to search a person's home without his or her knowledge and gain access to the records of potential terrorist targets, including records of books checked out at their local library. (The Inspector General of the FBI announced in March 2007 that up to 3,000 letters were issued improperly.) The Patriot Act was debated while workmen were still clearing debris from Ground Zero in New York. Few lawmakers challenged the bill's provisions, because either they supported expanded government power, or they were too politically intimidated to put up a fight.

Democrats partnered with a few libertarians and conservative Republicans in Congress to successfully attach language to the bill mandating that the extended powers for federal agents in the Patriot Act be subjected to review and a new vote after five years. In addition, Democrats were able to strip a provision from the act that prevented the federal government from hiring workers at salaries below the prevailing union wage for regional jobs at the newly created Department of Homeland Security, which was also established by the Patriot Act.

One of those senators responsible for removing the prevailing wage issue from the bill was Georgia's Democratic senator Max Cleland, a highly decorated, triple-amputee veteran of Vietnam. It was this effort to provide decent wages for workers that would cost him his Senate seat in the 2002 election.

Republicans, using familiar campaign tactics, would make masterful use of Cleland's opposition to this one provision. Cleland was a beloved figure among Senate Democrats. Perpetually cheerful in spite of his ravaged body, he was always ready to help a fellow senator.

His Republican opponent in the election was Congressman Saxby Chambliss, who, like Vice President Cheney, had avoided Vietnam through a series of draft deferments. That didn't stop Chambliss from running ads suggesting that Cleland opposed the Patriot Act, leaving a none-too-subtle suggestion that Cleland was soft on national security and the war on terror. Bush and Cheney picked up on this message while campaigning for Chambliss in Georgia. For Democrats, Max Cleland's defeat was what Robert Bork's defeat had been for Republicans fourteen years earlier.

George Bush used the same "weak on national security" message against other Democrats in the 2002 midterm elections. With these demagogic attacks, he all but severed ties with congressional Democrats, sending polarization to new heights. What infuriated Democrats was that a strong majority of them had supported both the war-on-terror resolution and the USA Patriot Act. Then the president, in the midst of his "weak on national security" attacks on Democrats, had the gall to accuse Democrats of politicizing the war on terror! The tactic worked for the Republicans. They actually gained seats in both the House and Senate in 2002.

In the spring of 2003, George Bush asked Congress for authority to take the country to war against Iraq. He cited three compelling reasons: Saddam Hussein had weapons of mass destruction that posed a severe security threat to the United States and its allies; Saddam Hussein had tried to buy enriched "yellow cake" uranium to restart Iraq's nuclear weapons program; and, most ominously, intelligence proved that agents from Iraq had met with the al-Qaeda planners prior to 9/11 in Prague. It was a compelling case and it convinced a majority of Democrats in the House and Senate to vote for war authority. (It also persuaded me to write a column for the conservative newspaper the *Washington Times* in support of the war, a position I profoundly regret.)

Some of America's allies, notably France and Germany, opposed a war with Iraq and attempted to derail a UN Security Council resolution supporting American action. Secretary of State Colin Powell, by far the most widely respected American on the world stage, was dispatched to the UN to make the case for action against Iraq. It was a masterful presentation that lasted three hours. Powell produced intelligence information, including photographs, that purported to show Iraqi mobile WMD labs.

Although the UN failed to vote for a specific war resolution, President Bush believed he had the authority under previous UN resolutions with which Iraq had failed to comply. Bush attempted to build a "Coalition of the Willing." The first to sign up was America's strongest ally, Great Britain. It was quickly joined by Canada, Italy, Spain, Poland, and various former republics (now countries) of the Soviet Union. Japan, South Korea, and Australia also joined the coalition, along with smaller countries from Latin America. With the exception of Britain, these other countries had minimal combat operations in Iraq. The main force consisted of the United States and Britain.

A year earlier, the United States had led a larger coalition against the Taliban in Afghanistan. After forcing the Soviet Union out of Afghanistan in 1989, the Taliban had taken control of the Afghan government and provided shelter to al-Qaeda and its leader, Osama bin Laden, who claimed responsibility for 9/11. The United States and its allies, working in coordination with anti-Taliban forces called the Northern Alliance, routed the Taliban, established a new government, held national elections, and came close to capturing bin Laden.

The Afghan war was a success and had the strong backing of the American public. President Bush was riding a well-deserved wave of popular support when he asked for authority for war against Iraq. Neither Congress nor the public had reason to doubt the intelligence the president presented as the rationale for war. As he pointed out at the time, Congress had access to the same intelligence. Presumably they had reviewed it and also reached the conclusion that war was necessary. It would take almost two years for the intelligence to be discredited.

The invasion of Iraq began in March 2003. Initially, the war went well. The British force defeated the Iraqis in the south of Iraq to secure the country's vast southern oil fields, while the Americans went north to take Baghdad. Iraq fell quickly; Saddam Hussein fled, and his two notorious sons were killed in a firefight with American forces. The Iraqi military put up little resistance and most fled to the countryside.

Signs of trouble soon emerged. Vice President Cheney had predicted, prior to the war, that the American military would be treated like liberators by the Iraqi people. Instead, they were greeted by insurgent gunfire. The American force was relatively small—about 130,000 troops. The number had caused serious disagreement among officers at the Pentagon, Defense Secretary Donald Rumsfeld, and his civilian deputies. Rumsfeld favored a smaller force that could win with speed and just as quickly leave once the country was secured.

The problem was that the country had not been secured. It remains unsecured at this writing, over four years after the initial invasion. U.S. war dead in Iraq would pass the three-thousand mark on New Year's Eve 2006. Two days before, on December 29, Saddam Hussein was hanged after having been convicted of mass murder by Iraqi courts. It became apparent that there were sufficient troops to drive Hussein's government out of power and immobilize his military, but not enough to secure the peace.

It took a long time for this reality to settle in. After Baghdad fell, President Bush copiloted a jet fighter to a landing on the aircraft carrier USS *Lincoln*. The president declared that major combat in Iraq was over. A huge banner appeared behind him with the words MISSION ACCOMPLISHED.

Despite a string of bad news from Iraq, President Bush went into his reelection campaign in 2004 with a solid advantage on national security issues over his opponent, Senator John Kerry of Massachusetts. Voters were not happy with the Iraq war, but they still believed it was part of the war on terror. Memories of 9/11 were fresh in American minds, and voters remained sufficiently traumatized by those memories to reelect George W. Bush. The president and the Republicans once again hauled out their favorite theme: "The Democrats are weak on national security." Once again, voters took the bait.

By 2005, events had turned against the Republicans. Despite brief periods of hope after the capture of Saddam Hussein and successful national elections, news from Iraq worsened by the day. Over 3,390 American soldiers had been killed by the middle of May 2007 and over 25,000 injured. More than 70,000 Iraqi civilians were dead. The insurgency grew in strength as the new Iraqi army being trained by the United States was not yet prepared for independent combat.

In the words of President Bush, "When it [the new Iraq army] stands up, we will stand down." The Iraqi army isn't close to standing up. The new Iraqi government was unable to control sectarian violence as the country descended into civil war between Shiites and Sunnis.

Back home, Republicans faced a series of scandals involving a lobbyist named Jack Abramoff. House Majority Leader Tom DeLay was indicted for money laundering in Texas, albeit by a partisan district attorney. George Bush's poll ratings were terrible, but not as terrible as the ratings for the Republican Congress. Democratic contributors smelled blood in the coming midterm elections and poured millions into individual campaigns and party committees.

The ever-optimistic president pulled out the national security card again, and his attacks became more shrill and acerbic. He accused Democrats of "cutting and running," of "waving the white flag of surrender," and, most egregious of all, he suggested, "If Democrats win, the terrorists win." Once again, Bush accused Democrats of politicizing the war! This time, voters weren't listening. Republican candidates fled from Bush, repeatedly refusing to appear with the president.

Voters had concluded that Bush and his administration had mismanaged the war. They also believed the war in Iraq was separate from the war on terror. Exit polls in the 2006 election indicated that voters thought the Bush administration had lied about the intelligence used as the rationale for invading Iraq. It may take time to prove who lied, or if anyone deliberately misled the public. One thing is clear: the selling of the Iraq war will go down as one of history's great con jobs.

The public was told that Saddam Hussein had weapons of mass destruction. He did not. They were told by Vice President Cheney on *Meet the Press* in the spring of 2003 that Iraqi intelligence officials had met with al-Qaeda in Prague prior to the 9/11 attacks. The meetings never took place. Bush himself suggested that Saddam had a robust nuclear weapons program. He did not. Despite pleas from the military for more troops for the war, Rumsfeld refused to send them. Postwar planning was chaotic and led to Iraq dissolving into civil war. As you read this, more soldiers have now died in Iraq than civilians in all three attacks on 9/11.

President Bush desperately tried to keep up the illusion that Iraq was central to the war on terror. In some respects, he was right. Most experts believe Iraq was not a haven for terrorists before we invaded, but it is today. Democrats turned the war issue against the Republicans in the 2006 campaign. It turned out not to be necessary since the public, in its wisdom, had turned against the Iraq war before most Democrats had the courage to do so. Nevertheless, Democrats were the beneficiary of the public's wrath over Iraq and the polarization of Washington politics, and they took control in both the Senate and the House in 2006.

WHAT FOLLOWS IS CAL'S VIEW OF IRAQ.

No less an authority than Osama bin Laden has said that Iraq is the central front in what he considers a world war. Should he not be taken at his word?

Saddam Hussein did have weapons of mass destruction. He used them against the Kurds and was charged with mass murder by the elected government that replaced his dictatorship. Saddam had plenty of time to hide or transport his WMDs out of Iraq before U.S. troops invaded. A top Iraqi air-force official, General George Sada, made that charge in a book he wrote titled *Saddam's Secrets: How an Iraqi General Defied and Survived Saddam Hussein.*

Most of our allies had access to the same intelligence President Bush saw regarding Saddam's weapons—the ones he had and the ones he was developing. (Remember "Chemical Ali," a female scientist in charge of his biological and chemical weapons manufacturing unit?)

If it were only this simple: accurate and real-time intelligence, proper oversight by Congress, and a president who had the impeccable foresight of a biblical prophet.

I recall British prime minister Margaret Thatcher's insightful remarks in the late 1970s. Thatcher said we in the West make a mistake when we "transpose our morality on those who do not share it."

This is the serious flaw in Western thinking: that what the United States and what remains of its Western allies do, or don't do, affects what our enemies do, or don't do. Rarely, if at all, in world history has the behavior of radical Muslim fanatics been determined—or their objectives deterred—by Western actions, unless those "actions" are, in fact, inactions, or ineffective actions.

That's because this is a religious war, no matter how many times President Bush, the State Department, and then–British prime minister Tony Blair have denied it. The prize is world domination. The radicals say it and they prove it by blowing themselves up and killing others, which their doctrines teach is their only guarantee of entering heaven. How do Western militaries fight and Western diplomats negotiate with such fanaticism? How do we sit at a table with people who believe their God wants us dead? Do we say, "Okay, we'll give you this sliver of land; now will you please not kill us?" They reply, "We'll take your sliver of land and we will continue killing you until you give us all of the land, which belongs to us anyway."

Apologists say the fanatics are a minority of the world's more than 1 billion Muslims, possibly "only 10 percent." Ten percent of one billion is one hundred million, which is enough to destabilize any government and to seriously impair any economy. And how do we know there are "only" 10 percent of them? As they infiltrate and attempt to dominate France, England, the Netherlands, and Germany, and already dominate the Arab world and Indonesia—as well as making inroads in some African countries—there are no "moderate" Muslims rising up to turn them in or to obstruct their "jihad." Few, if any, authoritative Muslim clerics speak publicly about the "heresies" of the radicals. Is it because they fear being killed, or because they quietly agree with their objectives? Either way, the killing continues. If the radicals do not represent "authentic" Islam, why, then, doesn't "authentic" Islam do something about them? Authentic Christians and Jews seek to isolate those who speak wrongly in their names.

This is a war that was destined to come. Can those who claim that terrorism is the result of the United States invading Iraq and toppling Saddam Hussein answer the question of who, or what, was responsible for terrorism before the United States entered Iraq this time, or the time before? The fact is, modern terrorism has been occurring in the Middle East since Israel's restoration in 1948. Before that, Muslims and Arabs killed one another and supported Adolf Hitler in his "final solution" to exterminate the Jewish people. Every peace offer by Israel has been rejected. Every concession has gone unrewarded. Every peace agreement has been violated, not by Israel, but by her enemies. Every one. Still, the State Department in Republican and Democratic administrations pressures Israel and claims the "key" to peace and stability in the Middle East is solving the Israel/Palestine problem. By this is meant a Palestinian state, which will surely be used to wipe Israel from the map and eliminate the Jewish people from the region. That is their pledge in sermons from mosques, in newspaper editorials, in editorial cartoons, on state-controlled television, and in their behavior. This is no secret. They have made their plans abundantly clear to anyone with eyes to see and ears to hear.

There is something else: had the United States not enforced sixteen UN resolutions requiring Saddam Hussein to demonstrate that he was not a threat to international peace and security, he and his sons would have continued to oppress, murder, rape, and torture the Iraqi people. And the war would have come elsewhere. Liberal Democrats like to say that the real war on terrorism should have been in Afghanistan, which the Taliban used as a training and ideological base for the fanatics who hijacked airplanes and flew them into the World Trade Center and the Pentagon on September 11, 2001, and would have hit the Capitol or the White House had not those brave passengers retaken United flight 93 and crashed it into a Pennsylvania field in this war's first counterattack.

Islamofascism, as President Bush correctly labeled this movement, is confined to no borders and follows no rules. There are no elected officials to whom one can speak. There are no capitals to which one might travel for summit meetings. This is a spiritual war that is different from any we have ever fought. The old rules and ways of warfare do not apply. If we seek to fight this war with the same tactics we have used in previous wars, we will lose. That's why it is ludicrous to be concerned about "torture" and human rights with people who practice one and ignore the other. The most often heard criticism is "we can't behave like them." I agree. We must be worse than them and so humiliate, decapitate, and eradicate them that those who remain will not think of trying anything like this for centuries to come. The United States was once feared and respected. A major reason the world is in such turmoil with so many simultaneous threats is that we have not done enough recently to instill fear in those who would harm us.

If our good behavior made our enemies behave like us, I would say let's be better than we are. But it doesn't and so the only way to win—if winning is our goal (anything less is defeat)—is to outdo them. Does that offend? It offends me more to have these people jerk our chain. It offends me more to wait for the next attack, preceded by an ultimatum issued by hundreds of people who illegally entered our country, or who may have been born here and were radicalized in Wahaabi schools subsidized by the Saudi Arabian government, our "ally" in the war on terror. The only reason we pay any attention to them is that they sit on massive amounts of oil that we want. If our politicians were serious about energy independence, and we weren't drunk on oil, we might be able to liberate ourselves from their clutches.

The Islamofascists see no "innocents" in this war. They tell us that all Americans are combatants because a majority voted for President Bush. Therefore, even civilians can be targets. Does anyone believe the terrorists won't use a nuclear weapon on American cities if they can get their hands on one? Iran is rapidly pursuing a nuclear weapon. Does anyone think they won't use it, or at least threaten to use it, on Israel and, if they get the long-range missiles, on us? Maybe they'll partner with North Korea, which has been developing nuclear material and long-range missiles. If terrorists can smuggle nuclear (or chemical, or biological) weapons into our cities, who doubts they would threaten us with mass murder if we don't bow to their demands? Could any president tolerate millions of casualties?

Faced with such a threat, President Bush's "doctrine" of getting them before they get us is the right approach. I only wish he had pursued it with the same resolve he displayed immediately after 9/11.

We may like our "peace" songs and we may like to view ourselves as more civil and humane than others, but any war in which the good side (that's us, which many have forgotten) plays with one hand tied behind its back and a ball and chain on its leg, while the other side has no restrictions and can fight and kill by whatever means it chooses, is bound to result in the bad guys winning.

These are not pretty choices, but we didn't create them. Our enemies did. When political opponents once engaged in duels to defend their honor, one person got to choose the venue for the duel and the other the weapon. If the person who had his weapon chosen for him was not experienced in its use, he had two options: take a crash course, or die.

The United States didn't choose this war, nor did it choose the weapon of suicide and insurgency following three free elections in Iraq. Pulling our punches won't win this war. Throwing at them with all the power we have, will.

CAL AND BOB ARE NOW BACK ON THE SAME PAGE.

Shortly after the 2006 election, George Bush invited the new Speaker of the House, Representative Nancy Pelosi, to lunch at the White House. Pelosi was the first woman to be elected Speaker, which put her third in line to become president. After their meeting, the president emphasized the need to seek common ground for the good of the country. Bush used these two words at least half a dozen times that day. Pelosi agreed wholeheartedly.

The political world had not heard such talk between a Democrat and a Republican in decades. Polarization appeared to be lessening.

They both appeared to be sincere, not only because seeking common ground was a higher calling, but because it had become a political necessity. The public was tired of the bickering, and politicians sometimes respond to public concerns, at least until they stop paying attention. If George Bush hopes to salvage his legacy after Iraq, he'll need Democrats to help him by finding an honorable (and successful) end to the Iraq war and forward movement on at least a few domestic issues.

The Democrats understand that their performance as the majority in Congress will determine whether the public is willing to put a Democrat in the White House in 2008. Watching Bush and Pelosi that beautiful fall day brought back memories of how American politics sometimes used to be when bipartisanship was not a synonym for wishy-washiness, consensus made for good politics, and polarization was seen as bad manners.

PART IV

The Way We Were

19

A CHANGE OF CULTURE

IF YOU BELIEVE THAT CHANGE IS NOT POSSIBLE IN WASHINGTON, you're not alone. A few decades ago, Washington seemed to have vaccinated itself against change. It is an isolated place where fresh thinking and departure from convention are about as welcome as the August heat. Washington may be the only place in America where new thinking and innovation are punished, while those committed to maintaining the status quo receive the Presidential Medal of Freedom.

There are no Martin Luthers with a tack hammer in one hand and new ideas in the other. Nor is anyone like Martin Luther King Jr. marching over the Fourteenth Street Bridge singing "We Shall Overcome" and demanding change. The only outsider who would feel welcome in Washington is Rip Van Winkle because he could wake up after twenty-five years and the only thing that would have changed is the traffic. There would be more of it.

In politics, meaningful change almost always comes through the ballot box, and then only when the people have had enough. The 1980 and 1994 elections were like that. So was the one in 2006. The problem is that when the new replaces the old, the new often starts behaving like the old it replaced. That was true of many Republicans who vowed revolutionary change in the 1994 election. However, as history reveals, the new bunch may promise "the most ethical administration" in the nation's history (Bill Clinton) or "the most ethical Congress ever" (Speaker Nancy Pelosi) but they usually end up like all the others, ensnared by temptation and entangled in scandals of their own making.

Sometimes policy causes the electorate to "throw the bums out." Sometimes it is disgust over the general state of affairs with no one issue as the cause. In the 2006 election it was some of each. Democrats and independents were driven to the polls by growing frustration over Iraq, a series of ethics violations by Republicans, and spending on new and existing entitlement programs by Republicans that grew government and deepened the deficit. Many voters saw Republicans trying to maintain power for its own sake—a type of political entitlement—rather than using power to advance the country's agenda. They thought the Republican Congress had lost its way and did not deserve to remain in the majority.

But each of these separate domestic issues stems from polarization. Deficits, entitlements, earmarks, all are about keeping power, and the way that power has been maintained over the last twenty-five years is by keeping polarization alive. Stay in power long enough in Washington and a sense of entitlement sets in, which leads politicians to believe they are untouchable and immune from the rules of conduct the rest of us must follow. That was why, in part, Mark Foley thought he could repeatedly contact former pages, and Bill Clinton thought he could have an affair in the White House. It was why Republicans used government programs and projects (once the exclusive purview of Democrats) as an insurance policy to keep power.

History tells us that politicians can abuse power for limited periods before the public loses its patience. Once voters reach a "tipping point," no amount of projects or political commercials will change people's minds. When voters decide to make a change, they are generally replacing the party in power in either Congress or the White House, or both.

American voters do not often make major changes, so parties can stay in power for long periods. We are not like other democracies whose governments can change every few years or even every few months. We like stability. That may seem surprising with today's nonstop political combat and never-ending election cycles, but our country still has a strong desire for political stability. This is due in part to the large number of immigrants who come here from unstable nations and oppressive regimes. They craved stability in their native lands and never got it. When they settled in America, they voted for stability.

That may also explain why two major political parties have continued to dominate American politics. While third parties have occasionally been formed (the Bull Moose Party of Theodore Roosevelt in 1912, the American Party of George Wallace in 1968, the independent candidacy of Ross Perot in 1992 and 1996, and the Green Party of Ralph Nader in 2000), none has developed into a serious alternative to the Democrats or the Republicans.

Democrats trace their roots to Thomas Jefferson. The Republican family tree was planted by Alexander Hamilton, though the Republican Party was not formally organized until the 1850s. For our purposes, we'll focus only on the parties from the twentieth century to the present. Much has changed in their philosophy and demographics over this period, but the two parties' domination of the political system has not changed.

For the first third of the century, voters went back and forth between Democrats and Republicans in the White House and Congress. Republicans Roosevelt and Taft held the White House for twelve years (1900–1912). Republicans held Congress for the first ten of those years, and then the Democrats took the House the last two years (1910–1912). Democrats took the White House for the next eight years under Wilson (1913–1920); Democrats controlled Congress until the last two years of Wilson's second term (1918–1920), when Republicans took the Senate. Two years later, the White House would go to Republicans for twelve years (1920–1932) under Harding, Coolidge, and Hoover. Republicans controlled Congress until the last two years of that period, when the Democrats won the House (1930–1932), followed two years later by the Democrats taking control of both the White House and Congress.

Please excuse the social studies class, but it illustrates a point. Voter stability gave one party control of the White House and Congress for long periods of time. When the party in power lost favor with the voters, they sent a warning two years before each "wave" election by putting the opposition in power in one or both houses of Congress. Two years later, the party in power lost both the White House and Congress. The story repeated itself for thirty-two years. The conclusion was that voters liked stability, but when they turned, they did so in a crushing wave (hence the term *wave election*).

That voting pattern changed during the second third of the century, from 1932 through 1952. The Democrats, with a few exceptions, controlled the White House and both houses of Congress. Republicans managed to win enough seats in 1946 to have a congressional majority, but that lasted only two years. So "normalcy" was defined as Democrats running the White House and Congress, especially the House of Representatives.

In 1954, however, the era of divided government became the rule rather than the exception. For forty of the next fifty-four years, Congress and the White House were divided between the parties. It seemed that voters liked the idea of checks and balances between the legislative and executive branches. Each time voters put one party in control of both branches during this period, a wave election ended one-party control (1980, 1994, and 2006). Each of these elections occurred as the polarization of American politics intensified.

20

WHEN ADULTS WERE IN CHARGE

The reason there are so few female politicians is that it is
too much trouble to put makeup on two faces.
—Maureen Murphy

BEFORE ANALYZING THE TWO PARTIES, IT'S WORTH LOOKING AT THE geography, people, and philosophy of the parties today as described by humorist Dave Barry. Residents of the mythical red states are "ignorant, racist, fascist, knuckle-dragging, NASCAR-obsessed, cousin-marrying, road-kill-eating, tobacco-juice-dribbling, gun-fondling, religious fanatic rednecks."

The mythical blue-state residents are "godless, unpatriotic, pierced-nosed, Volvo-driving, France-loving, left-wing Communist, latte-sucking, tofu-chomping, holistic-whacko, neurotic, vegan weenie perverts." The best satire contains some truth, and Barry's list shows how some people on one side view those on the other side. It might be fun to read, but is it helpful to the country if it is viewed as accurate? How can anyone find common ground with the "other side" if their side takes such a view?

America's political activists are in general agreement about what defines the parties. Republican activists say Democrats are the liberal party. Democrats are pro-union and antibusiness, pro-abortion and pro–gay rights, including same-sex marriage. Democrats are for big government, love welfare programs, and oppose foreign wars and maybe even God. They're also against free trade, favor high taxes, and are isolationists. Ann Coulter and other pompous polarizers are making a fortune sticking these labels on Democrats.

Democratic activists say Republicans are pro-business and anti-union. Republicans favor the smallest government possible with the fewest regulations, and they believe in using the military to exert American influence around the world, in the process getting us into wars we have regretted. They oppose tariffs, dislike government regulation of business, and favor lower tax brackets, which disproportionately benefits wealthy Americans. The Republican Party is against all abortions, and opposes gay unions and legal benefits for same-sex couples. Republicans want to seal our borders to keep immigrants out and open the church-state border to let God in, making them religious fanatics in the eyes of Democrats.

These are the views of the political and media elites, but a majority of Americans don't see either party entirely this way. The historical record during most of the twentieth century provides little support for the picture today's activists paint of each other. We will avoid another social studies lecture here, but we also must point out some facts that provide a strikingly different narrative of the Republicans and Democrats both before, and at times during, the current period of polarization:

- William Howard Taft of Ohio was both president and chief justice of the Supreme Court. Until Reagan, Taft was the embodiment of the century's Republican Party, much in the way FDR defined the Democrats. As president, Taft ordered the breakup of Standard Oil and American Tobacco, two of the country's largest monopolies. As chief justice, he ruled in favor of the minimum wage, and affirmed the federal government's right to regulate the railroads.
- Republican president Herbert Hoover sided with the union movement by supporting legislation that prevented judges from issuing injunctions, at the request of big business, to stop workers from striking.

- Republican president Dwight Eisenhower warned Americans about the potential for fraud and abuse from the few powerful companies that supplied weapons to the military, calling them the "military-industrial complex."
- Republican president Richard Nixon created the Environmental Protection Agency, and opened the door to diplomatic relations with Communist China.
- Republican president George W. Bush created the largest new entitlement program since the 1960s when he supported adding prescription drug benefits to Medicare.

None of this seems to fit the Dave Barry/liberal polarizers' description of Republicans, does it?

- The first president to publicly criticize welfare (or, as he called it, "the dole") was not Ronald Reagan, but Franklin Roosevelt.
- For most of the century, it was Republicans who supported tariffs and Democrats who strongly opposed them.
- Speaking of opposition, Republicans after World War II opposed increases in the defense budget, while Democrats strongly supported increases in military spending.
- Democrat John Kennedy attacked the Eisenhower/Nixon administration for allowing a "missile gap" to develop between the United States and the Soviet Union. He said the United States was on the wrong side of the gap. Although the gap didn't really exist, JFK made it a centerpiece of his 1960 campaign.
- Democrat Jimmy Carter established the Defense Department's Central Command for the Middle East. It was under this command that George H. W. Bush and George W. Bush launched two wars against Iraq.
- Democrat Bill Clinton negotiated and signed a welfare reform act that dramatically lowered the number of people on welfare by putting them to work.

None of this sounds like the Dave Barry/conservative polarizers' definition of Democrats, does it?

We can hear the polarizers (left and right), the media, the political science professionals, and the ever-ready pundits saying, "Nice try, Cal and Bob, but you're talking about Republicans and Democrats as far back as a hundred years. Get with it, the world of politics has changed. There aren't many Republicans or Democrats like that anymore!"

Yes, there are. Moreover, there are a lot more of them than all the polarizers—left and right—combined!

The 2000 and 2004 presidential campaigns ended in virtual ties. The polarizers, and their polarizing sympathizers in the press, academia, and lobbying and pundit communities, declared that the results proved just how polarized the country has become. Ridiculous. The vast majority of voters in both elections were neither polarizers nor polarized. For example, the vast majority of voters who supported George Bush favored strong environmental regulations, as did those who supported Al Gore. The vast majority of voters who supported John Kerry supported a strong national defense, as did those who voted for George Bush.

This brings us full circle to the fundamental thesis of Common Ground. *The country is not polarized. Polarizers and their amen corner in the press and among political elites are the ones who are polarized, and who have much to gain from continuing to stir the pot.*

To go back to our examples of the roughly 100-million-plus voters in the presidential contests of 2000 and 2004; the majority of these voters, no matter who they supported, want a clean environment and a strong defense. By suggesting voters are divided on these and other issues, the polarizers are foolishly saying that half the voters would be happy to have more toxic waste sites, or that the other half is not in favor of a strong military to protect their families from terrorists.

How have polarizers gotten away with selling the idea of country-wide polarization? It is because they control the levers of politics, and spend hundreds of millions of dollars to maintain control.

For a long time in national politics, both political parties believed consensus made for good policy (and politics) and that no simplistic definition (or color, for that matter) could be applied to such a diversity of interests that was embodied in America.

Do supporters of each party differ in their policy approaches to solving the nation's problems? Of course they do. Do the majority of supporters of the two parties insist that the answer is either black or white, as the polarizers insist? Of course they don't. Do the overwhelming numbers of supporters of both parties believe that finding consensus and a common ground solution on virtually all issues (including abortion) confronting the country is preferable to no solutions based on intractable polarizing agendas? Absolutely they do.

There are many political analysts who have used exit polls from the 2006 election to suggest that America is divided. In those polls, however, voters were provided with only two choices—for example, "Do you favor or oppose gay unions?" Forced to answer only one of two ways, the voters were split on the issue. But if the following option had been included in the question—"Do you believe that reasonable people on both sides of the gay union issue could and should find a consensus opinion?"—the vast majority of respondents, we believe, would have supported consensus.

Therein lies the fundamental point about the corrupting influence of polarization. Polarizers insist on black and white (or red and blue), while the country much prefers a reasoned shade of gray (or purple). But you can't raise money on kindness and consensus, and actual achievements are death to one's fund-raising goals. One must always have an enemy if the money is to flow. And that's why the polarizers have done so well. Polarizing has worked . . . for them and their candidates, but not for the country.

21

BIPARTISANSHIP

Bad officials are elected by good citizens who do not vote.
—George Jean Nathan, drama critic, 1958

IF WE LOOK BACK AT THE IMPORTANT EVENTS AND LEGISLATIVE achievements of the twentieth century, one political reality stands out. Virtually all successful solutions to issues foreign and domestic depended on bipartisanship. Putting partisanship aside was never easy, but when the times demanded consensus for the general welfare, Democrats and Republicans rose above party and ideology. That didn't mean partisanship ceased to exist or that there was no polarization. What it meant was that bipartisanship was a powerful factor in politics, and, when exercised, overwhelmed the forces of polarization.

From regulating monopolies to protecting workers, from confronting the Great Depression to expanding trade, from world wars to rebuilding Europe, from civil rights to women's rights, Republicans and Democrats mostly found consensus. Bipartisanship required compromise that was at times both painful and politically dangerous.

Today's Democrats and Republicans rarely find bipartisan consensus on anything, mostly because they don't look for it. Cooperation across party lines is now regarded as a sign of weakness and disloyalty. Parties constantly prop up "the base," which is supremely ideological and fundamentally unforgiving of anything it regards as compromise.

The reigning philosophy of both parties can be summed up this way: better to go down in defeat while standing on principle than to achieve at least part of the objective through consensus and live to fight another day.

Why is bipartisanship seen as a weakness today, but for most of the last century it was thought of as good politics and even courageous? It is mostly because ideology (or faux ideology) has replaced reason, and reasonableness has given way to fighting (which raises more profiles in the 24/7 cable-news era, as well as more money). Republicans and Democrats are so divided along stark ideological lines that consensus and bipartisanship are nearly impossible to achieve.

In the past, a broad spectrum of ideologies existed within each party that led to natural coalitions between the parties. Coalitions of like-minded Democrats and Republicans produced a significant body of bipartisan public policies, and laws to enforce them. Finding common ground on policy tended to produce laws that represented the thinking of a larger share of the American political demographic, and as a result more Americans benefited.

A Bipartisan Success Story

The Panama Canal Treaties, negotiated in the Ford and then Carter administrations, were simultaneously an important foreign-policy issue and an explosive domestic one. The Canal Treaties required sixty-seven votes in the Senate for ratification. Bob Beckel was in charge of the White House effort to ratify the treaties in the Senate.

President Carter called a group of us—including the chairman and ranking member of the Senate Select Committee on Intelligence, Daniel Inouye (D-HI) and Barry Goldwater (R-AZ)—into a rare Saturday meeting. The subject of the meeting was drug trafficking by Samuel Torrijos, the brother of Panamanian head of state Omar Torrijos. A top secret CIA cable had leaked, which revealed that a sealed indictment against Samuel Torrijos for facilitating shipments of cocaine to the United States, had been handed down. Carter (nor anyone else in the meeting) was aware of it.

Samuel Torrijos had resigned as Panama's ambassador to Spain and was returning on a ship scheduled to dock in the Panama Canal Zone, then a United States territory. American officials were waiting to arrest Torrijos, but he had been tipped off and his ship diverted to Panamanian territory, where the United States could not touch him.

The drug revelation could not have come at a worse time. Carter asked the senators for help. Goldwater told the president that he opposed the treaty, but he opposed leaking intelligence even more, and he did not want the treaty to fail on the basis of selective leaks.

Barry Goldwater was nothing like the Goldwater portrayed in the '64 campaign. He was razor sharp, courteous, and above all a patriot. For Goldwater, partisanship had no place in the affairs of state, especially when it concerned national security.

I walked Goldwater to his car, and thanked him for his help, especially since he opposed the treaty. He stopped, put his arm around me, and said, "Bob, Carter is my president and commander in chief, too. This [the leak] is not right. Don't thank me; just promise me if something like this ever happens to a Republican president, you'll stand up for him."

Goldwater did as he promised. He rebuked treaty opponents, and secretly threatened to vote for the treaty if any more intelligence leaked. The drug issue caused a major upheaval that almost destroyed ratification. It did not in the end because Barry Goldwater kept his word.

The Panama Canal Treaty passed the U.S. Senate 68 to 32.

22

THE POWER OF THE PARLOR

He who travels the high road of humility in Washington will not be troubled by heavy traffic.
　　　　　—former Wyoming Republican senator Alan Simpson

THERE WAS SOMETHING ELSE AT WORK DURING TIMES OF BIPARTI-
san consensus that had nothing to do with where members of Congress came from or what ideology they held. It had to do with
attitude, gratitude, and latitude.

With occasional and notable exceptions, the political culture in
Washington prior to the current period of polarization was more
civil than today. Friendships between members of opposing parties
were encouraged and often necessary. Members of Congress spent
weeks, at times months, together in Washington, unlike today's
forty-eight-hour "work" week. At the center of old Washington's
social life were the hostesses who opened their homes for social
events that were not just pleasant gatherings, but also often served
as places where "hothouses" flourished. Many important issues
were dealt with under the watchful eye of these quietly influential
women. And they *were* influential, not because of any office they
held (none did), but because they had the ability to actually make
Washington work.

Is this nostalgia in overdrive? The political past—even the recent
political past—was no golden age. But there were political and social

rules one was expected to follow and these rules worked for every-one, regardless of party or persuasion.

A Suitcase Town

When Tony Hall arrived in Washington in 1979 as a first-term Democratic congressman from Ohio, House Speaker Thomas "Tip" O'Neill told him to bring his family with him. "No one heeds that advice anymore," Hall told us. "Washington has become a suitcase town." He meant that members of Congress spend so little time in Washington they don't have to unpack their suitcases.

House Minority Leader Steny Hoyer echoed the same feelings when we spoke with him prior to the 2006 elections that would pro-pel him to majority leader: "The Tuesday–Thursday sessions are bad news. We're going to have to lengthen them just to get the work done. And frankly, most of the Tuesday–Thursday sessions are spent on fund-raising."

Hoyer told us that if he became majority leader after the 2006 election, the short workweek would change: "They'll need to come in Monday night and leave Friday."

True to his word, after he became majority leader in December 2006, Hoyer announced that starting in January 2007 the House would be in session Monday through Friday. Shortly after the an-nouncement, he started hearing complaints from many Republicans and quite a few Democrats who liked the old way.

Hoyer made one other comment worth mentioning. It concerns the much-maligned issue of congressional travel and why it helps blunt polarization: "When you travel overseas in a bipartisan group, an interesting thing happens. The plane takes off from Andrews [Air Force Base] and you get into the air and you're not a Republi-can or a Democrat, you're an American." Some might wonder why Republicans and Democrats can find common ground in the sky, but not on earth.

Congressional wives had their own way of building bridges across party lines. That so many were in D.C. also had the benefit of holding down the number of "bimbo eruptions" one sees with more frequency today.

Veteran party giver Esther Coopersmith, a staunch Democrat, is famous for putting together people who might have remained strangers had it not been for her hand-addressed invitations and her social graces. She agrees with Tony Hall, but goes a step further: "Not only do they come to town Tuesday and leave Thursday, they come mostly to have fund-raisers, not to legislate." She recalls that when she used to host fund-raisers, the person for whom the money was being raised attended, staying the evening, dining with the guests. "Now they use professionals and it's 'Give me your check, or even better, just send it,'" she says. "The legislation they get around to is flag burning and gays."

Coopersmith remembers being told by one of the Republican Senate wives, "Esther, if it wasn't for you, I wouldn't know any Democrats."

"I couldn't believe it," Coopersmith said. "In order to get anything done, you need both parties to work together. Right now, I look at Congress and say, 'That's my tax money doing nothing.'"

Coopersmith is an endangered species, and Washington and the country are worse off because of it. While a lifelong Democrat, she has the grace (and wisdom) to have Republican friends. Coopersmith, who arrived in Washington from her native Wisconsin in 1954, is part of a bygone era in which one did not see members of the other party as enemies to be wiped out like termites by an exterminator, but as valued fellow citizens, who might occasionally have ideas worth considering.

She is from an era in which people wrote thank you notes for gifts and kindnesses provided. She still prefers hand-addressed party invitations, and notes in longhand, eschewing the impersonal convenience of e-mail.

Letitia Baldrige was Jacqueline Kennedy's chief of staff. She often writes on social deportment. Presiding over many of those grand social occasions that made Washington come alive in the early 1960s, she provided an atmosphere that people from both parties wanted to be a part of. Born and reared a Republican, Baldrige said she was somewhat surprised when the Kennedys asked her to come to the White House.

Reflecting on today's tone in politics, she said similar behavior in her day would have gotten a politician blackballed from the social circuit. "If you showed venom," she said, "it showed you were a total loser."

Baldrige recalls members of Congress greeting one another in the hall or on the street. "There was tremendous affection because they were part of a group: the Congress of the United States. There was tremendous civility. They would call each other up for favors."

Tony Hall agrees: "I established a pattern, as many other members did, of going home only twice a month. So I got to know other congressmen. You might play cards together, have dinner with each other. Your children knew each other. If you start to build a relationship, you begin to trust the other person. Then it's a little difficult to beat each other up on the floor of Congress."

Baldrige believes the loss of these relationship patterns of effectively working with strangers is a major reason "we're going through a period of nastiness." She also charges, with much justification, that the unpleasantness "is aided and abetted by the press." She thinks the media focus too much on "celebrities," instead of accomplished people. When she was growing up, her heroes were people like Arthur Vandenberg, a Republican senator from Michigan, and Robert Taft, a Republican senator from Ohio. These were people, she says, who voted according to their principles. "We talked about principles and people like this at the family dinner table," she recalls. "Today, there is no family dinner table and people don't seem to vote according to their principles anymore."

Clare Crawford-Mason is a journalist, television producer, and author. She was a founding editor and Washington bureau chief for *People* magazine and reported on the White House from the Kennedy through the Reagan administrations. She remembers those years as "vastly, vastly different" from today. She also recalls the importance of Washington parties. "The most important thing in Washington was to be 'club-able,' which means the ability to get along with other people," she said. 'You've got to go along to get along' was a popular slogan of those times. It wasn't that you passed up what you believed in, but everybody mostly had the same aim: to enhance life in America. People didn't have separate agendas, like getting rich. You came to Washington to help the country become 'the greatest and best country.'"

Crawford-Mason becomes even more passionate when she adds, "You could do good without doing well. There were people who had money; there were moneyed families, but it wasn't like a story I read in the *Washington Post* which told of someone in Alexandria, Virginia, paying $140,000 to put a spa in their bathroom. Back in the 1940s, there were people who were glad to have two bathrooms in their homes and those who still remembered having outhouses."

Crawford-Mason recalls interviewing Pearl Mesta, who was known in Washington as "the hostess with the mostest" and subsequently became an ambassador to Luxembourg. "I said, 'Mrs. Mesta, tell me about these parties.' And she said, 'These parties are very good. We provide a place where people can get together and talk about what's going on in our country.'"

Crawford-Mason continued: "That place is missing. We try to get the Israelis and Palestinians to talk. Why can't we get the people who run our country together to talk?"

Today, what social glue there is—and there isn't much—is produced not by hosts or hostesses, but by lobbyists who throw parties for influence and for money.

THE JULY 12, 2006 *WASHINGTON POST* CARRIED A STORY BY JEFFREY H. Birnbaum about forty-year-old Jeffrey S. Shockey, the deputy chief of staff of the powerful House Appropriations Committee. Birnbaum reported that Shockey collected nearly $2 million in severance payments from his former employer, "a lobbying firm that specializes in winning benefits from the committee he now serves." Previously, Shockey worked for Representative Jerry Lewis (R-CA), who was at the time a member of the committee and subsequently became its chairman. In that role, Lewis gets to assist members with "earmarks," which are special projects for the member's home district. Getting reelected back home, not serving the public, is the main objective in today's Washington.

No wonder this sort of behavior is called the "revolving door" in Washington. The lobbyist is all-powerful, and Shockey was merely being compensated for his value to the firm and the anticipated business he will bring in for its clients.

But it shows that when objectives change, the means for reaching them also change. The "pursuit of happiness" has replaced the pursuit of honor, civility, virtue, and integrity. If Jonas Salk were around today his cure for polio would have to compete for magazine cover space with Angelina Jolie and Brad Pitt, and most likely Salk would find himself on an inside page.

The media feed our lower natures by focusing on the superficial and the unimportant, but the media wouldn't if they weren't responding to what so many of us seem to want.

Another contributing factor to the general contentiousness is the failure of anyone in modern politics to take responsibility for anything and the obsessive need to blame someone else. And citizens, focused on their own pursuit of happiness and wealth, don't take the time to explore complex issues, and so instead rely on the spoon-feeding given to them by the media. It is easier to blame, than to understand; easier to watch a sound bite on television, than to read a book.

To paraphrase Peter, Paul, and Mary, "Where have all the leaders gone? Long time passing."

President George H. W. Bush famously dismissed what he called "the vision thing." But as the proverb says, "Without a vision, the people perish" (Proverbs 29:18).

PART V

Common Ground

23

COMMON GROUND: SLOGAN OR CHOICE?

I believe on a lot of issues we can find common ground.
I do believe we have an opportunity to find some common ground.
I believe we can find some common ground with the Demo-crats.
> —President George W. Bush answering questions at a press conference the day following the 2006 election

Extending the hand of partnership to the president—not partisanship, but partnership . . . [I] say let's work together to come to some common ground where we can solve the problem in Iraq.
> —Nancy Pelosi (D-CA), November 8, 2006

Now let's work and find the common ground, move forward with the kind of policy that makes sense for this country's small businesses, working families, and we all win in the process.
> —Senator-Elect Jon Tester (D-MT)

Yes, we have differences, but we are not divided. We ad-dress the issues, but we don't attack each other. We fight over our causes, but in the end we find common ground.
> —Governor Arnold Schwarzenegger (R-CA)

WHEN WE STARTED OUR "COMMON GROUND" COLUMNS FOR *USA Today* in May 2005, those two words were rarely heard in political circles. By fall 2005, the occasional "common ground" began appearing in the press and sporadically in political speeches. But as the 2006 midterm election drew closer, the term became a staple in campaign rhetoric across the country. After Labor Day—when politicians and the public traditionally pay the most attention to campaigns—"common ground" spread like the common cold in a third-grade classroom.

From political debates to campaign ads, from the blogosphere to the op-ed pages, everyone seemed to be talking about seeking "common ground." Following the election, politicians were tripping over one another to declare the results a clarion call for bipartisanship. The quotes at the beginning of this chapter are all public statements recorded the day after the 2006 midterm election when voters put Democrats in control of the House and Senate, ending the Republicans' twelve years in the majority.

At the beginning of 2006, few predicted the election would so dramatically alter the political landscape. Republicans expected to lose seats in the House and Senate, but they were not prepared to lose the majority in one, much less both. They believed they were invincible.

Incumbents have good reason to feel that way. Incumbents are provided free mail, video conferencing, and unlimited e-mail accounts, allowing them to keep their names constantly before the voters. Election years add thousands of miles to an incumbent's frequent flyer account as the pace of trips home increases exponentially during the campaign season. Incumbency also gives them a huge fundraising advantage, as lobbyists line up, checks in hand, to pay homage to the "masters of the Hill."

Then there was the issue of redistricting. After the 2000 census, congressional district lines were redrawn to make incumbents safer than they had ever been; more than 95 percent of all incumbents were reelected in 2002 and 2004. In 2006, despite poll numbers that showed public approval of Congress at record lows, Republicans remained confident of maintaining their majority, if for no other reason than their safe gerrymandered districts. Confidence turned to concern as the election approached.

With each campaign trip home, incumbents found an increasingly angry electorate. Like most political observers, incumbents attributed voter anger to the war in Iraq, or President Bush's job ratings, or scandals, or Congress's failure to deal with virtually anything. They were also getting an earful about the polarizing climate in Washington. All but the most partisan voters hated it. Still, incumbents had been through elections with angry voters before, and they believed that tenure and experience would help them survive.

Republicans avoided talking about President Bush, while Democrats never stopped talking about him. Incumbents told voters about the spoils they sent home, while challengers talked about what was spoiled in Washington. Even the most strident supporters of the war in Iraq began to talk about reassessing the mission. It became popular, even among some Republicans, to call for Secretary of Defense Donald Rumsfeld's resignation. (Rumsfeld was fired the day after the election.) Scandals were attributed to a few bad apples. Each party blamed the other for lack of progress on important issues. However, the public wasn't buying any of it.

Incumbents deluded themselves by looking to the 2002 midterm election, when voters were still in an angry mood after 9/11 yet Republicans still gained seats in both houses of Congress. But even the most optimistic recognized that the voters were fed up with the polarizing climate that enveloped Washington. In response, they simply blamed the other side for the bitterness. This time it didn't work. The lack of progress in Iraq and polarized inaction on virtually anything, coupled with Republican scandals, was just too much baggage.

In the end, it was obvious that Republicans had been in denial. They never seemed to grasp the depth of voter anger. A poll released shortly before the 2006 election confirmed that voters were not only reacting to a list of issues, but were questioning the entire political structure. A poll of 1,021 voters in October by Opinion Research Corporation for CNN found that an astounding 78 percent of the electorate believed "Our system of government is broken."

The politicians had been right about one thing: voters did want to see a change in direction. However, the voters decided to change policy makers, along with policy. They concluded that the government they had was not the government they needed. Voters sensed, correctly, that the polarized climate in Washington was less about issue differences between the parties and more about holding on to political power.

This doesn't mean issues weren't polarized in the 2006 election. Clearly, they were. The war in Iraq was polarized with the choice of either "staying the course" or "cutting and running." Stem-cell research was polarized. One side argued for doing anything to cure diseases; the other declared, "Not if it means killing unborn babies." Immigration reform was polarized. One side said allowing illegals to stay meant granting them amnesty and "tolerating lawbreaking"; the other said deporting them was xenophobic, heartless, and racist.

The last Congress was so polarized that over two years it was in legislative session fewer than 250 days. The fewest days in session in fifty years, according to Thomas Mann, a congressional scholar at the American Enterprise Institute. Major changes in immigration reform, restructuring Social Security, rewriting the tax code, easing the cost of health care, ethics reform, and an increase in the minimum wage—all bogged down. Only three of eleven appropriations bills to fund the government for 2006–2007 had been approved by the time of the election.

After 9/11, President Bush's message to world leaders was "You are either with us or against us," but he turned that into a frontal polarizing attack on Democrats who opposed his policies in Iraq. Some Democrats responded by calling Bush "incompetent," "a fool," and "a liar." Polarization, already bad, got uglier in 2006. As the election neared, incumbents decrying polarization looked increasingly disingenuous.

The voters' anger wasn't solely focused on the polarization between the parties. They were also angry about what polarization was doing to the relationship between politicians and the voters. In an earlier chapter, we quoted economist Robert Samuelson, who got the villain right: "The real polarization in American politics is not between the politicians themselves; it is the polarization between the politicians and the rest of us." Our system of government calls for those who govern to govern with the consent of the governed. This time, the voters withdrew their consent.

The voter rebellion in 2006 was reminiscent of the elections of 1980 and 1994. The issues were different in the three elections, but there were many similarities. All three changed the political landscape dramatically. All were dominated by unpopular presidents. All three took place when one party controlled Congress and the White House. All three elections resulted in divided government, and after each, politicians responded with a call for common ground.

In the aftermath of the 2006 election, they didn't have much choice. Faced with divided government and an angry electorate tired of polarized infighting, politicians had felt compelled to call for common ground and embrace bipartisanship. That was the easy part; making it work (assuming they really wanted it to work) was going to be much harder. Trying to revitalize bipartisanship, after two and a half decades of polarization, was swimming against the political tide.

How productive the calls for bipartisanship and common ground were after the wave elections in 1980 and 1994 is open to argument. Certainly there was genuine bipartisan progress on multiple fronts in the second Reagan term, until Iran-Contra and the Bork hearings in 1987 ignited a fierce period of polarization. Even following those events, some legislative progress was made during the Bush 41 administration. And, despite an accelerating polarizing climate, there were even some bipartisan successes between Bill Clinton and the Republican Congress after the 1994 election.

During the Reagan years, with Democrats controlling the House, major changes in the tax code, including major rate reductions, a new budget policy, Social Security and Medicare reform, and immigration reform were enacted. Under Bush 41, again, with Democrats controlling Congress, the savings and loan bailout was enacted and a minimum-wage increase was passed. A major clean-air bill also became law.

With Clinton in the White House and Republicans in control of both houses of Congress, the first major overhaul of federal welfare programs was achieved, as was a sweeping trade agreement with Mexico and Canada—the North American Free Trade Agreement. "Deadbeat dad" legislation, bringing the federal government into the enforcement of delinquent child-support payments, became law. In the first two years of the Bush 43 administration, with Democrats controlling the Senate, major education reform, No Child Left Behind, was enacted.

None of these significant policy changes came easily. Not only was bipartisanship essential for enactment, but finding intraparty consensus was also necessary (and given the large numbers of extreme partisans in both parties, never easy). But most telling was that these legislative achievements were approved under divided government. During times of one-party control (two years under Clinton and four years under Bush 43), virtually nothing of consequence was achieved. Norman Ornstein, a congressional scholar at the American Enterprise Institute, told the *Washington Post*, "United government in an age of fierce partisanship and sharp ideological polarization between the parties does not work very well for very long."

It's too early to tell (especially with the current bitterness over Iraq) if bipartisanship will emerge in the years following the 2006 election. After talking to many politicians who are genuinely frustrated with today's climate of polarization, we believe much of the talk about common ground is more than sloganeering. Given the choice between bipartisanship and polarization, all but extremists would opt for common ground.

However, there is evidence that the tide is turning. Shortly after the new Democratic Congress convened on January 4, 2007, Democrats in the House passed several bills in the first one hundred hours, as they had pledged to do during the campaign. A bill to increase the minimum wage and another cutting student-loan interest rates were among those passed with large numbers of Republicans crossing over to vote with Democrats.

In his state-of-the-union speech on January 22, 2007, President Bush called on Congress to work in a bipartisan spirit, saying, "The American people don't care which side of the aisle we are on." That remark ignited the longest sustained applause of the night. One got the sense that there was a real yearning on both sides to end the long partisan war. (Nevertheless, the other war, in Iraq, has continued to widen the partisan divide, making efforts at consensus difficult at best.)

There has also been some progress among Washington institutions. The Business Roundtable (representing most major American corporations), the AARP (representing millions of senior citizens), and the Service Employees International Union (one of the largest unions in the country) had been on opposite sides of every health care proposal over the last two decades. In a rare coming together of these special interests groups, they announced on January 16, 2007, an agreement on the outlines of the new health care reform proposal. Their message was remarkable given that each of these groups has contributed mightily to polarization over the years. To hear these three combatants call for a consensus approach was music to the ears of common ground supporters.

Missing the point, cynics were quick to point to the barriers facing health care reform. Of course health care reform will be difficult, and these three groups may yet find themselves on opposing sides of the issue. Nevertheless, the mere fact that these special interests were sharing the same podium and uniting behind a set of health care principles spoke volumes about the commitment to roll back polarization in the aftermath of the 2006 elections.

Nor was that the only coming together of special interests who were historically on different sides in Washington debates. Beginning in early 2007, lobbyists for the conservative U.S. Chamber of Commerce and the Business Roundtable met with their liberal counterparts from the Education Trust (an advocacy group for poor and minority children), the Citizens Commission on Civil Rights, and the National Council of La Raza, an advocacy group for Hispanic issues. Their agenda was to coordinate efforts to reauthorize and increase funding for the No Child Left Behind law.

Despite these and other favorable developments, however, few politicians believe that these efforts at common ground will endure. What a testament to the hammerlock polarization has around the neck of our national politics! Yet there is a lingering awareness in Washington that the voters' impatience with polarization may be deeper and will last longer than in past years. "Wave" elections are happening with more frequency, and the political cycle is speeding up (there has been no "downtime" when politicians gave themselves and the public a rest between the 2006 election and the start of the next cycle).

For most of the last century, voters behaved like carmakers. They were reluctant to make radical "style changes" in government. No more. Who can doubt that the voters in 1994 had run out of patience with the long period of Democratic dominance of Congress? Who doubts that a similar fate decimated Republicans in 2006? How much longer can the evils of polarization continue to destroy our political system? Not much longer.

The eloquence of Dr. Martin Luther King Jr. reaches across the years to provide an answer. The day before he was assassinated, King spoke to a frustrated black audience in Memphis, Tennessee, that was demanding to know how long the political powers would ignore their civil rights. King answered in his unique rhetorical style, "How long? Not long. I may not get there with you, but I have been to the top of the mountain and I have seen the other side. How long? Not long."

King knew that the tide would turn against segregationist politicians. In time, those same politicians, believing their power was secure, would miss the rising tide and be washed away. Today's politicians should pay heed to those words, and remember that voters today don't have the patience of King and his followers in the 1960s. The American electorate is becoming increasingly impatient with dysfunctional, polarizing politics. The short time between the waves of 1994 and 2006 will only get shorter.

Those elected officials who called for common ground in the wake of the 2006 election may find that there are indeed political rewards in bipartisanship and consensus. Perhaps events spinning out of control around the globe, including terrorism and the development of nuclear weapons in countries hostile to the United States, are causing voters to demand more order here at home. Maybe this time voters will be watching more closely and rendering a judgment at the polls more quickly.

The question for elected politicians is: Should they wait? Should they tolerate the continued domination of politics by the polarizers, and hope that another (and inevitable) voter wave does not wash them away? Or should they look at the results in 1980, 1994, and 2006 and conclude that common ground is a message they can run on, and not an example of rhetorical sleight of hand? Will "common ground" be just another slogan after this wave, or a choice to govern in a bipartisan climate? Can a campaign that emphasizes common ground be successful? We believe it can.

24

COMMON GROUND: A CAMPAIGN GUIDE FOR 2008

If God wanted us to vote, He would have given us candidates.

—Jay Leno

MICHAEL DUKAKIS STOOD AT THE PODIUM ON A SWELTERING Atlanta night in 1988 to accept the Democratic Party's nomination for President of the United States. The overflow crowd stood shoulder to shoulder on the convention floor, gasping for what little cool air blew from the overworked industrial air-conditioning. Thousands more were in the streets, denied access to the convention center by the Atlanta Fire Department. A beaming Dukakis, dressed in a blue pin-striped suit, looked cool and very presidential—at least to Democrats.

"This campaign is about competence, not ideology," the former Massachusetts governor said, attempting to draw on his successful tenure as governor and broaden it into a national campaign message. It was widely accepted, even by Republicans in Massachusetts, that Dukakis had revitalized his state's economy from one dependent on outdated heavy manufacturing to the leading high-tech economy in the Northeast. Dukakis was also credited with turning the huge budget deficits he had inherited into real surpluses by the time he left. The press dubbed it "the Massachusetts Miracle."

Democrats saw the "competence not ideology" message as a solid defense against the predictable Republican attack on "tax-and-spend liberals" while the media—looking to keep the latest scandal story alive—saw it as an attack on the Reagan/Bush mismanagement of the Iran-Contra mess. Both would be disappointed when Dukakis squandered a double-digit lead in the polls following the convention and suffered a near-landslide loss to George H. W. Bush in November.

The Dukakis implosion is widely blamed on any or all of the following: a poor campaign operation, the infamous Willie Horton ad, an ill-advised photo of Dukakis in an army tank, and a less than forceful response during a debate to a hypothetical question about whether the rape of his wife might alter his opposition to the death penalty. Amid this, Dukakis's message about competence, not ideology, took a pounding from the critics.

The message ultimately failed because Dukakis tried to sell the right product at the wrong time. A message of competence over ideology was a good product, but by 1988 polarization was growing into an even stronger political force than in the previous two national elections when Ronald Reagan was the Republican candidate.

After the last two years of the Reagan administration, burdened by the Iran-Contra debacle, Republicans wanted to avoid a competence test. They much preferred to make the fight about ideology, hence the Bush campaign's mantra that Dukakis was a "card-carrying member of the ACLU." Twenty years ago, ideology mattered. Politics forced most Americans to take sides.

As the Chinese calendar names years after an animal (year of the rat, snake, dog), so 1988 was the year of polarization, when the concept of divide and conquer took hold of our national political life and would not let go. The Christian Coalition emerged as a political movement. The labor movement was in decline. Liberals were trying to define a new post-FDR identity. The Cold War was thawing and with it the one enemy (the USSR) that had united Democrats and Republicans on national security. The movie *Wall Street* highlighted the lifestyles of the nouveaux riches; crack and crime was ravaging inner cities, terrifying the mostly white suburbs (as well it should have, for their turn was coming soon). Nineteen eighty-eight was the year of labels: liberal/conservative, big government/small government, free markets/government regulations, left/right.

There was little room for middle ground, let alone common ground. It was a time when expanding the party's voter base with polarizing rhetoric was the hot new strategy for winning elections, while competing for voters in the middle was a zero-sum game. After twenty years of worsening storms, followed by a brief lull at mid-decade, America looked at the new political landscape and saw the powerful front of polarization overtaking them. No wonder ideology trumped Dukakis's message of competence.

Why spend time on a losing twenty-year-old message? Because that message, in the hands of a good candidate, running with a companion message of common ground, is exactly the right message for 2008. The victor in that campaign will be the candidate who causes the public to see him or her as the most competent and the least ideological.

American politics has come full circle in the twenty years between 1988 and 2008. Competence and results are "in," while polarization appears headed back to the political fringes. In today's political environment, voters want less cross fire and more cease-fire; fewer arguments and greater results. A modern candidate would be nuts to call his opponent a "card-carrying member of the ACLU," or to use another version of LBJ's "Daisy" ad. Trying to replicate a winning message from a different time is no guarantee of success, while ignoring good messages from losing campaigns can be missed opportunities.

A good campaign plan (and accompanying message) should reflect the political tone of the times. Campaign plans are not timeless, nor are they available in political science textbooks. A good plan should begin with a set of assumptions about current voter attitudes on domestic and national security issues, the state of the nation, voters' personal and financial security, the degree of confidence in the future, and their assessment of how much change is necessary in leadership and governance to address the challenges facing the country.

All these have been factors in past presidential campaigns, and will be in one form or another in future ones. However, it is the degree of importance voters attach to these issues *in the current political climate,* and which candidate's *style and approach to governing* best suits that climate, that will guide persuadable voters. (Note: "Persuadable voters" are self-identified weak partisans or independents who, unlike partisan Republicans or Democrats, enter an election year undecided or "leaning" toward a candidate.)

A candidate's character is the one factor that is timeless and vital to voters. But character is more than virtue and honesty (although if voters sense a deficit in either it can be a deal breaker). Personality, style, comportment, and manner also figure into the equation. Jimmy Carter's seriousness and virtue suited the post-Watergate environment, just as Ronald Reagan's optimism was viewed as an asset after the grim decade of the 1970s. John Kennedy's character was ideal for a country eager to move on to a new generation of leaders, just as the bigger-than-life characters of Lincoln and Roosevelt were so vital in times of crisis.

The results of the 2006 election and recent polling provide a good snapshot of voters' attitudes as we approach the 2008 election:

National security issues are dominated by the war in Iraq. A strong majority wants the United States out of a war they perceive as unwinnable. Voters also understand the pitfalls of withdrawal and will expect presidential candidates to be specific about their plans to accomplish a pullout safely, while leaving Iraq with at least a chance to avoid a bloodbath and survive as a country (and therefore some comfort that our soldiers did not die in vain). They are tired of the right screaming "cut and run," and just as fatigued with the left saying our soldiers died for no reason other than a Bush/Cheney secret plan to control Iraqi oil.

The public doesn't think leaving Iraq ends the war on terror. They will want to know a candidate's plan to continue that war after Iraq. That had better include a plan that no longer leaves voters with the impression that the United States is going it alone. The right-wing polarizing mantra, "we have to fight them over there so we don't have to fight them over here," is no longer going to cut it. No more grounded in reality is the left-wing polarizers' claim that only a tiny percentage of Muslims wants to terrorize the West, and we should be tolerant of every new mosque and Islamic charity being created in America (at a rate that should alarm more of us).

President Bush's call for democracy around the world in his second inaugural address was moving and idealistic. Voters are wary, however, of using U.S. forces in attempts to install democracies abroad. That is especially the case in countries with no history of democracy and with political, religious, and economic systems foreign to our own. They don't believe we have the resources to police the world. Iraq has forced many foreign policy idealists to become realists.

Domestically, the economy is a major concern. That's a surprise given the low unemployment and inflation of recent years, but that good news is countered by stagnant wages. According to the Congressional Budget Office, the average middle-income worker has actually lost purchasing power over the previous decade. The polarizers in the business community, who seem to be quite content with soaring CEO salaries, are not going to get away with the old "that's the free market, and if you don't like it, you're a socialist." Nor will liberal polarizers convince voters that the United States must stop all trade with countries that don't have strong environmental or labor laws.

The growing cost of health care, combined with concerns about Social Security and Medicare solvency, is dampening voter optimism, especially among baby boomers. The old partisan Democratic polarizing line that we can't touch the "third rail of American politics" (Social Security and Medicare) is becoming tiresome; nor will an updated version of "Harry and Louise" (from the TV commercial in the early nineties that helped sink the Clintons' health care reform plan) kill health care reform. That scam was played out by the polarizers fifteen years ago, effectively paralyzing the debate. Unfortunately, the situation has gone from bad to worse.

The voters' view on the state of the nation is best explained by the much-tested question, "Is the country headed in the right or wrong direction?" The available data was unanimous in mid-2007 that most voters by a substantial margin see the country headed in the wrong direction.

On political leadership, President Bush's average job-performance numbers are over 60 percent negative to 30 percent positive. Although the Iraq war certainly impacts the president's approval numbers, the government's failure to respond effectively in the aftermath of Hurricane Katrina still haunts the Bush administration. The Democratic Congress, although still viewed more favorably than the Republican

Congress that preceded it, has lost all of its post-2006 election glow.

Finally, among the so-called social issues (at the heart of polarization and the red state/blue state, "culture war" divide), neither abortion, gun control, gay rights, church/state separation, stem-cell research, nor flag burning reaches double digits in polls measuring issues about which voters are concerned. A few, like flag burning, rate less than 1 percent. The lack of concern over the big culture issues is a mighty blow to the polarizers and the fund-raisers who have successfully picked the pockets of polarized voters in the "culture war" for twenty-five years. If they can't fuel the fires of the culture war, how are they going to perpetuate the red state/blue state divide they have come to depend on to justify their existence?

The evidence, taken together, points to competence, not ideology, as the foundation for a successful campaign in 2008. To succeed, a candidate must be seen as a competent leader, rather than a partisan ideologue. A leader capable of forging bipartisan consensus at home and meaningful diplomatic relations around the world. That is a compelling portrait for a general-election presidential candidate. But how does a candidate emerge from either party in a nominating process still heavily influenced by partisan ideologues?

There are indications that the nominating process in 2008 will not be as dominated by polarizers as in past elections. The number of voters who declare themselves "strong Democrat" or "strong Republican" is giving way to an increase in "weak Democrats" and "weak Republicans." Although self-identified "strong Democrats" and "strong Republicans" will still account for a substantial percentage of primary and caucus voters, their percentages are shrinking. Presidential polls survey only voters who say they are "certain" or "almost certain" to vote in primaries or caucuses. More "weak Democrats" and "weak Republicans" are indicating to pollsters that they intend to participate in larger numbers in 2008. If so, the polarizers' domination in the nominating process is no longer absolute.

There is another factor in 2008 that will help more pragmatic, less ideological candidates to emerge from both party's nominating process. The absence of clear front-runners and no incumbent president seeking reelection makes the race for the White House in 2008 very unpredictable.

The stakes are high for both parties. The Democrats have been shut out of the Oval Office for the last eight years (and twenty of the last twenty-eight). In that time George Bush has filled two Supreme Court seats and hundreds of other federal judgeships. The Democrats can ill afford to see the courts move further to the right.

For the Republicans, it could be argued that the stakes are even higher. If history is a guide, it is unlikely that Republicans will regain the House or Senate. Following the second term of an unpopular president (even popular presidents in most cases) his party usually loses seats in Congress. Republicans are terrified that they may once again be a minority in Congress *and* shut out of the White House.

With so much at stake and the outcome so uncertain, primary voters (even very partisan primary voters) are likely to be less dogmatic, and more inclined to support the most electable candidate. By definition, the most electable candidate is likely to be the less ideological candidate.

Casting a vote for president is serious business. On average, more than twice the number of voters will turn out in a presidential year than in a midterm election. In the 2006 midterm, approximately 41 million people cast ballots, just one-third of the 126 million who voted in 2004. Large turnouts in presidential races diminish the impact of polarized voters by drawing more moderates and independents who are less aligned with a party or ideology. We expect, given that so many remain angry about politics and politicians, that turnout in 2008 will be higher than in 2004—bad news for polarizers, good news for "the rest of us."

The Republican presidential campaign of former New York City mayor Rudy Giuliani provides more evidence of the declining importance of the so-called culture issues. Giuliani is pro-choice. As mayor, he enforced strict gun-control laws and favored equal benefits for gay couples. At the height of the polarization era such a record would have automatically disqualified Giuliani for the Republican nomination. In 2006 many pundits predicted that the Giuliani record, when it sank in with GOP primary voters, would do just that.

Nevertheless, within weeks of announcing his White House bid in early 2007, Giuliani became the GOP front-runner. By May 2007, despite broad dissemination of his record (mostly by his GOP rivals), Giuliani had lost some support, but remained the front-runner. There was unanimous agreement among political observers that the mayor's performance in the aftermath of 9/11 is driving his candidacy. The competence shown by "America's Mayor" (a moniker attached to Giuliani within days of 9/11) was trumping ideology, even among GOP primary voters.

This is not to suggest any less commitment to cultural issues among Republican activists. The strong Evangelical Christian base is not enamored of any of the three GOP front-runners (as of summer 2007), who include, in addition to Giuliani, Senator John McCain and former Massachusetts governor Mitt Romney. Unless efforts to recruit a credible "values" candidate are successful (Senator Sam Brownback, former Arkansas governor Mike Huckabee, and former Virginia governor Jim Gilmore are way back in the pack), it looks as if the GOP choice may be limited to these three, or to former Tennessee senator Fred Thompson, who declared his candidacy in July. That once would have been considered "early." Not in this election cycle.

MOST OF THE POST 2006 ELECTION ANALYSIS FOCUSED ON THE voters' rejection of hyperpartisan politics, and fueled much of the early rush to embrace "common ground" by leaders in both parties. However, as the battles in Congress over Iraq and the Democrats' pursuit of missteps by the Bush administration escalated in 2007, many pundits began revising their initial analysis. In their insatiable need to appear "current," pundits are now suggesting that Congress and the president did not get the voters' message; or (and this is the "current" analysis) that maybe the election results were all about Iraq and had nothing to do with polarization.

This assessment has, of course, been embraced by the polarizers (and also by some political leaders), but it is foolish and shortsighted. Of course the Iraq war (like any controversial armed conflict) is leading to strong partisan feelings, but the fallout from it is obscuring two important realities. First, since the new Congress convened, there has been more cooperation between the parties on several fronts unrelated to the war. And second, the hyperpartisanship surrounding the war is increasing the voters' desire to move past polarization and begin to find consensus and common ground on the war, as well as other concerns.

The question is which candidate will read the signs correctly and ride the voter wave against polarization. There are not many politicians with the foresight to grasp the antipolarization sentiment. Very few of them believe that a common ground message will get them elected, despite evidence that polarization has cost votes, and is a dangerous strategy.

Politicians will concede that some losses in 2006 could be attributed to polarization. However, they are not yet willing to accept that the resulting victories were a response to calls for common ground. "What about Joseph Lieberman?" Critics argue that Lieberman's contest was unique. They argue that (1) he lost the primary because of his position on the Iraq war, and (2) he ran statewide as an independent in a state that has a history of electing independents. Moreover, they believe that Lieberman's campaign against polarizing liberals attracted Republicans as well as independents. Therefore, his success had nothing to do with a call for common ground. In effect, they believe that polarization beat polarization!

It's always difficult to change the conventional wisdom in the campaign business about what works and what doesn't. Candidates are generally afraid of an untested strategy or message. This kind of thinking is why most of the high-profile campaign contracts are distributed among a few well-known political consultants. Candidates fight over the hottest campaign talent, chasing the ones who have been involved in successful (and preferably high-profile) campaigns.

Political consultants are a surprisingly cautious breed. They tend to use the same formulas that have worked for them since they entered the political game. They should look at the previous election for clues to voters' thinking and adjust their game plans accordingly. Instead, they are like old football coaches who use the same plays every season, despite having a new team with different skills going against different opponents. At least in football the dimensions of the playing field don't change. That is not so in politics, where voters' attitudes can alter the playing field.

We believe the 2008 election will usher in a new era in American politics that will reward competence and reject ideology. The people have already provided the clues. If a person woke up from a thirty-year coma in 2006, he would not have missed the following: (1) the voters were very angry, (2) much of that anger was directed at polarization and gridlock in Washington, and (3) the biggest issue was a war that was going badly, while all the politicians could do was fight among themselves and question one another's patriotism.

Despite our criticism of Karl Rove's base strategy, it worked for him in 2002 and in 2004. He decided that polarization was necessary to turn out the Republican base in both elections. Voters bought it. But polarizing elections lead to polarizing government, because politicians, who run as polarizers, govern as polarizers. Polarization does not have an on/off switch. In 2006 Rove and company continued to embrace the strategy that had been successful for them in previous campaigns. This time the voters altered the playing field, making Rove's base strategy inoperable.

Political polls generally include a question that measures the degree to which voters feel estranged from their government. The nonpartisan Pew Research Center presented the following yes/no statement to 2,017 adults in the aftermath of the 2006 election: "Most elected officials care what people like me think." Only 34 percent of the respondents agreed with the statement. That answer explained a lot about voter anger in 2006.

Voters concluded that politicians had become blind to the realities of their everyday lives. They didn't see politicians listening to people like them. Rather, they saw politicians interested in retaining power. People heard a political debate lost in a flurry of insults and sound bites. They saw the big picture, while politicians focused on the small scenes. In 2006 voters went to the polls to give their answer to the question of whose interests politicians were looking out for. Clearly, they decided, it wasn't theirs. We believe voters will bring this same skeptical attitude into the 2008 presidential election.

The winning candidate will be the one who best understands the voters' mood.

Presidential nominations and general-election campaigns often turn on one or two moments that convince people that a candidate is on their wavelength. In 1980, Ronald Reagan caught the public's mood with one line: "Are you better off now than you were four years ago?" That changed the campaign's focus from concerns about Reagan's brand of conservatism and lack of experience to Jimmy Carter's failures. Carter lost because voters concluded that they were worse off than they had been four years earlier. Despite their doubts about Reagan, they thought he understood how they felt.

Reagan found one of the most important formulas to success in politics: he minimized both his weakness (lack of experience) and Carter's strength (incumbency). He maximized his strength (relating to voters) with the sense that he understood their problems, and in doing so maximized Carter's weakness (that he was contributing to their problems). In the process, Reagan accomplished the most important thing a politician can hope to achieve . . . he exceeded expectations.

There lies the key to a common ground victory in 2008. In the next chapter, we will tell you how a common ground campaign can maximize the strength of a consensus message and the weakness of polarization. It will require departures from conventional campaign methods and rhetoric, and it will require a candidate with the substance and courage to challenge polarization and force it back to the fringes of politics where it belongs.

Political observers call 1980 a "hinge" year in American politics, an election year when voters closed the door on a difficult period in our history and moved on. In that year, after nearly two decades of discord and pessimism driven by years of war and racial and cultural divisions, they were looking for something different. Certainly they wanted a change in policies, but they also wanted change in the current political environment that was dividing the country. We think 2008 has all the ingredients to be another hinge year.

25

SELLING COMMON GROUND

Politicians are the same all over. They promise to build a bridge even where there is no river.

—Nikita Khrushchev

AT THE BEGINNING, WE PROMISED TO PUT POLARIZATION ON TRIAL. We presented evidence of the damage this insidious disease has done to our system of government and how it has grown to dominate our political system. We named the culprits, past and present (ourselves included), and the myths, tactics, and scams of polarizers. In addition, we looked back to what bipartisanship, with all its imperfections, had accomplished at crucial periods in our history.

But this trial was different than most because the jury had already reached a decision. The voters had cast guilty verdicts on polarization in the elections of 1994 and 2006. As early as 1980, voters convicted polarization much like contagious disease, giving a much-ignored warning that left unchecked, it could become an epidemic.

Polarization may have lost a round or two at the polls, but it still holds power over our national politics. It may continue to do so for some time, unless bipartisanship and consensus are accepted as a strong political counterforce to the tactics that have been the weapon of choice for two decades.

There are legitimate questions whether common ground can emerge as that competing strategy. Could common ground, which until now has been little more than a meaningless campaign slogan, become a powerful enough message to win a national campaign? Could it then become a governing mandate for the victors?

How can common ground compete with polarization, especially in light of the vast amounts of money polarization has been effective in raising for thousands of interest groups and politicians? (In 2006, $2.6 billion was spent by special interests on federal lobbying alone, excluding campaign donations, according to the Center for Responsive Politics.)

Is common ground a relic of the past, like the drive-in movie or a five-cent Coke, cherished in retrospect but not practical in today's world? And if not, how would common ground work in today's political climate? How can politicians benefit from a common ground message when they have been grounded in the dark arts of polarization?

Before we answer these questions, let's begin by saying what we do *not* believe common ground will accomplish. We are not suggesting that Republicans and Democrats will sit around a campfire, sing a few choruses of "Kumbaya," and pledge to study political war no more. There are reasons we have a two-party system. Too many countries have only one party, and if the people are allowed to vote at all, the system is rigged so the dictator and his cronies are always reelected.

Common ground is not a theory or an issue, and it's not a mealy-mouthed, let's-split-the-difference message. Nor is it a strategy that is at odds with either party's ideology. By seeking common ground, politicians are not required to abandon their deeply held beliefs. More important, common ground is not a new nonpartisan movement. In fact, common ground can't realistically work without partisanship.

Common ground, which is a governing strategy based on consensus and bipartisanship, is not a new idea. For much of our history, it has been the political rule rather than the exception. At times, it has given way to great polarizing periods, such as the Civil War, the civil rights movement, and Vietnam; all driven by deeply-felt ideological differences. As divisive as these polarizing events were, they differ from the special-interest, power-driven polarization era of the last thirty years.

If progress is to be made on the important issues facing America, then common ground is necessary in a system of government dominated by two major parties that have conflicting ideas on most issues. Fortunately, in this period of voter unrest, a few politicians in both parties are beginning to recognize the need to find some consensus before another voter wave crashes over them. Common ground is a means to that end, not the end itself.

We don't expect that a common ground climate will settle on Washington overnight, or that it will completely replace polarization. Polarization, to some degree, will always be with us because polarizers will always be among us. We believe that common ground can compete with polarization, and that it will be accepted by a new generation of politicians as a strategy to win elections.

What follows is the case for common ground as a viable political strategy for a 2008 presidential campaign and beyond. The messages, tactics, and ideas we offer can be integrated into the campaigns of candidates from either party or an independent third party candidate. Much like polarization, whose tactics have operated across party lines for years, common ground is a "nonpartisan" strategy.

THE PLAYING FIELD: 2008 IS THE PERFECT YEAR FOR A COMMON GROUND MESSAGE

The 2008 presidential campaign is the most wide-open race in recent history. For the first time since 1924, neither a president nor a current or former vice president is competing for either party's nomination. At the same time, both parties are facing an identity crisis: Democrats are adjusting to their new status as the congressional majority party, while Republicans face a presidential season without their traditional party-establishment front-runner.

For the first time in two decades, polarization is under fire. Both parties are experiencing internal battles between pragmatic party operatives and their ideological wings over the dangers of continuing polarizing tactics. While Democrats try to control their partisans on the left over Iraq, Republicans are attempting to develop a less "values"-driven strategy that can attract crucial independent voters, many of whom have abandoned the party. They will need them if they are to hold the White House and gain congressional seats. This must be done without alienating GOP supporters on the right, a difficult task.

This "soul-searching" is complicated by the absence of a recognized leader to impose party discipline and establish a consistent message. That role will be filled by each party's presidential candidate, a process that will take months to sort out. Meanwhile, Democratic congressional leaders are torn between confronting the Bush administration over policies ignored under a Republican-controlled Congress and trying to pass legislation promised in the 2006 election. Republicans are finding it difficult to put space between themselves and an unpopular president while still supporting him (thus far at least) on the war in Iraq.

The early presidential front-runners sit atop the polls more as a reflection of name recognition than as candidates with a base of loyal supporters. The situation is so tenuous among Republicans that talk of potential candidates entering the battle in the summer was being taken seriously in the spring of 2007. The Democrats' field is more settled, but it is dominated by current or former members of the Senate, which has not sent a candidate directly to the White House since John Kennedy, nearly fifty years ago.

There is general agreement among operatives of both parties that voters signaled a message for change in the 2006 election. The question remains whether they were signaling a midcourse change in the current political cycle (which has lasted for twenty years) or signaling the beginning of a completely new cycle. How the presidential candidates and their handlers answer that question will determine their choice of a message and strategy for 2008.

One signal from 2006 seems to be accepted by most of the presidential candidates: polarization as a central campaign message is not a strategy that will win this election. That doesn't mean polarizing tactics are going away, but campaigns will not be as eager to highlight them, nor will the press simply accept such tactics without much criticism, as was the case in the presidential campaign of 2004.

How much of a role polarization will play in 2008 goes back to the question of a new political cycle. Those candidates who believe a new cycle is beginning will be very wary of using polarizing tactics. Those who reject the new-cycle theory realize the need for "midcourse" change in strategy, but are not sure what changes will work. We predict they will eventually fall back on polarization because they prefer the familiar to the new, especially when the familiar has a twenty-year track record of success.

We believe a new cycle has begun, and that a common ground message is in sync with that cycle. Even the election calendar favors a common ground strategy. With several large states moving their caucuses and primaries to early 2008, the nominating process is now so front-loaded that most of the campaigning for the nomination is taking place in 2007.

It's now likely that each party will select its nominee very early in the campaign year, allowing the winning candidates to switch from campaigning for the partisan voters necessary for the nomination to swing voters who will most likely decide the election outcome in November. In previous presidential nominating contests (with the exception of those in which incumbent presidents were seeking a second term), the calendar and a crowded field have forced candidates to tailor their message for partisan party voters, sometimes deep into the election year.

The sooner a candidate who adopts a common ground message can distance himself from party polarizers, the sooner he can make polarization an issue. That's one reason 2008 is favorable to a candidate who adopts a common ground message. If the nomination is indeed determined early in the year, common ground is a fresh strategy that can sustain a protracted general election. Trying to maintain a campaign with polarizing tactics will be especially difficult in 2008.

Every reliable indicator points to voters fed up with the current cycle and ready to move on in 2008. But the desire for a new political direction comes at a time when voters are more uncertain about their own futures, and the future of the country, than at any time since the Vietnam War. Most political observers believe that an uncertain electorate makes the selection of a strategy difficult. We think the level of uncertainty provides a perfect climate for a common ground strategy and message.

Uncertain times demand more predictable and stable politics. Voters will be looking for a president who can begin to calm some very turbulent waters. In times like these, we believe, voters will be looking for the most competent and least dogmatic leader. They will be looking for a candidate open to new ideas, who can unite the country. In other words, they will be attracted to a candidate whose message is about competence, not ideology.

If this is the climate in 2008 (and we have no doubt it will be), then common ground is clearly not a pipe dream, but an opportunity. What follows are suggestions for maximizing that opportunity. To better explain common ground in the context of a presidential campaign, we offer suggestions for how a candidate might articulate a common ground message by using parts of several "fictitious" campaign speeches. Neither of us has been a speechwriter, so please take what we suggest as more of an outline than actual speech recommendations.

Campaign Recommendations

1. CAMPAIGN AGAINST POLARIZATION.

Polarization is not a strategy to campaign on, but an issue to campaign against. Our travels around the country have shown us that people are longing for a candidate who is willing to confront polarization. They want a candidate who can articulate the case against polarization, and who understands that to the voters, polarization is no longer an isolated battle between parties in Washington. They believe polarization has strained the relationship between the people and their government to the breaking point and they want it to stop.

The people we met want to embrace common ground as the alternative to polarization, but wonder if politicians will ever make the necessary sacrifices so that consensus politics is possible. We met one particularly cynical voter in March 2007, in Grand Rapids, Michigan. This fellow sarcastically asked if we expected politicians to embrace common ground because it is "nicer" than polarization. We agreed that politicians don't change to "nicer" strategies unless they are winning strategies.

Let's be clear about the common ground campaign message and

strategy we are suggesting here. It is not some Pollyanna-ish, good-government exercise in taking the political high road (although taking the high road in politics would indeed be nice). Polarization is an evil but powerful force in politics, and driving it off center stage is going to take guts and determination. It will require a strategy of confrontation and hardball politics. It is not a strategy for the faint of heart. In that context, common ground is not a "nice" strategy.

Voters will respond to a common ground message, but they will do so cautiously. Keep in mind that voters are more suspicious than ever of politicians, and for good reason. The credibility gap between politicians and voters is not easily bridged after twenty polarizing years. A candidate's commitment to a battle against polarization will be tested by voters who, like the cynics in Washington, have "heard it all before."

They will expect a candidate who campaigns against polarization to name names, and to not be afraid to name the polarizers in his or her own party. Take health care for example. If you are the Democratic nominee, you have no credibility if you attack doctors and don't bring the malpractice excesses of trial lawyers to the debate. If you're the Republican candidate and pitch the old "we have the best health care system in the world," but don't attack the health care providers and the insurance industry (which block meaningful reform while reaping big profits from the status quo), you, too, will have a credibility problem.

Similarly, if you're a Democrat and minimize the threat of Islamic terrorists (yes, call them what they are) and think, because of Iraq, the public has backed off the war on terror, you're deluding yourself. If you're a Republican and roll out the G. W. Bush/neoconservative line about using military power to spread democracy around the world, while belittling diplomacy and rejecting our allies' advice . . . count on getting your vote, maybe your spouse's, and those of a few true believers. Idealism is out in foreign adventures, and pragmatic diplomacy is in.

Here are just a few examples of common ground attack points to consider:

"We have lived through too many years of small and destructive politics. It has been a politics that seeks to divide

Americans against Americans, and communities against communities. It is a politics that raises money and secures votes by cynically pitting the values of one group against the values one another. It is a politics that encourages people to challenge others' patriotism and character. That politics is the politics of polarization and the extreme ideologues and institutions that perpetuate it."

"Polarization is undermining the very foundation on which our system of government rests. Polarization promotes the politics of personal destruction; it drives our citizens away from the voting booth; and it pollutes our political debate with incendiary rhetoric and baseless allegations. Polarization is not about principle; it is about keeping power and making money and it will be stopped."

"It is time to move beyond the evil era of polarization and the paralysis it breeds to a new era of common sense and common ground, an era that seeks consensus and not constant confrontation, an era that seeks to find what is in the common interest of most of us rather than promoting the narrow interests of a few."

"We stand on the hallowed soil of the American spirit. It is the common ground I share with millions of my fellow Americans. It is ground where 'we the people' stand, and to those who promote polarization we say simply . . . it is time for you to move to other ground."

2. DO NOT CAMPAIGN AS THE DEMOCRATIC OR REPUBLICAN CANDIDATE FOR PRESIDENT, BUT AS A COMMON GROUND CANDIDATE FOR PRESIDENT OF THE UNITED STATES.

The two major political parties are dinosaurs. They are seen by the vast majority of centrist voters as corrupt institutions where polarizers mimic one another and where big campaign money is handed out (with instructions on how to use the money and what message the money should buy); and they are seen as places of convenience, more than incubators for new ideas. For most self-described "weak" Republican and Democratic voters, a party represents no more than a list of candidates on the ballot in descending order of importance.

Of course party affiliation still matters to most people who vote in a caucus or primary to choose their party's presidential nominee and it certainly matters to the candidates seeking the party's presidential nomination. Both parties have histories, traditions, core values, and heroes, and candidates for the nomination will be expected to adhere closely to the spirit of each. However, in 2008 candidates will have fewer ideological restraints because the outcome is so uncertain. The desire to win in an unpredictable year tends to give candidates more room to maneuver.

That's a good thing, because if ever there was a time when party labels mattered less and competence mattered more, it is now. The old stereotypes thrown at each party by the other will matter less, and a serious political discussion will matter most. A campaign based on ideological grounds will be no match for a campaign of fresh ideas.

A campaign void of as much partisan rhetoric as possible will be important to success in 2008. The polarizing battles between Democrats and Republicans over the last two decades have done much damage to the reputations of each. We would strongly suggest that a candidate avoid lines like "The Democratic [Republican] Party has a long tradition of standing up for blah, blah, blah."

A common ground approach would read more like this:

> *"I am the nominee of a party for president, and I am grateful to my party for that honor. I sought this nomination as a member of my party, but I seek the office of president as a citizen of America. For too many years, both political parties have tried to attach simplistic and often derogatory labels on each other, labels that were meant to bring one candidate down while building the other up. The result has been a vicious climate of polarization. It is time for that to stop.*
>
> *"I have no interest in labeling my opponent, and I will not*

allow labels to be attached to me. Simplistic labels are meant to divide us. They have too often succeeded. But in the end, the polarizers who attach the labels will be the losers. They will lose because we are first and foremost Americans, and that is the only label that matters."

3. MATCH RONALD REAGAN'S BET, AND RAISE IT.

Ronald Reagan said he believed in an "eleventh commandment": never speak ill of a fellow Republican. In a common ground general election, we would broaden that to "speak as little ill of your opponent as is reasonable and politically practical."

This suggestion is aimed particularly at the use of negative ads, which have dominated the polarization cycle over several decades. The voters consistently, and with increasing intensity, say they hate negative ads. To which media consultants respond, "Voters always say they hate them, but they pay attention to them." The reality is not quite so clear. A better (and less biased) observation is that voters hate negative ads more and more, and are influenced by them less and less.

That is another overlooked (purposely by political consultants) lesson from the 2006 campaign. Negative TV commercials had very little impact on closely contested races (with a few exceptions).

When Pennsylvania Republican senator Rick Santorum fell behind his Democratic opponent, Bob Casey, in the summer and early fall of 2006, Santorum spent millions on an anti-Casey campaign ad blitz, spread over several weeks. When it was over, Casey had increased his lead. Santorum lost the election.

When Democratic challenger Jim Webb was gaining ground on Virginia incumbent senator George Allen (after numerous Allen missteps), Allen unleashed a thirty-day, multimillion-dollar negative television barrage against Webb. When it ended, Webb had a slight lead. Furthermore, with the Virginia race dead even going into the weekend before Election Day, Webb chose to end his campaign with a positive TV and radio message. Webb won.

The candidate who campaigns more on substance and less on the shortcomings of his or her opponent will find a far more receptive audience. The candidate willing to challenge the conventional wisdom of the last few presidential elections, which suggests that to win, a candidate must drive their opponent's negatives up, is likely to fare better. Here's a radical thought that is certain to upset expectations about politicians: look for opportunities to say something nice about your opponent and mean it. Polarization has driven the last remnants of civility from politics, and voters resent it.

Presidential campaign debates in the polarizing era have grown increasingly contentious. As a rule, pollsters bring preselected voters together in focus groups to watch presidential debates. They use the responses to prepare their candidate for the next debate. In 2000 and 2004, pollsters reported that many voters felt uncomfortable with the level of confrontation between the candidates. It is human nature to want to avoid confrontation, but that apparently has been lost on political operatives who think confrontation makes a candidate appear strong.

Here are a few suggestions for a common ground approach to presidential debates in the 2008 campaign.

CANDIDATES ARE USUALLY ALLOTTED BETWEEN TWO AND THREE minutes for opening statements in a presidential debate. Instead of using the entire three minutes to applaud yourself (although you should save time for some of that), or attack your opponent (although some of this may be necessary, it should be done with civility), why not use one minute and say something like this:

"Before we start tonight, I want to take a moment to say something about [opponent's first and last name]. Running for president is an honor, it is rewarding, but in recent elections, running for president has dissolved into unnecessarily harsh rhetoric. Neither of us want that. I have known my opponent for many years [or whatever fits], and he/she is an honorable person who is a dedicated public servant. As you will see tonight, there is much we disagree on, but before we

speak of our differences and possibly some agreement, I want to say to [use opponent's first name] how much I appreciate your service, and to thank you for joining me tonight in this debate. We will disagree on some, perhaps many, things, but I am confident we will do so agreeably."

Before a candidate listens to some political consultant dumb down this suggestion, consider this: if you can say something positive about your opponent and mean it, even the cynical media will have a tough time finding an angle to attack. If your opponent happens to be a polarizer at heart, what is he going to say?

"I have known you a long time, too, and you are a no-account low-life."

That may be what he is thinking, but most likely the opponent will simply say thank you. More important, if the millions watching on TV believe the candidate is sincere, that candidate will exceed expectations and reap the benefits.

Just consider how different the 2004 election might have been if John Kerry had said, in the first debate with George Bush, "Before we begin, I wanted to thank President Bush for his leadership and healing words in the difficult days following 9/11." Then, with Kerry's convention salute still fresh in people's minds, he could have turned to the president, saluted, and said simply, "Sir, the American people thank you, and I thank you." The Swift boat ads might have been a little less believable.

4. GIVE YOUR OPPONENT CREDIT WHERE CREDIT IS DUE; AND IN THE PROCESS GET CREDIT FOR GIVING CREDIT.

How many times have we heard a presidential candidate, after listening to his opponent's answer to a policy question in a debate, feel compelled to say, "I agree with that answer," while exhibiting an expression that conveys torture? Here's what a common ground response would sound like:

"[Opponent's first name], I think that's a good point, and I agree with you." [Then pick out one idea your opponent has campaigned on that you think is smart and workable, an idea that she has used successfully in her campaign, and is perceived by the press and public as "owning." Why not give your opponent credit for something for which she has already been given credit?]

"You have made a proposal in this campaign that I think would be good for the country." [Short description of the proposal.] "I'd like to make a deal with you tonight. If I win this campaign, and I believe I will, I'd like you to help me turn your idea [whatever it is] into policy after the election. Your idea would be good for the country, and I want to see it become law."

Again, before you let your overly cautious political consultants tell you it would be crazy to give your opponent credit for anything substantive (he is probably still getting over your opening statement), consider this: your opponent has already made the idea his own, it is a very good idea, it will get your opponent votes, and you can't steal it from him at this point without the media calling you a plagiarizer.

Trying to attack the idea is dumb—after all, it is a good idea. You might as well recognize that, and at least get credit for a magnanimous gesture. More important, it would be good for the country, your opponent can help sell it to his or her side if you win, and it sets a model for what common ground governing is about. Everybody wins, most especially the country.

5. MR. LINCOLN AND MR. DOUGLAS HAD A GREAT IDEA; USE IT.

Speaking about debates, virtually every candidate for president from both parties has used a version of Hillary Clinton's call for a conversation between candidates and voters. She has actually made it a campaign mantra: "Let the conversation begin." We are not suggesting that other candidates use that line, but rather that they (including Hillary Clinton, if she is the nominee) agree to put the concept into action (with a twist) during the general-election campaign.

Presidential campaign debates matter. In some cases (Kennedy, 1960, and Reagan, 1980), they may well have decided the election. The television audience is huge (close to 100 million watched the first Bush–Kerry debate in 2004). Debates are the only real chance voters get to see the candidates side by side, and they give voters a chance to assess the content of a candidate's message as well as measure his character.

The problem is modern presidential debates are too scripted. There are too many artificial barriers to allow for a serious debate. The moderators and/or questioners are from the political media. They are forever trying to create a "gotcha" moment. The time to answer or respond to the opponent's answer is too short. The few times real voters are allowed to participate, their questions are screened and they are rarely allowed follow-up questions. Worst of all, the candidates don't get to ask each other questions, or get into a serious discussion of an issue, beyond a thirty-second "rebuttal."

In 1858, the Democratic candidate for the U.S. Senate, Stephen Douglas, and the Republican candidate, Abraham Lincoln, agreed to tour regions of Illinois together and debate. They took questions from the audience, and they did this for hours at a time. People brought picnic baskets and stayed to listen and ask questions. The only other person on the stage, besides Lincoln and Douglas, was the man who introduced them. There were seven debates during the campaign. Lincoln lost the election, but from the debates he gained national recognition that he used to win the presidency two years later.

If you have ever read the debate transcripts, you can't help but be impressed with the substance, the amount of detail, and a sense of the character of both men. We are not suggesting debates of that length (the TV networks would never cover them), nor are we suggesting as many debates. But even a few of these real debates would provide voters with more useful information than contemporary faux debates could ever give them. For one thing, these types of debates would be more spontaneous and revealing of the candidates' character, and the candidates would be freed from the straitjackets negotiated for them by political consultants.

Bob Beckel negotiated debate details in 1984 with only one thing in mind: "make as little room as possible for my candidate to 'screw up'" (the political consultant's version of the Hippocratic Oath, "First do no harm"). By now, your political consultants are in convulsions, begging you to put down this book. Pay no attention to them.

Most presidential candidates we have known are fairly confident of their debating skills, believe they would be the best president, have political courage (or wouldn't run for president), and secretly detest the restraints put on them by their handlers. There are endless accounts (several spoken directly to us from the source) of candidates exploding after debates because the format was too restrictive and their responses too scripted. This comes from candidates who were generally regarded as winners of the debate.

There will no doubt be critics of this idea from the "do no harm" crowd (political consultants) and the "unemployed questioner" crowd (the press). The consultants will argue that one candidate could sandbag the other with a question, for example, about an ex-mistress. In today's climate, that kind of attack would be seen by the public as the worst kind of polarization and the candidate who asked it would lose the debate.

The consultants might ask, "Who is going to referee this?" Come on. This isn't professional wrestling. These people want to be president. If they can't control themselves, they shouldn't be running for president in the first place. The press will fret that the two candidates will get too substantive and not give television, radio, and headline writers a good sound bite. The press will secretly be saying, "Without us, who's going to trick these two into a 'gotcha' moment?" The media don't want a draw, and will rebel against this format, thinking it might not produce a winner.

For a candidate running on a common ground message, at least calling for this type of debate is essential. It would underscore the point that a new era in politics, short on ideology and long on substance, has begun. If your opponent refuses, the public will wonder what it is he is hiding. Contrary to current debate wisdom, it would be far less dangerous than the intense pressure candidates are under in the current formats, with time constraints and rules that offer no margin for error, or time to recover from an honest mistake.

A common ground campaign message calling for more open debates would be ideal at the end of a nominee's acceptance speech at his or her party convention:

> *"This year marks the 150th anniversary of the historic Lincoln/Douglas debates. In 1858, both were candidates for the United States Senate from the great state of Illinois. It was a time of fierce polarization in our nation over the issue of slavery, an issue that would lead a few short years later to the Civil War.*
>
> *"Lincoln and Douglas agreed to a series of debates across Illinois that year. There were seven, some lasting for many hours. Voters by the thousands came to hear the two men. There was no television or radio. There were no moderators, or panels of reporters asking questions. The two men debated face-to-face, asking each other questions and taking questions directly from the voters. They were substantive and civilized discussions, free of personal attacks and rancor.*
>
> *"Today, our political debate is mired in polarized rhetoric, perpetuated by those who seek to divide our nation. Our political discourse is no longer an open and honest exchange of ideas; it is an exchange of insults, allegations, and innuendo. It is about scoring political points. It is no longer a debate about ideas to secure our future; it is about sound bites to secure a spot on cable news.*
>
> *"On this anniversary of the Lincoln–Douglas debates, I ask my opponent to join me in the spirit of those meetings. Let's go before the American people, not in scripted formats designed to minimize mistakes and maximize sound bites, but in a free and open exchange of ideas. No moderators, no*

media intermediaries between the voters and us. Let's commit to an open and honest discussion, without props or gimmicks. Let's question each other, not about our motives, but about our ideas. Let us commit to a vigorous, but civilized conversation that will be judged on the depth of the whole of our ideas, not on the basis of a single sound bite.

"Let's debate once in the North and once in the South, once in the East and once in the West, and let's have a final discussion in Illinois at one of the sites of the Lincoln–Douglas debates to honor their contribution to the political discourse. Let's allow the people, not the pundits, to decide which of us is the right candidate at this moment in our history. And let us not engage in polarizing rhetoric to further expand the political battleground, but rather let us engage in a civil exchange of ideas in an attempt to find common ground."

[Alternative close] *"And after the debates are over, let it be said of us that we did not seek to expand the battleground with more polarizing rhetoric, but rather by a free, honest, and civil exchange of ideas we helped put America once again on the road to common ground."*

Candidates from the polarizing school will detest this, because their clever canned attack lines would be subject to a response in a Lincoln–Douglas format. They'll also hate it because success would depend on substance, not sound bites. They might hate it, but how can they reject it?

6. A COMMON GROUND CANDIDATE SHOULD PROMISE (SINCERELY) TO INCLUDE MEMBERS OF THE OTHER PARTY IN THE NEW ADMINISTRATION.

Every administration in recent memory has included a token member of the opposition party in the cabinet, or some other visible job, usually in a president's second term. At times, these appointees actually have had some influence with the president, but usually they were window dressing meant to convince the press and the public that this was an "inclusive administration." Some were appointed because the administration saw in the token appointee an opportunity to sell a policy to the opposition. The strategy rarely worked because the opposition party (and also the token appointee) was never included in the formation of policy.

There are important reasons for the next president to include a significant number of appointments from the opposition party (so long as they do not have profound ideological objections to the president's policies and will pledge not to undermine those policies). The margin between the majority and minority party membership in Congress is small, and it looks to remain so for several years, if not decades. As a result, polarizers in both parties have been able to use procedural hurdles, especially in the Senate, to stop legislation on important issues from passing Congress.

No legislation of consequence can hope to gain approval unless it is the product of bipartisan consensus. If the minority believes that members of their party are seriously involved in the administration's policy-making process, the chances for passage of the resulting legislation will increase significantly.

How many times have we witnessed important policy legislation dismissed as "dead on arrival" when it reached Congress. (Think the Clinton health care reform, the Cheney energy plan. Policies developed by one party without input from the other are roadkill for polarizers. The tougher the issue, the more essential it becomes to develop an early bipartisan policy approach. If it is seen as a partisan policy dressed up to look bipartisan, it will fail, and everyone loses, especially the public. The winners are the status quo crowd, filled with polarizers.

That is why the only successful strategy in Washington is a common ground strategy, which calls for both parties to come to the table with their ideas at the beginning, not the end, of the process. Partisans argue that if their side has its brand on a common ground proposal, it gives too much credit to their opponents if they (the opponents) initiated the proposal. As opposed to what? No one gets credit if nothing is accomplished and each ends up blaming the other for failure, when in reality, both have failed. Did it ever occur to these rabid partisan troglodytes that sharing credit is still getting some credit, but it is also the right thing to do?

7. A COMMON GROUND CAMPAIGN MESSAGE SHOULD NOT INCLUDE COMMON GROUND SOLUTIONS.

In order to secure at least a chance for a common ground governing mandate, a candidate running on a common ground message will have to convince the voters, and a skeptical press, that it can be done. The explanation will be particularly scorned by polarizers, since finding common ground consensus on issues that have been polarized (and therefore paralyzed) is the polarizers' greatest fear. However, they have been successful at keeping these issues polarized by keeping politicians terrified. Politicians may secretly wish for consensus, but they dare not campaign on consensus, for fear of being targeted by polarizers in their own party.

So why should a common ground candidate campaign on specific consensus solutions and risk losing their party base, which could potentially cause a drop in turnout? The answer is they shouldn't. A common ground candidate will undoubtedly take issue positions that do not stray too far from their party's traditional ideology, and for good reason; he or she believes them, or it is unlikely they would get the nomination. What a candidate considering a common ground campaign must understand is: *a common ground campaign does not require offering common ground solutions.*

The two presidential candidates in 2008, whether running on common ground or not, will still represent positions that are left of center (the Democrat) or right of center (the Republican). Hopefully, the candidates will offer fresh and/or less conventional ideas, but these are not common ground ideas. *Remember, common ground is not a set of ideas; it is a process for governing that can break the paralysis that has set in after two decades of polarization.*

This may sound contradictory to our point above about not running as a party candidate. Running with a message that strategically emphasizes country and deemphasizes party does not mean running away from what the candidate and his or her party believe. In any event, a presidential nominee is automatically associated in the voters' mind with the historical political philosophy of his or her party. This is a critical point that must be understood if a candidate runs on a common ground message. *We are not making the case that a successful common ground candidate must run in the ideological center.*

What will draw centrist voters to a common ground candidate is not common ground solutions. What will attract votes is a commitment to common ground governing, and the willingness to do battle against polarization.

CG Governing Principles

The following is an example of a message that explains a candidate's position on common ground governing:

> *"My life in public service has been guided by principles and values that are at the soul of my being. They define the ideal that is America. When I attempt to find a common ground solution to the problems facing our nation, those principles and values will be in the chair with me because they are me. I wish I could convince everyone charged by the voters to find solutions to our problems, that my principles and values are the right ones, and I will continue to try to do just that.*
>
> *"But I am also guided by my responsibilities to the people who put me in office. They didn't elect me to say, 'It's my way or no way,' although I assume, because they elected me, that they prefer my way. But in the end, it is every elected person's responsibility to try the very best they can to find solutions for our people's needs, and not get up and walk away because they don't always get their way. That does not serve the interests of the country.*
>
> *"Every American, on almost any day, has got to make some concessions. Whether it's dealing with a person at work who has different ideas from yours, or it's finding an open*

spot in a crowded parking lot at the same time as another driver sees the spot—you have to decide whether to give the spot to the other person or take it yourself. Do you try to find common ground with the person at work, or do you insist on your idea and walk away if you don't get your way, leaving the problem unresolved and as a result hurting your business? Most reasonable people would try to find common ground.

"If the person in the other car is elderly and you are young and alone, you have to make a value decision. Do you accept that the other person needs the spot more than you and you look for another? Or, do you rush into the spot, refusing to concede it? Most good citizens would give up the spot, not because they didn't have a right to it, but because it was the right thing to do.

"For too many years now, most politicians in Washington have not been willing to accept any compromise in their position. They seemed to believe they are always right, and the other side is always wrong. They try to punish another point of view by turning the person holding it into an evil person. For too long now, politicians have left the table to head for the battleground rather than stay at the table to find common ground. Worse yet, many of these polarizing politicians don't want solutions; they come to the table looking for a fight. In the end, the losers are the American people.

"Our government is in a state of paralysis because of the evil climate of polarization inflicted on it by polarizers. You ask what I mean by common ground governing? It's very simple. It means meeting the other party at the table, bringing my values and principles with me, in an honest effort to seek common ground on issues that can no longer be ignored. I may not get everything I want, but I will stay at the table to seek consensus. Politicians have to make concessions, too, not because they like to, but because it is the right thing to do.

If I leave that table and refuse to concede anything, and walk away leaving the job unfinished, then I really will have left my principles and values at the door."

A candidate with a common ground message will be asked to explain how a common ground governing strategy would work. The following is a set of principles that are essential if consensus is to emerge on any significant issue.

CG GOVERNING PRINCIPLE ONE: THERE MUST BE AGREEMENT THAT A PROBLEM EXISTS, AND AGREEMENT ON WHAT GOAL NEEDS TO BE REACHED TO ALLEVIATE THE PROBLEM.

Let's use a local example before we look at federal issues. Raleigh, North Carolina, has five public school districts. Three have an average class size of thirty students; the other two average fifty students per class. Let us assume the school board in Raleigh is divided between liberal and conservative members. They agree that the two districts are overcrowded. They then agree that the goal is to bring the two districts in line with the other three districts. What is left is to agree on a solution.

The scenario may appear straightforward, but in Washington, it is rarely that easy to even agree that there is a problem. Without an agreement on what the problem is, no goals can be reached, and therefore no solutions are necessary.

There are certain issues on which both sides recognize a problem, but feel so strongly about the issue that consensus is nearly impossible. Banning handguns is an example. One side sees owning handguns as an absolute right under the Second Amendment and the only problem is the side that wants to ban the weapons. The other side thinks the Second Amendment is no longer valid and so government can—and should—ban all handguns, except those in the hands of the police and the military.

There is little chance here for common ground, so principle one is inoperable. On issues like this, where consensus is improbable it is better to back off. Doing so may well prevent emotions from governing the debate or spilling over to issues where common ground might be reached.

CG GOVERNING PRINCIPLE TWO: FOR A CONTROVERSIAL ISSUE TO BE RESOLVED IN A COMMON GROUND CLIMATE, IT MUST CONTAIN ELEMENTS OF THE HISTORICAL ORTHODOXY OF BOTH PARTIES.

If a new president hopes to succeed at finding common ground on difficult issues, paradoxically, he will have to stake out a position during the election that is true to his core philosophy. As we mentioned above, that is necessary to win the election, but also necessary for common ground governing. Assuming principle one is in place—that is, that both sides agree there is a problem, and the goal is to solve the problem—then a president must come at the problem with a solution that ensures his party in Congress is with him.

Let's look at a problem that reappeared in American politics in the aftermath of Hurricane Katrina—poverty. Both candidates in the 2008 presidential contest are likely to accept that poverty is a continuing problem that must be addressed, despite its becoming somewhat less visible two years after the massive storm ravaged the Gulf Coast.

The candidate who is the Democrat might say this about poverty, and the role of the federal government in addressing it.

"Let me be clear on my position about what must be done to help the poor in this country. I have always believed that the federal government must continue to play a major role in alleviating poverty in this, the wealthiest country in the world. To have 37 million of our fellow Americans still living in poverty in the year 2008 is unacceptable. Government can't walk alone on the path to ending poverty; neither can it walk away from the problem and leave the burden totally to charities or the private sector.

"Past government programs to alleviate poverty, although well intentioned, have often failed because government tried

*to go it alone, or failed to offer incentives to the able-bodied
to escape poverty. In the last decade, however, we have seen
the private sector finally begin to step in and help.*

*"Any successful antipoverty program in America today
must involve government and the private sector working together to find common ground solutions to this daunting
challenge. Therefore I propose [see poverty below]."*

The emphasis on the government's staying involved is clearly a
long-standing Democratic position, but the door is open for government to work with the private sector, while also promoting individual initiative, responsibility, and accountability.

Here's what the candidate who is the Republican might say:

*"Poverty, as we witnessed after Hurricane Katrina, is still
with us, and it is still unacceptable. We cannot abide 37 million of our fellow citizens living in poverty in the wealthiest
nation on earth. The government programs, as well intentioned
as they may have been, have failed to solve the problem.*

*"I don't believe we can afford to launch another govern-
ment program that is likely to fail. It is not fair to raise the expectations of those in poverty who have been promised relief in
previous programs, only to see them disappointed again. Besides that, with a multibillion-dollar federal deficit, we cannot
afford a new program. Our only hope is to bring the private
sector to the poverty battle, while ending those programs that
have clearly failed to achieve their stated objectives. Maybe it's
time for the federal government to reach out to the private sector and see if solid business practices might provide the key to
help people out of poverty."*

Common ground principle one is met: an agreement that poverty is
indeed a problem and something needs to be done about it. The candidate who happens to be a Republican has stayed true to his party's
belief that the free market can solve problems the government can't. In
the process, the candidate has left the door open to a common ground

governing approach. Both sides agree that the poor must be responsible and accountable.

In an attempt to explain how common ground principles applied to the governing process might work, we have picked out a few issues that have traditionally caused polarization between the parties. We have attempted to illustrate some old and new ideas that might provide the basis for a common ground solution.

Before we begin, a word of caution. For common ground to work, both sides must agree there is a problem. We have to begin with a few assumptions: the parties involved genuinely want to make progress on the issue; the parties agree that continued polarization on the issue helps no one; that no attempt to seek progress could result in another voter revolt similar to 1994 and 2006; and, the toughest assumption of all, the press must not only encourage progress, but also watch and expose any polarizing elements bent on obstructing progress.

As we have noted, a common ground governing strategy does not begin with a specific proposal, but rather with an agreement on the problem and goals. After agreeing on problems and goals, a solution needs to emerge. It helps to bring some creative ideas to the table that have not already been beaten down by the polarizers, which leads to:

CG GOVERNING PRINCIPLE THREE: THE CHANCES FOR CONSENSUS ON A SOLUTION INCREASE DRAMATICALLY WHEN FRESH IDEAS TO ADDRESS THE PROBLEM ARE BROUGHT TO THE TABLE.

Each of the areas we explore here has been—and remains—at the heart of much political debate. Each of them has been used by political consultants and fund-raisers to energize and mobilize their respective political bases. None of them has been adequately addressed because too many politicians and consultants would rather exploit the issue than see it resolved. On most controversial issues, both parties have returned over and over again to old solutions they have been wedded to for years.

Trying to find consensus by beginning with one party's old position will not work. On any of these issues, there are solutions that have been proposed outside the party structure that can be used as a starting point. What's important is to use an idea that satisfies principle two—that is, it contains some aspects that both parties can reconcile with their values.

We begin with a problem our hypothetical candidates addressed above.

POVERTY

Though it can be argued that the poorest American is still "richer" and has more access to government programs and private charity than almost any other country in the world, that does not excuse our inattention to the poor. According to the Census Bureau, there were 37 million people (nearly 10 percent of our population) in poverty in 2004, up from 35.9 million in 2003. This is—or ought to be—intolerable for a rich nation like the United States. Lyndon Johnson's "War on Poverty" sounded compassionate, even noble, but the big bureaucracies involved in that war proved incapable of offering the type of incentives necessary to help people actually climb out of poverty.

Perhaps it isn't a big program the poor need, but a small one.

A number of conservatives say many in poverty are lazy and are addicted to drugs or alcohol, people who insist on making the kind of decisions that doom them to a life of poverty. Liberals say that most of these unfortunates were born in poverty and have no options. Each side's position has just enough conventional wisdom in it to polarize the poverty issue.

However, whether the position of the left/right is more or less accurate is irrelevant to the millions in poverty who are desperate for a way out. Many poor people harbor entrepreneurial dreams and, with the right incentives, could realize those dreams by creating their own businesses. One of those incentives is the microloan program introduced by the 2006 Nobel Peace Prize winner, Muhammad Yunus, thirty years ago in the impoverished country of Bangladesh.

Mr. Yunus, an economist, convinced some doubtful financiers to provide funds to Yunus's Grameen Bank, which he created to provide very small loans (a few hundred dollars or less) to people in poverty who wanted to start their own businesses. These small loans are then used to purchase a cow, kitchen utensils and a cart for mobile snack-food services, or hair dryers to start an in-home beauty parlor, etc. Interest rates are moderate to high, but are provided with no collateral beyond the borrower's will to succeed.

The program has been a raging success, and in thirty years has spread to sixty countries, including the United States. The worldwide default rate on the loans has averaged less than 2 percent. In the United States, 13 million "micro-entrepreneurs" have received loans of $500 to $25,000 at rates that average 20 percent. The rates are high, but these borrowers don't usually qualify for standard bank loans. AcciónUSA, a nonprofit organization that helped start the microloan program in the United States, has been followed by major lending institutions that see microloans as good business.

Both of us like the microloan approach. We believe ownership of a successful business is the best road out of poverty. Both of us believe there are millions of people currently in poverty who have, or might acquire, if they had the opportunity, the entrepreneurial spirit to be successful businesspeople. We further agree that these people, without a creative idea like microloans, have little chance of getting the capital they need to get started. Bob is further willing to agree there is little chance that the federal government will provide capital directly through a new government program.

From a common ground perspective, this idea meets most of the assumptions for a common ground success. We believe the problem of poverty is terrible and must be addressed; we believe the voters want a successful antipoverty program, and because it involves poor people, the press might be supportive; and we know the polarizers are unlikely to be satisfied with a compromise on the issue. (In this case, we will assume that even polarizers think poverty should be relieved.)

Cal loves the idea because the government is not involved (beyond perhaps helping to spread the word about microloans) and it is a pure private-sector initiative (both basic conservative orthodoxies). Bob loves the idea because it will help the poor (as does Cal), but Bob thinks the government has a role to play in making the program available to more people in poverty. His position is the same as that of the common ground candidate we mentioned earlier—that is, to provide incentives to lenders and to substantially lower the interest on the loans (20 percent is better than the Mafia, but not much). He believes the federal government should guarantee at least half the loans' repayment in exchange for lenders lowering interest to a maximum of 10 percent (basic liberal orthodoxy).

If microloans were brought to the common ground table, both parties' ideologies could be part of the solution. We are not going to suggest what consensus might emerge from this common ground approach, but the chances of reaching consensus are far better than, for example, Democrats trying to push through a poverty program on their own. If a microloan program funded by the private sector, but with government support, were to be instituted, most Americans would support the idea. Polarizers on the right wouldn't because of government involvement, no matter how minimal, and polarizers on the left wouldn't because they don't believe the private sector wants to help the poor unless they can gouge them with exorbitant interest rates.

As microloans have grown in country after country, the concept has received increasing support from the business community, the United Nations, respected economists, financial writers, the *Wall Street Journal, Forbes,* and many others. With each new endorsement has come credibility, and favorable opinions have given the program stature, as well as protected it from detractors. That brings us to another essential weapon in the common ground arsenal.

CG GOVERNING PRINCIPLE FOUR: A COMMON GROUND STRATEGY FOR GOVERNING MUST BE PROVIDED WITH THE MAXIMUM POSSIBLE AMOUNT OF POLITICAL COVER.

The increase in the federal minimum wage passed by Congress in 2007 followed many of the same common ground principles. First, there was general agreement that after ten years with no minimum-wage increase, one was due. And by combining a substantial increase in the wage (a Democratic principle) with accompanying tax breaks for small businesses that would be impacted by the increase (a Republican principle), each party's orthodox principles were met. The consensus on the issue sent a chill through polarizers on the left and right. It wasn't just because they opposed the details (polarizers on the right were dead set against increasing the minimum wage, while left-wing polarizers screamed about yet more business tax breaks). The shock was that it had happened at all.

If a president is elected on a common ground message, and the opposition party begins to sense political advantages to consensus and bipartisanship, polarizers will go into overdrive to protect their monopoly. If a minimum-wage increase could set them off, imagine how they might fear a new anti-poverty program like microloans. With each common ground success will come a more vicious response from polarizers. As we said earlier, this crowd is not going quietly to the fringes of politics, especially after more than two decades in the center ring.

A common ground governing strategy needs to anticipate and respect the polarizers' counterattack, and respond by increasing the political cover for those legislators willing to seek consensus and compromise. A number of issues we touch on here will require strong political cover, and we believe one of the strongest methods of providing that cover has been used too sparingly. In a common ground governing climate, this idea needs to be better utilized.

SECOND OPINIONS

The concept of a second opinion in medicine is recognized by patients and doctors as beneficial because doctors are not infallible and a "second set of eyes" is in the best interest of the medical profession and most especially the patient.

We believe getting "second opinions" that come from outside the Washington war zone can not only help our elected officials do a better job, but will also help promote policies and actions that serve the interests of the most people, rather than the narrow and partisan interests of a select few.

As we have noted, many elected officials feel that if they extend their hand to someone on "the other side," they risk having it cut off by interest groups who are determined to keep them under their control. If that base sees a senator or congressman who has been identified as "going off the ranch," they will immediately denounce him as a compromiser and tell their base he lacks conviction. People are unlikely to send money to those who practice conciliation because they have been taught politics is an all-or-nothing game.

There are many experienced people who could be helpful in providing solutions—and political cover—on a number of contentious issues. For them to assist in the pursuit of common ground, they need to have the necessary stature to help the politicians who really do want to reach out to "the other side" to encounter as few obstacles as possible. To bring enough political muscle to the process, the group must be large enough to be seen as a strong political force, but small enough to be manageable.

This group of experts—equally divided among Democrats and Republicans—must be committed to finding common ground, no matter who controls the Congress or the White House. Among them should be former members of Congress or veterans of past administrations, and perhaps a former president or two who has not been too harshly critical of the currently serving president. Former members of Congress who are now lobbyists would be excluded, as would any other person with a financial or personal interest in a particular idea or policy.

The "second opinion" groups would be approved and funded by Congress through legislation, which, like any other law, would be signed or vetoed by the president. Each group would be asked to address a particularly pressing problem, and produce second-opinion remedies within six months to one year. This would not be another Washington commission whose final reports get one day of press and a thank-you from the politicians, and are then put on a shelf to gather dust.

Under a common ground approach to governing, second-opinion groups would come with different mandates for implementing their proposed solutions, which is why we don't call them commissions. In Washington, commissions are established by Congress. Since commissions are usually formed to find solutions to problems Congress considers politically difficult, it's no wonder that commission proposals are usually ignored. The only tool available to commission members to sell their proposed solutions to Congress is moral persuasion. When morality competes with politics, guess which usually wins?

There have been exceptions. Several commissions formed to address very big issues that the American people cared deeply about have not been ignored. For example, the bipartisan 9/11 Commission, which was fully funded and staffed, was composed of members who commanded respect and attention. It issued a series of recommendations on homeland security that are now law. These included the creation of the Department of Homeland Security, which was the largest reorganization of government departments and agencies in history. The 9/11 Commission had no force of law requiring Congress to act, but in this case, the proposals had the support of a large majority of Americans who demanded that they be carried out.

In a government committed to a common ground approach, traditional commissions would still be utilized on issues that have broad public support, as the 9/11 Commission had, because Congress would find it politically difficult to dither. But issues as big as 9/11 fortunately are rare, so stronger second-opinion formats should be developed. One would have the authority to force Congress and the White House to act; the other would not disband after its proposals were submitted. Both have precedents (with some slight differences) and both could be used to get second opinions on, for example:

BUDGETING, SPENDING, AND ABUSING THE TAXPAYERS' MONEY

The 1994 Republican "Contract with America" pledged that the GOP would change the way things had been done in Washington under the Democrats. Republicans promised to restore fiscal sanity and accountability; they would eliminate government waste, fraud, and abuse, and they would treat the taxpayers with more respect. It didn't take long before those promises were broken and Republicans began to outdo the Democrats with new entitlement spending and bigger deficits.

According to the Office of Management and Budget, Washington now spends nearly $22,000 per household, the highest amount (adjusted for inflation) since World War II. In 1990, federal spending was $20,000 per household. No matter which party controls Congress, or whether a Republican or Democrat occupies the White House, spending doesn't seem to end. In fact, federal spending by the administration of President George W. Bush has been twice that of his predecessor, Bill Clinton. For 2005, the federal government spent $21,878 per household, overall, taxed $19,062 per household, and ran a budget deficit of $2,816 per household.

While government revenue continues to increase, the rate of spending, especially since September 11, 2001, rises even faster. A good percentage of the increase has been due to the war on terror, but spending on entitlement programs—old ones and new ones, like the prescription drug benefit for seniors—and record amounts of pork-barrel projects for individual members pushed the deficit ever higher and deprived Republicans of one of their biggest issues against Democrats.

President George W. Bush once told Cal he didn't worry about the deficit because it helped hold down the tendency of Congress to spend. Unfortunately for those who care about such things, the deficit had no effect at all on Congress, which continues to find new ways to spend our money no matter who is in the majority. In the meantime, as the deficit steadily increases, the government must borrow to pay for increased spending.

Even more insane is that this is all happening just when retiring baby boomers, the most populous generation to date, are about to collect Social Security and Medicare benefits. As President Bush can attest, along with those before him, any politician who tries to reform these programs becomes a target for polarizers on the left. They know reform is necessary, but they would rather exploit the issue than find a solution.

There is a common ground way out, but it will require a president with a common ground mandate. It will require another second-opinion bipartisan group with a congressional mandate to deal with the long-term fiscal challenges, but unlike the 9/11 Commission, this group would get input from Congress, the executive branch, private-sector experts, and the public. All fiscal policy issues would be on the table. The group would then develop legislation on which Congress and the president would be required to act.

By passing legislation like this, Congress would be accepting common ground principles one (there is a real problem and it has to be fixed) and two (with a goal set to achieve fiscal sanity before the train wreck). Congress would vote on the legislation allowing only revenue-neutral amendments (any spending increases would have to be accompanied by spending cuts of the same amount). There is a precedent for second-opinion proposals that force the Congress and president to act. One is the Base Realignment and Closure Commission (BRAC).

Since 1988, Congress has enacted laws that provide for the closure of military bases, in part or in whole, and the realignment of other military related facilities. Since 1988, there have been four successive bipartisan Defense Base Closure and Realignment Commissions that recommended shutting down military facilities. The law establishing BRAC mandated that the number of military closures had to be voted up or down by Congress, implicitly recognizing that closing military bases facility-by-facility would be politically impossible. Making hard choices on other politically sensitive spending (particularly Social Security and Medicare) is impossible without a BRAC-type second-opinion, bipartisan group committed to common ground.

Fraud, waste, and abuse in government spending needs to be addressed by another category of second-opinion group, for which there is a precedent: the Grace Commission. Instituted by Ronald Reagan to ferret out unnecessary government spending and uncover fraud, the Grace Commission was and remains a good idea. If staffed by responsible Republicans and Democrats whose only agenda is the fiscal health of the nation, a similar group working in a common ground climate could succeed today. The Grace Commission proposed many reforms. Some were implemented, saving taxpayers millions of dollars. Others were not, ensuring that unnecessary programs and spending would continue.

When the Grace Commission disbanded, Congress felt it could return to its misspending ways. A common ground second-opinion group would keep their staff in town full-time to monitor the legislative reforms recommended by the group. Should Congress be inclined to disregard the recommendations, group members would be called back to Washington to use their stature to put public pressure on Congress to act. "But isn't this what Congress is supposed to do with its oversight responsibilities?" Yes, but with the power of lobbyists and the temptations dangled before lawmakers to ignore their oversight responsibilities, the overseers need to be overseen.

Second-opinion groups are critical to common ground governing. There is hardly an issue before government that could not be shaped by one of the three types of second-opinion groups (the third being the 9/11 big-issue-type commission). But unless a president is elected on a common ground message, it is unlikely that the Washington polarizing community will call for a second opinion.

There are already efforts at reaching common ground on several issues despite attempts by polarizers to kill them off. Some have withstood the pressure and have produced results. Below are two examples:

HEALTH CARE

It's peculiar to us that some members of Congress can't practice common ground until after they have left office. Apparently, the polarizers and other special interests have too strong a grip on them while in office, but once they're out, they feel liberated and can search for consensus.

Former Louisiana Democratic senator John Breaux has created a program and web page called "Ceasefire on Health Care." Here is Breaux's statement of purpose: "Ceasefire on Health Care is a campaign . . . to identify areas of common ground between the political parties by bringing together Republican and Democrat policymakers and key opinion leaders to ask meaningful questions about where compromise can be made."

When we accessed the page in the fall of 2006, the first podcast listed was titled "Individual Responsibility in Managing Your Health." Senator Breaux spoke with Peter Pitts of the Center for Medicine and the Public Interest and David Kendall of the Progressive Policy Institute about being "proactive in your health care regimen."

That's a refreshing change in attitude. Good health isn't the primary responsibility of the government. It's yours and ours. Good health begins with you and me making the right decisions about not smoking, not drinking to excess (or at all, if you're an alcoholic), eating right, and exercising. Government plays an effective role as an information provider. Indeed, an increased focus on wellness care, which can help you avoid health problems before they develop, is needed. For example, government-required labeling of food products has been very helpful for consumers in their choice of healthy foods. However, in order for the government to help us help ourselves, we must individually utilize such information.

What about health insurance? Here are the statistics from the Census Bureau:

> *The percentage of the nation's population without health insurance coverage remained unchanged at 15.7 percent in 2004.*

> *The percentage of people covered by employment-based health insurance declined from 60.4 percent in 2003 to 59.8 percent in 2004.*

> *The percentage of people covered by government health insurance programs rose in 2004, from 26.6 percent to 27.2 percent, driven by increases in the percentage of people with Medicaid coverage, from 12.4 percent in 2003 to 12.9 percent in 2004.*

> *The proportion and number of uninsured children did not change in 2004, remaining at 11.2 percent, or 8.3 million.*

It is true that under federal law, no one can be turned away from a hospital emergency room. This is usually the only option for the poor. Add to that the burden illegal aliens are placing on our health care system (some hospitals in California have been forced to close because they can no longer afford to provide increasing levels of free care) and it is easy to see why the burden on the health care system of so many people without health insurance can rightly be labeled a crisis.

Former Massachusetts governor Mitt Romney, a Republican presidential candidate in 2008, signed into law in April 2006 a bill requiring all Massachusetts residents to purchase health insurance. Romney portrayed the measure as a historic solution to health care costs, even as some questioned whether it would end up costing more than the state can afford. The measure makes Massachusetts the first state to treat health insurance like car insurance. The law requires every citizen of Massachusetts to have health insurance and fines anyone who does not. Some observers say the plan promises a huge array of low-cost health insurance policies for the uninsured to buy, all subsidized by the state, and in some cases covered entirely by state government.

While the devil is clearly in the details of this bill, and in how it will be paid for, the fact that Republicans and Democrats could address health insurance as fellow citizens and not enemy combatants is a welcome step forward. Even if the government fully pays for the measure and it subsequently proves impossible, legislators have demonstrated a spirit of cooperating on a controversial issue that could serve them and the people of Massachusetts in future endeavors, which is what politicians are supposed to do.

We don't pretend to have all the answers to questions about health care and health insurance, but we think we can safely say that we will never find any in a contentious atmosphere. Talking beats fighting, and Mitt Romney and Republican and Democratic legislators, as well as John Breaux, have shown the way.

GOVERNMENT CORRUPTION

All new majorities in Congress and new presidents entering the White House promise they will be more ethical than the people they are replacing. It rarely turns out this way. Every administration and every Congress seem to have someone—a presidential staff member, a cabinet member, a congressman or senator, and sometimes the president himself—who gets into trouble. A lot of this is due to the sense of entitlement on the part of public servants who forget that they are supposed to serve the public, not themselves.

The press pays attention to, and often incites, high-level indictments leading to resignation, impeachment, and prison, but much of the corruption in Washington is below the radar. For every Jack Abramoff trading for government contracts worth millions, there are hundreds trading favors for government contracts worth thousands. Writer Michael Kinsley famously observed that the scandal in Washington is not what's illegal, but what's legal. In other words, many of the practices that are permitted legally in Washington are nonetheless scandalous or corrupting.

Earmarks are one of the most outrageous and ethically questionable activities engaged in by both parties. Simply put, an "earmark" is a spending measure often slipped into a bill that serves a personal or special interest. Often, the earmark is unrelated to the main legislation to which it is attached. Virtually every member indulges in earmarks, and most members don't try to block another member's earmark for fear of retaliation when it comes to something they want. There are a few exceptions, such as Representative Jeff Flake, an Arizona Republican, who has been tireless in his so-far fruitless efforts to end the practice.

The 109th Congress (which ended in 2006) achieved very little, but one bright light was the Federal Funding Accountability and Transparency Act. The measure was sponsored by Senators Tom Coburn (R-OK) and Barack Obama (D-IL) and signed into law by President Bush. It creates a type of Google search engine and database that will allow anyone to find out how his or her money is being spent. An October 2, 2006, editorial in the *Washington Examiner* said, "The purpose of this Web site is simple and straightforward. Taxpayers have a right to know how their money is spent. By lifting the veil of secrecy that obscures government spending, taxpayers will find it easier to hold elected officials accountable."

This comes two hundred years after Thomas Jefferson said, "We might hope to see the finances of the Union as clear and intelligible as a merchant's books, so that every member of Congress and every man of any mind in the Union should be able to comprehend them, to investigate abuses and consequently to control them."

The new law is a perfect example of what can result when two people from different parties and political philosophies search for common ground on a subject that benefits the country. Taxpayers will be able to track $1 trillion in government contract and grant spending—including earmarks—by congressional district. This will empower taxpayers to hold their elected representatives and senators accountable for the way they spend our money. No longer should we have middle-of-the-night legislation getting through in secret. If ever the phrase *we the people* had any meaning, this law puts more power in the hands of individuals and less in the hands of Congress.

Another change we recommend is term limits, which we believe would go far to limit the corruption that affects too many members when they stay too long. Recycling trash and members of Congress is a good idea, because if left in one place too long, both begin to emit a foul odor.

The Founders never intended Congress to be a career. In the early days of our nation, people came to Washington to serve their country for limited periods of time; then they went home to real jobs. An example of what can happen when people stay too long and get out of touch with average Americans occurred when a friend of ours, former senator George McGovern (D-SD), lost his reelection bid in 1980. McGovern had been in public life almost since returning from combat in World War II. After leaving the Senate, he bought an inn in Connecticut, but it soon went bankrupt. Interviewed by the *Wall Street Journal*, McGovern said if he had known how difficult it was to run a business, he might have voted differently while in Congress.

It's a funny line, but there is a lot of truth there. Senators and representatives never have to make payroll, or do a balance sheet. They can raise their own pay and provide themselves with health care and retirement benefits. Washington is a place where one can quickly lose touch. Term limits would lessen the opportunities for giving in to the numerous available temptations. Unfortunately, members of Congress would have to vote for term limits, and there has never been a majority with sufficient interest in doing so.

We also think it is time to consider term limits on federal judges, including those who serve on the Supreme Court. Under the proposal, judges would be limited to fourteen-year terms. If, after fourteen years, a judge wishes to stay in office, he or she must be renominated by the sitting president, and then reconfirmed by the Senate. There are practical difficulties with this proposal, including the fact that each year several federal bench seats become vacant by promotion to another federal judicial appointment, or because of retirement, or death. However, because these are lifetime political appointments, judges are often the prime targets for polarizers.

SOCIAL ISSUES

Nothing can fuel polarization more quickly than social issues. As we have noted, the evidence suggests that social issues will play a smaller role in the 2008 elections than in previous campaigns. A common ground candidate for president will undoubtedly take positions on most of them in the course of the campaign. But to the greatest extent possible, a common ground message on social issues should emphasize that social issues should not be allowed to poison the climate for other common ground solutions.

The likelihood that these issues will come before Congress and the White House is remote. Almost certainly they will not be issues resolved in the course of common ground governing because social issues are so polarizing that agreement among the best-intended politicians is impossible, and these issues are issues in most cases that need to be decided by the various states and the courts.

We come at social issues from two perspectives.

Bob's Take:

Social issues, especially abortion and gay rights, have been the most incendiary and divisive subjects in recent years and they are used by polarizers on the left and right to raise money and fuel division. They have made Washington a stage for their confrontations. Each year there are large demonstrations by pro-life and pro-choice groups, and there are multiple gay pride parades that always lead to counterdemonstrations. Yet, with the exception of a limited number of Supreme Court rulings, neither issue is before Congress, nor has any president submitted legislation to ban abortion or gay marriage. Both are issues for states to deal with unless and until the Supreme Court overturns *Roe v. Wade*, or a constitutional issue over reciprocity for same-sex couples "married" in one state and seeking recognition in another state comes before the Court.

These issues only add fuel to an already explosive climate of polarization. Because they are highly emotional and the groups representing them are organized and flush with money, they have succeeded in pulling the White House and Congress into the battle. Each year members of Congress, most with very strong opinions on the issues, participate in demonstrations in support of each side. Understandably, they get emotional and some fall into the darkest kind of polarizing, which demonizes the other side.

When the demonstrations end, Congress returns to legislation that has nothing to do with abortion or gay rights. But the emotions at the heart of these issues sometimes affect relationships and the ability to work on other issues. When it comes to abortion and gay rights, there is no chance that Congress or the president is going to tackle them head-on. Which leads me to suggest another common ground governing principle:

CG GOVERNING PRINCIPLE FIVE: DO NOT PICK FIGHTS WHERE THE OTHER FOUR COMMON GROUND GOVERNING PRINCIPLES DO NOT AND CANNOT APPLY.

On the issues of gay rights and abortion, there is clearly a problem that both sides recognize, but the problem is the other side! There is no agreed-upon goal. There is no new idea that will lead to a solution because in the end these are issues of conscience. Trying to get a solution based on conservative and liberal orthodoxies is impossible because the positions are so deeply ingrained on both sides that there is no way to combine ideologies.

Certainly, there are things like parental notification and wider dissemination of information to pregnant women, such as the sonograms that Cal discusses next, or issues like information on benefits to gay couples. But these are all issues for the individual states to decide. Congress couldn't implement any of the aforementioned initiatives if it wanted to, and it doesn't want to. If we learned nothing else from the tragic case of Terri Schiavo, the Florida woman at the center of a battle over life-support measures, it was that Congress is the worst place to deal with these issues.

These issues can only make finding common ground in Washington on other issues much more difficult. Congress and the president have enough problems to deal with (and for which they might wish to find common ground solutions) without attempting to take on state issues that we cannot affect.

Cal's Take:

If only abortion and gay rights were left to the states, I might be content. However, the Supreme Court in *Roe* and various state courts—in Massachusetts, for example—have circumvented the will of the people and imposed their judicial will. In Massachusetts, the state judicial court ordered the legislature to grant same-sex couples the right to marry and have all benefits enjoyed by heterosexual married couples. Every state where this issue has been on the ballot and the people allowed to vote on it has rejected elevating same-sex relationships to the level of marriage, which has traditionally been defined as a contract between a man and a woman.

According to a Pew Research Center poll released in August 2006, entitled "Pragmatic Americans Liberal and Conservative on Social Issues," it is impossible to easily label most of us when it comes to these subjects. "The public's point of view," says the survey,

> varies from issue to issue. They are conservative in opposing gay marriage and gay adoption, liberal in favoring embryonic stem cell research and a little of both on abortion. Along with favoring no clear ideological approach on social issues, the public expresses a desire for middle ground on the most divisive social concern of the day: abortion.
>
> Social issues reflect our deepest and most strongly-held beliefs, which is why it is so difficult to change them. They go to the heart of who we are, what we believe, our view of God and other

transcendent considerations. This is why it has been so difficult for people on both sides to change minds and laws through the political system. Apparently, Americans value freedom to decide such things more than they do a top-down imposition of someone else's views.

Abortion continues to split the country more than thirty years after the Supreme Court's *Roe v. Wade* decision. Pew reports that while the issue continues to divide us, "there is a consensus in one key area: two out of three Americans (66%) support finding 'a middle ground' when it comes to abortion. Only three-in-ten (29%), by contrast, believe "there's no room for compromise when it comes to abortion laws. The desire to find common ground extends broadly across the political and ideological spectrum."

Abortion is the most divisive social issue since Prohibition. I believe it is the taking of human life. However, we both believe that the millions of human hours and millions of dollars that have been spent trying to reduce or stop abortion from the top have been mostly wasted. We prefer another approach.

Pro-lifers should begin a campaign similar to truth-in-labeling and truth-in-lending legislation, which mandate certain information be provided a person shopping for items at the supermarket or applying for a loan at the bank. Women should be fully informed, not only about abortion, but about the alternatives to the procedure. Many women with whom we have spoken and who have had abortions tell us they would have made a different choice had they had additional information.

We expect to get as much information as we can before making other important decisions—buying a house or car, or even where to take a vacation. Why shouldn't women expect to be shown a sonogram of the developing baby (some surveys have shown more than 90 percent of women choose to continue the pregnancy after seeing a sonogram)?

This isn't about restricting choice; it is about giving sufficient information so that the choice will be fully informed.

On same-sex marriage, the state offers all sorts of contracts to individuals and to associations of people. While I believe that marriage is a unique "contract" between a man and a woman, two men or two women who wish to enter into a civil contract for the purpose of buying a house, applying for credit, or simply for companionship should not be prohibited from doing so. On matters involving same-sex "marriage," and in extreme cases such as polygamy, the state has the right, even the duty, to proscribe such arrangements as outside the boundaries of permissible social structuring.

I also believe that heterosexual people who support what they call the "sanctity" of opposite-sex marriage should do a better job of shoring up their own marriages, given the high divorce rate. They might then have more credibility when telling others how to live their lives.

These and other issues related to personal behavior may be addressed by government at the margins, but most deal with the character, integrity, and virtue of an individual, something that is beyond the power of the state to create in any of us. These things are mostly reserved for parents and religious bodies.

FINALLY, WE HAVE SPENT MORE THAN TWO YEARS, EVERY TWO weeks, on dozens of issues and events, trying to find common ground for our *USA Today* column of the same name. Of course, ours are only opinions, but even trying to find a common ground opinion is sometimes difficult. We do not pass laws or regulations, or promote other government actions. Those are decisions politicians are elected to make. In writing this book and our column, we have come to appreciate just how difficult their job is in finding solutions to complex issues, especially in a polarized climate.

We both have enormous respect for the vast number of elected officials who come to their jobs every day wanting to do the right thing. Most do want to find common ground solutions to the nation's problems and given the opportunity to do so, free of polarizers and their endless pressures, we think they would succeed. But unless we can elect a president who campaigns and wins elections on a commitment to governing in a climate of common ground, other elected politicians are unlikely to succeed. Common ground requires a strong leader to give them the best climate in which to try.

That is why we wrote this book. We want to encourage a presidential candidate (or two or three) to include a common ground message in his or her 2008 campaign. We hope that we have provided a commonsense political case to do just that. This window of opportunity to confront polarization is short, but the timing could not be better. The voters are waiting for just such a person. We hope we have given potential common ground candidates the reasons (and some methods) to be that candidate. Any takers?

"Common Ground," Our USA Today *Column*

The following is an example of our "Common Ground" column in *USA Today*. We are happy to report that it receives overwhelmingly favorable feedback and virtually no negative responses.

In the wake of this election, politicians are vowing to work together for a change. Let it begin with a mixer, perhaps a nice dinner. If Democrats and Republicans would talk outside of the Capitol dome, perhaps they'd get more work done inside it.

Cal Thomas is a conservative columnist. Bob Beckel is a liberal

Play nice

Democratic strategist. But as longtime friends, they can often find common ground on issues that lawmakers in Washington cannot.

TODAY: *Democrats, Republicans should break bread to break their impasse.*
(Illustration by Sam Ward, *USA Today*)

CAL: Congratulations, Bob, on your Democrats' impressive electoral victory.

BOB: Thanks, Cal. It was a great victory, but now the real work begins. And despite all the mudslinging and nastiness of this election year, I took great comfort in hearing so many politicians proclaim their determination to seek consensus and common ground. That may be the silver lining in what was otherwise a dismal campaign.

CAL: In his postelection news conference, President Bush used the words *common ground* at least half a dozen times. Even the next Speaker of the House, Nancy Pelosi, spoke of "common ground."

BOB: I wish we could take credit for this sudden birth of comity, but voters deserve the real credit by making it clear that it's time to end the partisan gridlock.

CAL: There could be a problem, though. After the platitudes about cooperation and "working together" subside, Democrats and Republicans will face harsh political realities. Neither side has converted the other to its point of view. So when Pelosi speaks of rushing through a Democratic agenda, the political cease-fire might end right there.

BOB: Maybe so, but I'd like to be more optimistic. These are not stupid people on either side. Surely they cannot have missed the voters' message. The public is fed up with partisanship and wants those we elect to work together to promote the general welfare more than their own.

CAL: After every election, politicians dutifully say the right things. "We'll work together." "It's time that we put aside politics and do the people's work." You know the drill. Yet in today's Washington, it's been all talk.

BOB: Despite differences, Washington used to be more collegial, but those of late who arrive in the capital have taken on a bunker mentality.

CAL: That's right, Bob, and the most extreme ideologues on both sides not only fund their causes but pressure political leaders to draw a line and then demand that they not cross it.

BOB: And that's where we are today.

CAL: If the politicians are serious about finding common ground, they need to get to know each other. With many incumbents leaving Washington and so many new faces arriving, it's a chance for new members to get acquainted in ways that previous members did not. If they want to protect themselves from lobbyists and special interests that descend on Washington like locusts, they need to pursue an active social life and spend time together. It's difficult to denounce someone as a danger to America when you've just had dinner with him or her. Personal relationships used to count for a lot more than they do today, and their loss has been a major reason why politics has turned ugly.

BOB: When we spoke with former congressman Tony Hall, an Ohio Democrat, he said Washington had become a "suitcase town." Members come to work Tuesday and leave on Thursday. During those three days, they squeeze in a few fund-raisers with lobbyists. I was encouraged to hear Maryland representative Steny Hoyer, who is in the running to become House majority leader, say it was time for Congress to return to a Monday–Friday schedule, as it was several decades ago. I hope they use some of this "extra" time to get to know each other on a personal level.

CAL: At parties and social occasions in Washington, Democrats and Republicans used to reach agreement on contentious issues, and the public was the beneficiary. President Reagan and Democratic House Speaker Tip O'Neill would sometimes quarrel during the day. By night, though, Reagan would invite O'Neill to the White House for drinks. They would try to work out their differences. Sometimes they did, sometimes not. But they had a healthy respect and even admiration for each other. Those days have vanished.

BOB: You make a valid point, Cal. Few members know each other beyond the party or ideological label applied to them. How can we expect people with different political views to find common ground if they don't know, or trust, members of the other party?

CAL: If anything is clear from this election, it's that the public is paying attention. As a result, lawmakers were destroyed by ethical challenges and other afflictions that can come with protracted incumbency. The public must keep the pressure on their congressperson; otherwise, the lobbyist buzzards will pick them apart like roadkill, and these newly elected "reformers" will come to resemble all of the other carcasses who have come here and met political death.

BOB: I was happy to see more people voted in this election than in most "off-year" elections, but fewer than half of eligible voters turned out. Just like the buzzards in Washington you mentioned, who move in when the people tune out, extremist voters dominate elections when mainstream voters fail to participate.

CAL: And then only the shrillest voices are heard.

BOB: Here's another thought. If the public wants our leaders to pursue common ground, they will have to practice it themselves. If you're a Democrat, invite a Republican to dinner (and ask him to pick up the check!). If you're a Republican, invite a Democrat (I know, you think he'd pay with a government check!). This is how we became friends, isn't it?

CAL: It is, indeed. Now let's go to lunch. It's on me.

26

THOUGHTS AND CONCLUSIONS

BOB: I come away from our last two years on the "common ground trail" with some contradictory thoughts and mixed emotions. After traveling thousands of miles; talking to several thousand people; and interviewing politicians, party activists, pundits, polarizers, members of the press, and hundreds of voters from every region of the country, I am more convinced than ever that an authentic grassroots revolt is building against polarization, and that voters are ready to embrace consensus and common ground. What troubles me is that polarization is so ingrained in our politics, I'm not sure if a presidential candidate will seize this moment. Politicians tell us they yearn for common ground, and in the next breath say, "Don't put that in your book." Cal wrote a popular book called *Blinded by Might*. There were times I thought we should rename this book *Blinded by Polarization*.

We mentioned the classic *Wizard of Oz* film early in the book as a metaphor for the polarizing bullies who intimidate the political establishment in Washington. We know who they are—heck, we used to be in the gang—and we know they are like the little man playing the big bad Wizard in the movie. Pull back the curtain on the big bad polarizers, and you'll find the same thing: small-minded, little people, using smoke and mirrors to convince us of their power and invincibility. Ironically, that's why I'm optimistic, because it is a scam, and eventually scams, like bad marriages, don't hold together. Cal, what's your take on the Wizard?

CAL: I agree, Bob. Polarization is an addiction. It is addictive for politicians who think they have to smoke the stuff in order to win, and it is addictive for the people who make money and gain influence for themselves so they will be hired for future campaigns; it is addictive for the public, many of whom don't know any other way in modern politics because most are too young to remember anything approaching reasoned debate. As with most strong drugs, it will be difficult to break the habit. The public must demand this for the good of our politics and the good of the country. Destroying one's opponent solves not a single problem faced by this nation. Leaving one's opponent with a level of credibility and humanity allows him or her to participate in the discussion that follows an election. That is good for the winning and losing candidate; it is good for the political process and it is good for the country, which too often seems to take a backseat in the quest by a few for power, prestige, money, and influence.

You have courageously battled your own addictions and have conquered them. Am I off base comparing political polarization to drugs and alcohol?

BOB: The only difference is that polarization is not a physical disease, but the psychological addiction is the same; dependence on a way of living, the inability to accept responsibility for the damage created, the refusal to listen to any alternatives, isolation, anger, it's all there. One other similarity between polarization and chemical addiction is that they both fit the same definition of insanity; doing the same thing over and over again and expecting a different result. Addicts come in all shapes and sizes. I was struck by how many different types of polarizers are contributing to polarization; ideologues driven by one issue; profit-driven polarizers and the interests they represent; polarizers dependent on one party to protect their interests; party polarizers, including party apparatchiks and political consultants; for-profit individual polarizers; policy polarizers operating out of hundreds of tax-exempt think tanks; and finally the "bottom-feeders" who promote polarization to sell books, get lucrative speaking engagements, or sell tickets. And of course there is the media. For observations on this crowd, I turn to my coauthor. Cal?

CAL: The media are hypocrites about this. I know I've said it before, but it bears repeating. On the one hand, they editorialize about the "politics of personal destruction." On the other hand, they invite the personal destroyers on their news and talk show programs for the simple reason that it brings them high ratings and big profits. Then, having had them on, they tsk-tsk about the depraved political discourse. There is a certain self-fulfilling prophecy in the media these days. They claim no one will watch serious programs, so they focus on stories like Anna Nicole Smith, Paris Hilton, and Britney Spears on her latest trip to rehab. But this insults the American people. It is also a matter of conditioning. If people only have junk food to eat, they will eat junk food. But if you give them a gourmet meal and ask which they prefer, most people would say they prefer the good food. The public has a role in this. If they want a higher tone, they will have to stop watching TV shows and listening to radio programs that take a lower road. It's all about supply and demand. If large enough numbers of us demand something better, they will have to supply it. They think they're giving us what we want, but it's not what we need. The public can challenge them to do better and make them do better.

BOB: What seems to be the hardest thing for politicians to understand is that common ground is not a radical change in message or political strategy. It is a message that would work with any other message, as long as it's not a return to polarization. We have had the hardest time explaining that common ground is not a set of ideas; it does not force a candidate to abandon his or her principles; and it does not force a candidate to run as a milquetoast moderate. Common ground is two things: first, it is a message that will attract voters to a common ground candidate willing to take on polarization; and second, it is a process of governing with a goal of undoing the paralysis inflicted on Washington by years of polarization. I only hope polarizers haven't intimidated politicians to the point that common ground is not an option. Is there hope, Cal?

CAL: There's always hope. Common ground is not an end, but a means. It isn't a group hug and pretending that ideas and convictions don't matter. It is the realization that no one gets his or her way all the time, perhaps not even most of the time. By putting the nation's interest before personal interest, one serves not only the nation, but oneself. It is a curious formula. If you seek to elevate yourself, you often end up denigrating yourself. But if you seek to humble yourself, you are exalted by peers and the nation for your selflessness. That's not a formula often practiced in self-centered Washington. But if people try it, they will find that it not only works, but that it also produces the kinds of political benefits they seek, but rarely find, when their first and sometimes only priority is self.

BOB: Too many voters make demands on politicians that they do not make on themselves. The number of people who vote remains appallingly low. When people do vote, too many make choices based on sound bites or a "voter information" card placed on their windshield. Politics is a full-time profession for politicians, and it should consume more of the public's time and interest. Otherwise, politicians will think the public doesn't care, or is not paying attention. That changed in 2006. Voters were paying attention and voted; even some traditional nonvoters decided to show up. I'm convinced that among nonvoters there is an overwhelming number of common ground supporters.

As we travel around the country and speak on common ground, we always receive an enthusiastic reception. Hopefully in 2008, this enthusiasm will lead to participation at the voting booth. People need to vote, not just in general elections, but in primaries. And they should recruit like-minded people in their own community to support common ground and to vote.

Finally, if they are able, they should open their wallets and contribute to sensible common ground politicians. The more people who participate in politics, the less potent the polarizers. The number of polarizers hasn't increased; the number of sensible centrist voters has declined. Ironically, it is polarization that will bring them back.

CAL: What we heard from our interviews is that when Republicans and Democrats travel and otherwise spend time together, they, too, begin seeing the other person as someone other than the enemy of all things good and begin viewing him as a fellow human being, even a fellow American. Then, when they work together on a bill and compromise—not their principles, but their rigidity—and consider that the other person may have an idea worth trying, they produce something that neither side supports fully, but each side recognizes as better than getting nothing at all. The next time they disagree on an issue, they are more likely to repeat the pattern and find that common ground is not only good politics, but good for the country.

BOB: There is fear that a common ground candidate can't attract the enormous amounts of money needed to run for president because most of the money in politics today is controlled by polarizers. I mentioned that common ground supporters at the grassroots level might contribute to a common ground candidate for president, and saw some evidence of this in 2007. Senator Barack Obama's message in his presidential campaign is closer, so far, to a common ground message than that of any other candidate in either party. His bestselling book *The Audacity of Hope* sounds remarkably close to many of the message suggestions we have presented in *Common Ground*. In the first quarter of 2007, Obama raised an astounding $24 million (more than any other candidate's total contributions for a party nomination) from

150,000 contributors including more than $6 million over the Internet.

There are also groups of polarizers mentioned above who will contribute to any candidate who has a reasonable chance to be elected president, if for no other reason than to get a seat at the table in the next administration. By the way, the nice thing about writing a book with an archconservative like Cal Thomas is that you know this is not a sly way of supporting Senator Obama, right, Cal?

CAL: Arch? Who's "arch"? If I were "arch," I wouldn't be partnering with you! I like Obama's language, but I want to make sure it isn't a cover for liberal policies I could not support. On abortion, for example, what would be his middle ground? How about gay rights? What are his policies for fighting the terrorists without and within our country? Taxes? The size and reach of government? I want to know how he would negotiate on such things with a conservative like me. If it's more than talk and selling books, I would be happy to take him seriously. But you know how modern politics has been. Some consultant tells a candidate he can make hay with a theme like common ground because the voters are fed up with polarization. Then, once elected, that person reveals his true self. It happens a lot, and both Republicans and Democrats have their share of people who could be indicted for such behavior. But if we want to see common ground politics practiced, we have to do more than preach it, and I trust we have made a start on this in this book.

BOB: My final thought, Cal, is what a pleasure it has been to ride the "common ground trail" with you. I've come to realize that not all conservatives are fire-breathing dragons ready to do harm to all I hold dear. You come to realize that once you rise above stereotypes and get to know someone, you can find common ground. If you don't, at least you tried, and the climate is not so embittered that you can't come together on some other problem. This book has been a bit of a mea culpa for both of us. After watching polarizers operate over the last two years, I can't believe we used to be contributors to that insanity. Live, learn, and most important, don't forget. Cal, I hope this has been only a small part of the journey.

CAL: We're a good example of how common ground can work. Before we knew each other, we only knew "about" each other. I saw you as a liberal Democrat with "evil" ideas and positions conservatives associate with that label. You saw me as a conservative Republican with similar "evil" ideas and suspect friends. When we got to know each other and talked about politics, as well as personal and family challenges, we stopped seeing each other in stereotype and came first to respect and then (shock, shock) even to admire each other. The politics became less important than the relationship. And, most surprising of all, we found ourselves in agreement about quite a number of things, though we occasionally still differ on the best ways to achieve our common goals. But that's what journeys are for. You make a lot of stops along the way and you learn something at each one. You want to drive this time, or should I?

EPILOGUE

PLAGUES AND POLARIZATION CAN TAKE TIME TO CURE. POLARIZA-
tion and the toxic political environment it has produced won't end
quickly. Neither will it happen at all unless the voters understand
this is not a game like King of the Hill we played as children. This is
about the type of country we want to live in and desire our children
and grandchildren to inhabit.

We have too many enemies who want to destroy us from without to indulge in political fratricide and destroy ourselves from
within. Al Qaeda is our enemy, not the party to which we do not
belong.

Like a plague, the infected are either going to have to be moved
from the area of greatest contamination (through term limits), or
voters are going to have to tell their representative and senators they
are "mad as hell and not going to take it anymore." They will need
to support those who sincerely attempt to practice bipartisanship
with the objective of not winning power for its own sake, but instead acting in a way that promotes the general welfare and the
interests of their constituents.

Politics is a lot like television and the movie industry. When a new show or film is a hit, others seek to emulate it and numerous copycat programs and movies soon follow.

We believe that if just a few Republicans and Democrats begin building personal relationships that translated into progress on important issues—as they once did—the "fever" might spread, positively infecting other members who would like to see the climate change. But most are reluctant to take the first step for fear of being clobbered by the polarizers.

The alternative is more of what most people hate—legislative gridlock, out of control spending, including earmarks—an out of touch Congress that has little in common with average citizens and an attitude of entitlement for the seats they hold, rather than one of public service.

There are some hopeful signs. In May 2007, a bipartisan group of senators announced agreement on a major overhaul of immigration laws. The group had met quietly for months. Its members included liberal Democrats and conservative Republicans. The final product employed common ground principles; the group agreed there was a problem and agreed on common goals; the outcome included new ideas that had not been a part of previous immigration reform debates; the proposed legislation reflected the historical orthodoxies of both parties . . . bipartisan consensus at its best.

President Bush immediately endorsed the proposals, while both Democratic and Republican candidates for president, showing the courage of pigmies, immediately rejected the package or hid behind "extreme reservations." The polarizing community went into full combat mode. The right attacked it as "rewarding law breaking and amnesty"; the left called it "cold, heartless, and unworkable."

The immigration package may well be a victim of the 2008 election, but it is a start. At the minimum, we should show respect for the bipartisan effort and not simply dismiss it. More important, we should take note of the effort to address a major issue such as immigration reform and not ignore it like so many other things the government does on our behalf. We pay too little attention to what government is doing, and spend too much time, after the fact, complaining about what it has done.

Ultimately, it is up to all of us to stop treating politics and politicians as an irritant and start paying attention to what they are doing in our name and with our money. If we get the kind of government we deserve, we will be in worse shape than we thought. Clearly, we are not getting the government we are paying for, as more is spent—whether by Democrats or Republicans—and the same problems never seem to get resolved.

Americans have notoriously short attention spans, but we must pay more attention to our government and the politics and politicians who run it. Otherwise, things will only get worse, and it will be (as it is now) our fault for letting it happen.

So, what will it be: More combat, leading to more anger and a perpetuation of our broken political system, or common ground? The question should answer itself.

Does it?

If Bob Beckel and Cal Thomas—coming from complete opposites of the political spectrum—can find common ground, what's everyone else's problem?

A final word for polarizers who might be reading this. It doesn't hurt to change your ways; in fact, it is liberating. When we began this book, we had reservations about our chances of completing *Common Ground* without serious disagreements and "a failure to communicate" with each other. We had some disagreements, but we worked through them. You know what we discovered? It feels much better to give a little and get an agreement than to insist on our position and get nowhere.

Who knows, if you become a "born again" common ground person, you might actually get a whole lot more than you might think. One thing is certain: if you insist on being a polarizer, you will produce nothing but more frustration for everyone and a perpetuation of a broken system, which will lead to even more cynicism and less citizen participation in the nation's political life. And that will mean even fewer people will be in control of a greater number of us. Does anyone believe that is a good thing?

ACKNOWLEDGMENTS

The authors want to thank all those who shared their thoughts with us for *Common Ground*, especially former president George H. W. Bush, former House Speaker Newt Gingrich, current House Democratic majority leader Steny Hoyer, senator Joseph Lieberman, and former congressman and ambassador Tony Hall. Special thanks to Esther Coopersmith, Letitia Baldrige, and Clare Crawford-Mason for sharing their personal stories of life in Washington. In addition, thanks to Pam, Doug, Pete, and the hundreds of other voters who shared their hopes and frustrations with us.

Also to Henry Ferris, our editor, and friend, at HarperCollins, without whom this book would never have been possible. Thank you, Henry, for your advice and guidance. Even when you were traveling the world you made time for us. We want to thank the team at HarperCollins, including Peter Hubbard and Pamela Spangler-Jaffee, who put up with us. A special thanks to our superb agent, Margret McBride; and to our researcher, organizer, and protector, Tom Cain, without whom we would have been lost.

―――――――

BOB BECKEL WOULD LIKE TO ACKNOWLEDGE A GROUP OF CONSERvatives who helped him understand why conservatives think the way they do. First and foremost, thanks to FNC chairman Roger Ailes, who took a chance when others would not, and is a man with a big heart. To Sean Hannity, who is a pain on air and a prince off. Thank you, Sean, for your kindness during difficult times. To the executive producer of *Hannity & Colmes*, John Finley, who shared brilliant insights on the political landscape.

To pastors Rob Norris and David Stokes, who helped me find grace and gave me encouragement when it was most needed. To John Keyser for reading early drafts and giving much needed input. To Tricia Bakunas for her editing of edits.

Last, but far from least, to my coauthor and dear friend, Cal Thomas, who has been with me in good and often exceedingly bad times, a true Renaissance man, a superb writer, and a man of God.

INDEX

AARP, 190–91
abortion, 44, 78, 79, 81, 107, 119,
    198, 199, 242–43, 244, 245
  Reagan and, 105
  Roe v. Wade and, 82, 88, 95, 103,
    104, 105, 108, 130, 243, 244,
    245
  sonograms and, 243, 245
Abramoff, Jack, 2, 42, 53, 156, 240
AcciónUSA, 230
Adams, John Quincy, 50–51
Aesop, 143
Afghanistan, 21, 101, 154, 159
Africa, 141
Agnew, Spiro T., 96
AIDS, 112
Allard, Wayne, 76
Allen, George, 213
al-Qaeda, 153, 154, 157
American Enterprise Institute, 33
American Insurance Association
    (AIA), 138
American Medical Association
    (AMA), 138
American Solutions for Winning the
    Future, 34
American Spectator, 123
appropriations, 53, 100, 181, 188
Armour, Richard, 1
Armstrong, William, 76
Atwater, Lee, 122
Audacity of Hope, The (Obama),
    255

Baldrige, Letitia, 179–80
Barbour, Haley, 121
Barry, Dave, 169, 171, 172
Base Realignment and Closure Com-
    mission (BRAC), 236
base strategy, 34–35, 175
Begala, Paul, 7
Benn, Ernest, 151
Bernstein, Leonard, 17
Bible Belt, 92
bin Laden, Osama, 154, 157
bipartisanship and consensus, 174–76,
    177, 186, 189–90, 192, 198, 204,
    205, 206, 221
  See also common ground
Birnbaum, Jeffrey H., 181
Blackmun, Harry, 95
Blair, Tony, 158
blogs, 43, 70, 71, 126, 130
Bloomberg, Michael, 76
blue and red states, 43, 74–78, 80,
    198
Boehner, John, 147–48
Bork, Robert, 119–20, 124, 127, 128,
    129–30, 153, 189
bottom feeders, 6, 7, 41, 42, 43, 128,
    253
Breaux, John, 237–38, 239
Britain, 154
Brock, David, 123
Broder, David S., 49
Brownback, Sam, 200
Buchanan, Pat, 7, 78–79, 81

Burger, Warren, 95
Bush, George H. W., 74, 78, 79, 119,
   120–25, 129, 134, 182, 189, 194
 Desert Storm and, 122, 124, 134,
   171
 Thomas and, 123–24
Bush, George W., 7, 9, 74, 130,
   131–33, 146–50, 187, 188, 190,
   196, 197, 199, 200
 Afghan war and, 154
 on common ground, vii, 185, 248
 federal spending and, 235, 240
 Hispanic vote and, 58
 immigration issue and, 58–59, 259
 Iraq war and, 151, 153, 154, 155,
   156, 157, 160, 161, 162, 171, 188,
   196–97, 207, 210
 Kerry's debate with, 215, 217
 Medicare and, 52, 171
 9/11 and, 150
 No Child Left Behind reform of,
   147–48, 150, 189, 191
 as polarizer, 131–33
 in 2000 election, 11, 172
 in 2004 election, 8, 58, 75, 76, 155,
   172, 215
 taxes and, 148
 terrorism and, 150, 153, 155, 156,
   157, 160, 161
Business Roundtable, 190–91
Byrd, Robert, 49, 54

campaign funding, 66–67, 72–73,
   88–89, 100, 205
Card, Andy, 147
Carson, Rachel, 88
Carter, Jimmy, 32, 99–102, 104, 107,
   128, 134, 171, 196, 203
 hostage crisis and, 101, 109
 Panama Canal Treaties and, 100,
   101, 175–76
 polarization and, 99, 100
Carville, James, 6
Casey, Bob, 213
Casey, William, 118
Cavuto, Neil, 50
CBS News, 65
Center for Responsive Politics, 66
Chafee, Lincoln, 30–31
Chamber of Commerce, U.S., 191
Chambers, Whittaker, 127

Chambliss, Saxby, 153
Cheney, Dick, 33, 149, 153, 221
 Iraq and, 155, 157, 196
 Leahy and, 50, 51
Cheney, Lynne, 17
child support payments, 189
China, 88
Choctaws, 42
Christian Coalition, 42, 44–45, 120,
   194
Churchill, Winston, 103
Cisneros, Henry, 129
Citizens Commission on Civil Rights,
   191
civil rights movement, 87, 90, 91, 92,
   93, 105, 192, 205
Civil War, 87, 91, 205
class warfare, 43, 45
Cleland, Max, 152–53
Clinton, Bill, 7, 52, 125, 128, 129,
   131–33, 134–42, 143–45, 166, 171,
   189, 190
 federal spending and, 235
 impeachment of, 2, 3, 137, 144–45,
   146
 as polarizer, 131–33
 scandals and, 135–36, 143–45,
   166
 taxes and, 52, 136, 139
 Whitewater and, 135–36
Clinton, Hillary, 55, 57, 134–35,
   216–17
 health care and, 138–39, 221
CNN, 36, 79, 187
Coburn, Tom, 240
Coelho, Tony, 33
Combs, Roberta, 44
Commentary, 3, 8
commissions, government,
   233–34
Committee for the Survival of a Free
   Congress, 106
common ground, 9–10, 11, 12,
   25–26, 60, 62, 161–62, 185–86,
   189, 190, 191, 192, 200, 201, 203,
   204–6, 253–54
 bipartisanship and consensus,
   174–76, 177, 186, 189–90, 192,
   198, 204, 205, 206, 221
 competing with polarization, 205,
   206

points to remember, 40, 43, 45,
46–47, 48, 62, 65, 80
as process, not set of ideas, 222
2008 campaign and, 206–47; *see
also* 2008 presidential campaign
recommendations
common ground governing principles,
223–46
a common ground strategy for governing must be provided with the
maximum possible amount of political cover, 231–43
do not pick fights where the other
four common ground governing
principles do not and cannot apply,
243–46
for a controversial issue to be resolved in a common ground climate,
it must contain elements of the historical orthodoxy of both parties,
226–28
the chances for consensus on a solution increase dramatically when
fresh ideas to address the problem
are brought to the table, 228–31
there must be agreement that a problem exists, and agreement on what
goal needs to be reached to alleviate
the problem, 225–26
communists, 127
"competence not ideology" message,
193–94, 195, 198, 202
Congress, 48–54, 55–60, 63, 137,
167–68
Bush and, 132–33
campaigning for, 66–68
Clinton and, 132–33
committees in, 100
House Ways and Means Committee,
49, 55–58, 100
immigration issue and, 58–60
incumbents in, 186–87
redistricting and, 186
Connor, Bull, 91
conservative, Thomas on being, 23–26
Conservative Caucus, 106
Contract with America, 49, 234
Coolidge, Calvin, 167
Coopersmith, Esther, 179
corruption, 239–42
Coulter, Ann, 7, 42, 71, 170

Crawford-Mason, Clare, 180–81
credibility, 210
criminal furloughs, 122
Crossfire, 36, 79
culture war, 43, 78–83, 93, 198
Culture Wars (Hunter), 79, 81
Cunningham, Randy "Duke," 53

Daley, Richard, 94
Darrow, Clarence, 99
debates, 214–20
defense appropriations, 53
DeLay, Tom, 2, 3, 57, 149, 156
Democratic National Convention, 94
Democrats, 61–62, 167–68
bipartisanship and, *see* bipartisan-
ship and consensus
CBS/NYT survey and, 65
polarizers' view of, 169–73
red state/blue state myth and, 43,
74–78, 80, 198
2008 presidential campaign and,
211–13
Department of Homeland Security,
152, 234
Desert Storm, 122, 124, 134, 171
DiMaggio, Paul, 38, 39, 74, 81
Dionne, E. J., 67
Dole, Bob, 120, 121, 122
Donovan, Raymond, 32, 129
Douglas, Stephen, 217, 219, 220
Drudge Report, 126
Dukakis, Michael, 74, 121–22, 125,
134, 193–94, 195

earmarks (pork barrel projects),
52–54, 181–82, 235, 240, 241
economic equality, 18–19, 43, 45
economy, 52, 124, 197
education and schools, 22, 24, 45,
147
No Child Left Behind law and,
147–48, 150, 189, 191
overcrowded districts and, 225
prayer and, 22, 79, 81, 82
Education Trust, 191
Eilperin, Juliet, 148
Eisenhower, Dwight, 96, 171
elections, 11
of 1976, 98
of 1980, 188–89, 192, 203, 204

elections (*continued*)
  of 1984, 111
  of 1994, 139, 165, 166, 168, 188–89,
    191, 192, 204
  of 2000, 11–12, 132, 147, 172
  of 2004, 8, 9, 58, 75, 76, 130, 155,
    172, 199, 215
  of 2006, vii, 9, 11, 29–30, 35, 36,
    38–39, 43, 66, 130, 165, 166, 168,
    186–89, 191–92, 199, 200, 202,
    204, 205, 207, 213
  of 2008, *see* 2008 presidential cam-
    paign
  wave, 29, 101–2, 168, 191, 192
Emanuel, Rahm, 39–40
Emerging Republican Majority, The
  (Phillips), 95
environment, 44, 88, 93, 95, 171,
  172
equality, economic, 18–19, 43, 45
Ethics in Government Act, 128
Evangelical Christians, 104–5, 200

fair trade, 20
Falwell, Jerry, 44, 105–8
FBI, 152
Federal Funding Accountability and
  Transparency Act, 240–41
feminism, 88, 93
Ferraro, Geraldine, 111
Fight Club Politics (Eilperin), 148
Fiske, Robert, 135–36
flag burning, 81, 198
Flake, Jeff, 54, 240
Focus on the Family, 7, 36
Foley, Mark, 36, 166
Foley, Tom, 33
Ford, Betty, 104
Ford, Gerald, 97, 98, 100, 102, 104,
  107, 175
foreign policy, 100–101, 150
Fox News Channel, 141
Franken, Al, 6
free trade, 20
Frist, Bill, 59–60

gambling, 42
gay rights, 21, 44, 79, 81, 107, 173,
  198, 199, 242–43, 244, 245–46
Geneva Convention, 151
Gilmore, Jim, 200

Gingrich, Newt, 1–2, 3, 31–34, 57,
  110, 140–41, 144
  Rangel on, 49
Giuliani, Rudy, 76, 199–200
Goldwater, Barry, 88, 98, 107, 176
Gore, Al, 74, 172
government:
  corruption in, 239–42
  increased size of, 88
government spending, 234–37
  budget legislation and, 111, 117, 124
  earmarks (pork barrel projects) and,
    52–54, 181–82, 235, 240, 241
  Federal Funding Accountability and
    Transparency Act and, 240–41
  Grace Commission, 236
Grady, Rachel, 47
Grassly, Chuck, 76
Great Britain, 154
Guantánamo Bay, 151
gun control, 22, 127, 198, 199, 225

Hall, Tony, 178, 179, 180, 249
Hamilton, Alexander, 167
Handgun Control, 7
Hannity, Sean, 6, 135, 141
Harding, Warren G., 167
Harkin, Tom, 76
Harris, Katherine, 132
Hart, Gary, 76, 110–11
Hastert, Dennis, 57, 149
health care, 188, 190–91, 197,
  237–39
  Clinton and, 138–39, 221
  credibility and, 210
  insurance, 238–39
  Medicare, 52, 55, 171, 189, 197, 235,
    236
Helms, Jesse, 111, 136
Hill, Anita, 123
Hispanics, 58–59, 191
Hiss, Alger, 127
Hitler, Adolf, 49–50, 159
Hofstadter, Richard, 4
Homeland Security, Department of,
  152, 234
Hoover, Herbert, 167, 170
Horton, Willie, 122, 134, 194
House of Commons, 137
House of Representatives, 137
  committees in, 100

Ways and Means Committee, 49,
    55–58, 100
Hoyer, Steny, 178, 249
Hubbard, Frank McKinney, 131
Huckabee, Mike, 200
Hudson, Rock, 112
Huffington, Arianna, 71, 72, 126
Humphrey, Hubert, 90, 94–95, 100
Hunt, Jim, 111
Hunter, James, 79, 81
Hunter, Joel, 44
hunting, 22
Hurricane Katrina, 197, 226, 227
Hussein, Saddam, 122, 153, 155, 156,
    157, 159

ideology:
  common ground campaign and,
      222–23
  competence and, 193–94, 195, 198,
      202
  polarization and, 5, 41–42, 43, 253
immigration, 21–22, 58–60, 81, 188,
    189, 259
  Reagan and, 112, 117
Independent Counsel Act, 119
independent counsels, 119, 128–29,
    135–36, 139, 143
Ingraham, Laura, 141
Inouye, Daniel, 53, 176
Internet, 70–72, 130
  blogs on, 43, 70, 71, 126, 130
Iran, 160
  hostage crisis, 101, 109, 118
Iran-Contra, 32, 117–19, 120, 124,
    129, 189, 194
Iraq, Desert Storm in, 122, 124, 134,
    171
Iraq war, 4, 9, 21, 29, 36, 54, 60, 151,
    153–61, 162, 166, 171, 187, 188,
    190, 196–97, 200–202, 206
  Chafee and, 31
  Lieberman and, 8, 30, 201
  9/11 and, 21, 153, 157
IRS, 129
Islam, 158–61, 196, 210
Israel, 159, 160

Jackson, Andrew, 50–51
Jackson, Jesse, 110, 111
Jefferson, Thomas, 167, 240

Jeffords, Jim, 149
Jesus, 44
Johnson, Andrew, 137
Johnson, Lyndon, 90, 92, 94, 95, 107,
    149, 195
Jones, Bob, III, 107
Jordan, Vernon, 144
judges, term limits for, 241–42

Kendall, David, 238
Kennedy, Edward, 59, 101, 102, 120,
    147
Kennedy, Jacqueline, 179–80
Kennedy, John F., 3, 90, 95, 171, 180,
    196, 217
Kennedy, Robert F., 87, 93, 94
Kerry, John, 8, 75, 76, 130, 155, 172
  Bush's debate with, 215, 217
Khomeini, Ayatollah Ruhollah, 118
Khrushchev, Nikita, 204
King, Martin Luther, Jr., 87, 93,
    105–6, 165, 192
Kinsley, Michael, 240
Krauthammer, Charles, 69
Kucinich, Dennis, 6
Kuwait, 122

labor unions, 20–21, 43, 93, 170, 194
Lance, Bert, 32
Larson, Doug, 134
Latinos, 58–59, 191
Leach, Jim, 76
Leahy, Patrick, 50, 51
Lee, David, 137
Leno, Jay, 193
Lewinsky, Monica, 143–44
Lewis, Jerry, 181–82
liberal, Beckel on being, 17–22
liberal activists, 100
Lieberman, Joseph, 7–8, 30, 201
Limbaugh, Rush, 42–43, 70, 72,
    81–82, 124, 135, 141
Lincoln, Abraham, 23, 24, 90, 196
  Douglas's debates with, 217, 219, 220
Livingston, Bob, 2, 3
lobbyists, 66–67, 73, 88, 181–82,
    191, 205, 237

McCain, John, 30, 59, 200
McCarthy, Eugene, 94
McCarthy, Joseph, 127, 128

McCarthyism, 128
McGovern, George, 96, 110–11, 241
McInnis, Scott, 50
Mann, Thomas, 188
media, 69–72, 126, 182, 253
Medicare, 52, 55, 171, 189, 197, 235, 236
Meese, Edwin, 118
Meet the Press, 157
Mencken, H. L., 61
Mesta, Pearl, 181
Michael, Bob, 33
Michel, Bob, 140
microloans, 229–31, 232
Middle East, 88, 159, 171
military facilities, 236
Miller, George, 147–48
minimum income, 95
minimum wage, 36, 170, 188, 189, 190, 231–32
Mondale, Walter, 110–11
Moore, Michael, 7, 42
Moral Majority, 24–25, 106, 107–8
MoveOn.org, 7, 36
Moyers, Bill, 107
Murphy, Maureen, 169
Muslims, 158–61, 196, 210
myths
  of culture war, 43, 78–83, 93, 198
  of red states and blue states, 43, 74–78, 80, 198

Nader, Ralph, 167
Nathan, George Jean, 46, 174
National Council of La Raza, 191
National Enquirer, 135
National Rifle Association (NRA), 6–7, 127, 141
Newsday, 49
news organizations, 69–70, 71, 126, 141
New York Times, 53, 65, 135
Nicaragua, 117
  Iran-Contra, 32, 117–19, 120, 124, 129, 189, 194
9/11 attacks, 44, 60, 149–50, 154, 155, 159, 161, 187, 215
  Giuliani and, 200
  Iraq and, 21, 153, 157
  Patriot Act and, 151, 152
9/11 Commission, 234, 235

Nixon, Richard, 79, 94, 95–96, 100, 103–4, 127, 171
  Watergate and, 32, 88, 97, 98
No Child Left Behind, 147–48, 150, 189, 191
North, Oliver, 118, 119
North American Free Trade Agreement, 189
North Korea, 161
NOW, 127
nuclear power, 22
nuclear weapons, 160–61, 192

Obama, Barack, 11, 30, 240, 255–56
Obey, Dave, 54
O'Casey, Sean, 29
O'Connor, Sandra Day, 108, 119
oil, foreign, 88, 101, 196
O'Neill, Thomas "Tip," 141, 178, 249–50
Opinion Research Corporation, 187
Ornstein, Norman, 190

Palestinians, 159
Panama Canal Treaties, 100, 101, 175–76
"Paranoid Style in American Politics, The" (Hofstadter), 4
Patriot Act, 150, 151, 152, 153
patriotism, 17, 93
Pelosi, Nancy, vii, 57, 161–62, 166, 185, 248
pensions, 56
People, 180
Perot, H. Ross, 125, 132, 167
Pew Forum on Religion and Public Life, 80, 82
Pew Research Center for the People and the Press, 80, 82, 202, 244–45
Phillips, Kevin, 95, 96, 100, 106
Pitts, Peter, 237–38
Pittsburgh Tribune Review, 49
Pledge of Allegiance, 81
Poindexter, John, 118, 119
polarization, 3–13, 38–45, 46–47, 60, 166, 204, 206, 258
  addiction compared to, 252–53
  Bush and, 131–33
  Carter and, 99, 100

Clinton and, 131–33
common ground competing with, 205, 206
negative campaigns and, 68, 126–30, 213, 253
1988 as year of, 194–95
Reagan and, 99
in 2008 campaign, 207–8, 209–11
voters' feelings about, 29–37, 38–39, 187–89, 191, 202, 209
polarizers, 253
bottom feeder, 6, 7, 41, 42, 43, 128, 253
Democrats and Republicans as viewed by, 169–73
ideologically driven, 5, 41–42, 43, 253
intellectual policy, 6
party, 5–6, 253
secular, 41–42
self-interest driven, 5
political activists, 64, 65, 100, 169
political consultants, 67–68, 130, 201–2, 213, 218, 253
political fund-raisers, 72–73
political parties, 61–68, 167, 205, 211–12
See also Democrats; Republicans
pork barrel projects (earmarks), 52–54, 181–82, 235, 240, 241
poverty, 44, 45, 226–27, 229–31
microloans and, 229–31, 232
Powell, Colin, 153–54
Powell, Lewis, 119
"Pragmatic Americans Liberal and Conservative on Social Issues," 80, 82, 244–45
press (media), 69–72, 126, 182, 253

Rangel, Charlie, 49, 73
Reagan, Nancy, 112
Reagan, Ronald, 26, 32, 79, 98, 101, 102, 104–5, 107, 108, 109–13, 120, 134, 170, 171, 189, 196, 203, 213, 217, 249–50
abortion and, 105
Bork and, 119–20, 124, 189
Grace Commission and, 236
immigration and, 112, 117
Iran-Contra and, 32, 117–19, 120, 124, 189, 194

polarization and, 99
taxes and, 109–10, 111–12, 117, 124, 148, 189
red and blue states, 43, 74–78, 80, 198
Reed, Ralph, 42, 44
Rehnquist, William, 144
Reid, Harry, 58, 59
religious right, 43
Reno, Janet, 129, 135
Republicans, 61–62, 167–68
bipartisanship and, see bipartisanship and consensus
CBS/NYT survey and, 65
polarizers' view of, 169–73
red state/blue state myth and, 43, 74–78, 80, 198
2008 presidential campaign and, 211–13
R Factor, The (Schluter and Lee), 137
Rich, Frank, 55
Robertson, Pat, 44, 112, 120–21
Roe v. Wade, 82, 88, 95, 103, 104, 105, 108, 130, 243, 244, 245
Romney, Mitt, 200, 239
Roosevelt, Franklin Delano, 95, 101, 170, 171, 196
Roosevelt, Theodore, 96, 132, 167
Rostenkowski, Dan, 57
Rove, Karl, 6, 9, 11, 31, 202
Hispanic vote and, 58
Rumsfeld, Donald, 155, 157, 187

Sada, George, 157
Saddam's Secrets: How an Iraqi General Defied and Survived Saddam Hussein (Sada), 157
Sadler, Barry, 89
Safire, William, 96
Salazar, Ken, 76
Samuelson, Robert, 40, 74, 188
Santorum, Rick, 49, 50, 213
Sargent, Francis W., 122
Sargent, Claire, 87
Scaife, Richard Mellon, 143
scandals, 126, 129, 156, 166, 187
Clinton and, 135–36, 143–45, 166
corruption, 239–42
Schiavo, Terri, 244
Schluter, Michael, 137

schools and education, 22, 24, 45, 147
  No Child Left Behind law and, 147–48, 150, 189, 191
  overcrowded districts and, 225
  prayer and, 22, 79, 81, 82
Schumer, Chuck, 39–40
Schwarz, Joe, 63–64
Schwarzenegger, Arnold, 185
Scopes trial, 103
second opinions, 232–34, 236–37
Senate, 137
  immigration issue and, 58–60
Sentelle, David, 136
separation of church and state, 81, 106, 121, 198
September 11, see 9/11 attacks
Service Employees International Union, 190–91
Shockey, Jeffrey S., 181–82
Silent Spring (Carson), 88
Simpson, Alan, 177
Snow, Tony, 141
social issues, 242–43
  Pew survey on, 80, 82, 244–45
social occasions, 73, 177–81
Social Security, 55, 110, 111, 188, 189, 197, 235, 236
South, 90–92, 98
Soviet Union, 88, 154, 171
special-interest groups, 66–67, 141, 191, 233, 237
stability, 167–68
Stark, Fortney "Pete," 50, 56
Starr, Kenneth, 136, 143
stem cell research, 79, 188, 198, 244
Stevens, Ted, 53
Studio 54, 128
Supreme Court, 82, 95, 107, 134, 152, 199
  Bork nominated to, 119–20, 124, 129–30, 153, 189
  Roe v. Wade, 82, 88, 95, 103, 104, 105, 108, 130, 243, 244, 245
  term limits and, 241–42
  Thomas nominated to, 123–24
Sutton, Willie, 4

Taft, Robert, 180
Taft, William Howard, 96, 167, 170
Taliban, 21, 154, 159

Tancredo, Tom, 6
taxes, 19–20, 23–24, 52, 55, 65, 124, 188, 231–32
  Bush and, 148
  Clinton and, 52, 36, 139
  government spending of, see government spending
  Reagan and, 109–10, 111–12, 117, 124, 148, 189
term limits, 241–42
terrorism, 21, 150, 151–52, 155, 156, 157, 159, 192, 196, 210, 235
  nuclear weapons and, 160–61, 192
  Patriot Act and, 150, 151, 152, 153
Tester, Jon, 185
Thatcher, Margaret, 158
Thomas, Bill, 55–57, 73
Thomas, Clarence, 123–24
Thompson, Fred, 200
Tocqueville, Alexis de, 117
Torrijos, Omar, 176
Torrijos, Samuel, 176
Tower, John, 118, 126
Tripp, Linda, 143–44
Truman, Harry, 139
Twain, Mark, 62
2008 presidential campaign, 11, 12, 30, 64, 195–200, 202–3
  common ground message for, 206–47
2008 presidential campaign recommendations, 209–23
  avoid speaking ill of your opponent, 213–15
  campaign against polarization, 209–11
  campaign as common ground candidate, 211–13, 222–23
  for debates, 214–20
  don't include common ground solutions, 222–23
  give your opponent credit where credit is due, 215–16
  promise to include members of other party in administration, 220–22

unions, 20–21, 43, 93, 170, 194
United Nations (UN), 154, 159
USA Today, 9, 185
  "Common Ground" column in, 9, 185, 246, 247–50

values and morality, 77–78, 81, 100,
106, 206
culture war over, 43, 78–83, 93, 198
Vandenberg, Arthur, 180
Vietnam War, 87–88, 89, 91–93, 94,
95–96, 97, 99, 118, 134, 153, 205
Viguerie, Richard, 107
vision, 182

Wallace, George, 88, 167
Wall Street Journal, 241
Walsh, Lawrence, 119, 129
Washington, George, 146
Washington Examiner, 240
Washington Post, 47, 49, 63–64, 67,
74, 181, 190

Washington Times, 153
Watergate, 32, 88, 97, 98, 99, 100,
119, 126, 128
Webb, Jim, 213
Weddington, Sarah, 104
Weinberger, Caspar, 118, 119, 129
welfare, 171, 189
Weyrich, Paul, 106, 107
Whitehead, Sheldon, 31
Whitewater, 135–36
Wilson, James Q., 3–4, 8, 9
Wilson, Woodrow, 167
women's movement, 88, 93
Wright, Jim, 1–2, 3, 33

Yunus, Muhammad, 229–30